LOSERS <u>CAN</u> BE CHOOSERS!

Now you have the run of the supermarket with the reference that offers true choice and variety. Take your pick of:

- Salmon—18 listings from 120 to 180 calories per serving
- Vegetable Soup—31 listings from 25 to 180 calories per serving
- French Salad Dressing—16 listings from 2 to 70 calories per tablespoon
- Chocolate Chip Cookies—20 listings from 17 to 130 calories each

The choice is yours: 8,500 listings of nutritious, delicious foods with exact calorie counts to help you tailor any diet to your tastes and needs.

"PERENNIAL DIETERS! COMPULSIVE CALORIE COUNTERS! WEIGHT WATCHERS DROPOUTS! YOU ARE *MY* KIND OF PEOPLE AND THIS IS *OUR* LITERARY EVENT OF THE DECADE....WITH THE DEDICATION OF A SCIENTIST, CORINNE NETZER HAS PENETRATED THE CALORIC MYSTERY OF THE SUPERMARKET."

—*Gael Greene,* Life *magazine*

Also by Corinne T. Netzer:

THE BRAND-NAME CARBOHYDRATE GRAM COUNTER
THE LOW-SALT DIET COUNTER
THE DIETER'S CARBOHYDRATE GRAM COUNTER
THE DIETER'S CALORIE COUNTER
THE FIBER COUNTER
THE FAT COUNTER AND THE 22-GRAM SOLUTION

THE
BRAND–NAME
CALORIE
COUNTER

Newly Revised,
Expanded and Updated!

CORINNE T. NETZER

A DELL BOOK

Published by
Dell Publishing Co., Inc.
1 Dag Hammarskjold Plaza
New York, New York 10017

Dell® TM 681510, Dell Publishing Co., Inc.

ISBN: 0-440-10779-2

Printed in the United States of America

March 1986

10 9 8 7 6 5

W F H

To Joy Stevens,
with affection and appreciation

ACKNOWLEDGMENTS

This book would not have been possible without the cooperation and goodwill of the American food industry, and I would sincerely like to thank the many companies and dozens of people who spent so much time answering my constant barrage of requests for more information. I wish I could list them individually, but space does not permit.

In addition, I would like to thank my editor, Elaine Chaback, and my assistant, Margaret Sullivan, for their help and encouragement.

INTRODUCTION

Eating is America's favorite pastime. If you stop and think about it, you'll probably realize that a good number of your working hours are occupied with food. If you're not actually eating, then you're buying food, planning to buy it, preparing it, even fretting over its prices. It's almost impossible for any but the most iron-willed soul to escape the national food obsession.

It is, therefore, little wonder that 58 percent of our population is overweight, and that every month an estimated ten million Americans embark on that battle of frustration known as a *diet*.

As a perennial dieter, I can tell you that there is definite hope, that you *will* lose weight if you stick to your diet. But that's the problem. Most people "fall off the wagon" after only two weeks of reducing. The sameness and boredom of crispy carrot sticks, broiled skinless chicken and wedges of lettuce gets to them and it's all over very quickly.

The purpose of *The Brand-Name Calorie Counter* is to help you stay on your diet by relieving the tedium. For instance, you might want to substitute a slice of *Celeste* pepperoni pizza (115 calories) for that broiled chicken, or have an eight-ounce bowl of *Progresso* minestrone soup (130 calories) for lunch or reward yourself with a lovely slice of *Sara Lee* chocolate chip pound cake (130 calories). Dieting is not a pleasant experience, but I do believe the information contained herein can help to make it less painful by introducing variety—which is not only the spice of life but of dieting as well.

This is the fourth edition of *The Brand-Name Calorie Counter*, and I have had to make many revisions because the food industry is growing and changing. In addition, I have again included a bonus section on fast-food and chain restaurants so you may take your diet out to dinner. This section has also been updated, but if you don't find your favorites listed, it may be because the information wasn't available (the expense of nutritional analysis is enormous) or because the product varies too much from one franchise location to another.

I've received letters from readers who tell me that they compile their weekly marketing list based on the information in *The Brand-Name Calorie Counter.* You may not opt to use the book in that way—but you might decide to make substitutions on whatever diet you're following, or you may try a new food or change brands. You'll even find the data important in "maintaining" the new you after you've lost weight. Dieting is very personal, and how you choose to use this book is up to you, but with it you will have the information you need to plan your diet—and stay on it.

C.T.N.

CONTENTS

WHAT YOU SHOULD KNOW
ABOUT USING THIS BOOK

WHERE TO FIND WHAT

Most calorie counters list foods alphabetically. *The Brand-Name Calorie Counter* does not. It lists foods categorically. This means that all breads are grouped together; so are all frozen dinners, all candies, all vegetables and so on. For example—and more important, for convenience—if you want to find the caloric content of various soups, you don't have to hopscotch from A (asparagus) through W (wonton); you simply turn to Chapter 9, "Soups, Broths and Chowders," and there you will find all soup listings.

Occasionally, you may have trouble deciding what category a food belongs in; to locate such hard-to-categorize foods quickly, just flip to the index.

BE CAREFUL ABOUT MAKING COMPARISONS

It's only natural that you will want to use this counter to compare the caloric content of different foods and different brands. In most instances, you can make comparisons accurately by merely glancing at the listings. For example, all soft drinks are listed in the same measure (eight fluid ounces); therefore, you can easily compare the caloric content of *Coca-Cola* with that of *Dr Pepper,* or *Schweppes Bitter Lemon* or whatever.

To facilitate easy comparisons, categories have been listed in a uniform measure *whenever it was possible or feasible to do so.* However, it was neither feasible nor sensible to list certain foods in a uniform measure. For example, all data on crackers could have been presented in a uniform measure of one ounce, but that would mean you would have to weigh a *Triscuit* to learn its caloric content. For practicality's sake, crackers, cookies, bread, rolls and various other foods are listed by the piece—in the size packaged by the manufacturer. This means you can easily determine the calories in a single cracker, but you cannot compare different brands and varieties of crackers accurately. Why? Because, unless you weigh every cracker, you have no way of knowing if they are the same size.

To get the most from this book—and from your diet—you must recognize that similar foods are not necessarily packaged in the same or even similar sizes. Consider, for example, two brands of chocolate-covered marshmallow cookies, *Mallomars* and *Pinwheels*, both manufactured by *Nabisco*. All cookies are listed by the piece (one cookie, as packaged), and if you check, you'll find that a *Mallomar* has 65 calories, while a *Pinwheel* has 130 calories. However, while it is true that one *Pinwheel* has twice as many calories as one *Mallomar*, it is also true that by the pound or by the ounce the caloric content of the two is almost identical. The reason for this is simple: The size of one *Pinwheel* is more than double the size of one *Mallomar*.

The point here is simple but important. If you're not certain that products are the same size, *don't make comparisons— they may not be accurate.*

You can, of course, compare any foods that are listed in the same standard measure. You can compare the calories in a half cup of apricots with the calories in a half cup of prunes; or the calories in one ounce of Muenster cheese with the calories in one ounce of Swiss cheese. However, what you cannot do is compare foods that are listed in dissimilar units of measure. Because even doctors and home economists sometimes confuse measures by capacity with measures by weight, it should be noted also that you can't, for example, accurately compare four ounces of custard with a half cup of ice cream. Four ounces is a measure of how much something weighs. Half a cup is a measure of how much space something occupies. The units of measure are dissimilar and, therefore, not comparable. Think of it this way: Eight ounces of puffed rice cereal contains approximately 850 calories and fills the capacity of about 16 eight-ounce measuring cups; an eight-ounce cup of puffed rice contains about 50 calories and weighs half an ounce. Clearly, eight ounces of puffed rice and an eight-ounce cupful of puffed rice are not the same!

Sometimes, exactly eight ounces of a food exactly fills the capacity of an eight-ounce cup, but just as often it does not—which is why you shouldn't try to compare foods listed by weight with foods listed by volume. Just remember: The capacity of a standard eight-ounce measuring cup is eight *fluid* ounces, not eight *weight* ounces.

As noted before, you can compare foods listed in a similar measure—and you can, of course, convert a unit of measure to a smaller or larger amount. You may find the charts below helpful in making conversions.

EQUIVALENTS BY CAPACITY
(all measures level)
1 quart = 4 cups
1 cup = 8 fluid ounces
= ½ pint
= 16 tablespoons
2 tablespoons = 1 fluid ounce
1 tablespoon = 3 teaspoons

EQUIVALENTS BY WEIGHT
1 pound = 16 ounces
3.57 ounces = 100 grams
1 ounce = 28.35 grams

You don't have to know that there are 28.35 grams in an ounce to use this book, but you may find the information handy when shopping or comparing package sizes. By federal law, the net weight (or volume) of a packaged food must be printed on the food's container. Most containers list a food's net weight in ounces or pounds; however, labels now include the weight in metric measure, as well, and a few labels will give only the metric weight.

PAY ATTENTION TO PACKAGE SIZES

To get full value from *The Brand-Name Calorie Counter*, it's important to pay attention to package sizes. Specifically, whenever the caloric content of a food is listed by one ounce, you must check the food's label to learn how much the product weighs—and then multiply its weight in ounces by the number of calories per ounce. Cheeses, for example, are listed in a one-ounce measure. To determine the caloric content of an eight-ounce package of *Dorman's* American cheese, simply multiply eight by 106 and you will see that the entire package contains 848 calories.

Pay attention to weights, too, when a product is listed by the whole package. For example, the weight of *Green Giant*'s beef stew entree is currently nine ounces, and the data herein pertains to the full nine ounces. Should *Green Giant* increase or decrease the amount of stew in their frozen entree, the data should be adjusted accordingly.

PAY ATTENTION TO PACKAGE DIRECTIONS
You will find many products listed in *The Brand-Name Calorie Counter* that require some home preparation: condensed soups, salad dressing mixes, sauce mixes, potato mixes and many more. For convenience, the data on the majority of these products is given for the "finished" food when it is *prepared according to the package directions*. Should you make a change in a package recipe, bear in mind that you may also change the caloric content of a finished food. If, for example, a package recipe calls for a cup of whole milk and you substitute a cup of skim milk, the prepared food will have a lower calorie content than is listed here. There is no reason why you shouldn't vary package directions—the point is, if you do so, be sure to determine how the change will affect the caloric content of the prepared food.

SOURCES AND ACCURACY OF DATA

The caloric values in this book are based on data obtained from producers and processors of all brand-name foods, as well as from label information. Every care has been exercised to evaluate the data as accurately and fully as possible; every effort has been made to present the material clearly and usefully.

Consumers should be aware, however, that a variety of factors can, to some extent, affect the accuracy of any and all analyses of food. For example, apples grown in different regions of the country may differ slightly in composition; therefore, the calories shown for any product that contains apples must be considered average or typical. Seasonal changes can also affect the composition of an apple; so, too, can the maturity of a crop when picked. For these and similar reasons, and because there is no practical way to analyze every sample of a processed food, it is an accepted practice within the food industry—and within the United States Department of Agriculture—to present nutritional data that is typical or "proximate."

As this revised edition of *The Brand-Name Calorie Counter* goes to press, the data has been checked to see that it is as up-to-date as possible. However, just as you strive to vary or improve your recipes, so do home economists in the food industry. In addition, economic factors sometimes cause a difference in how a food is packaged (for example, the size of a candy bar may decrease or increase) and, therefore, the caloric content may change. For these reasons it is impossible to guarantee that some of the data won't change in time. As needed, corrections will be made in later editions of the book. Until then, you must be on the lookout for changes yourself. In particular, if you find that a favorite food is suddenly labeled "New" or "Improved," you may want to write the producer directly to ask if the food's caloric content has changed.

ABBREVIATIONS IN THIS BOOK

cond. . . . . condensed
fl. . . . . . , ... fluid
". . . . . inch
lb. . . . . pound
oz. . . . . ounce
pkg. . . . . package
semicond. . . . . semicondensed
tbsp. . . . . .tablespoon
tsp. . . . . teaspoon

Chapter 1

EGGS, PANCAKES, CEREALS AND OTHER BREAKFAST FOODS

EGGS
See also "Frozen Breakfasts"

---

	calories
imitation, fat-free	
(*Fleischmann's Egg Beaters*), ¼ cup	25
imitation, fat-free, w/cheese	
(*Fleischmann's Egg Beaters*), 4 oz.*	130
omelets:	
cheese, freeze-dried	
(*Mountain House*), 1.2 oz. dry	180
cheese, mix*	
(*McCormick/Schilling* Seasoning Mix),	
1 serving	168
Mexican, freeze-dried	
(*Mountain House*), 1.45 oz. dry	220
western, mix** (*Durkee*), 1 pkg.	170
western, mix*	
(*McCormick/Schilling* Seasoning Mix),	
1 serving	164
scrambled:	
precooked, freeze-dried	
(*Mountain House*), 1 oz. dry	180
mix** (*Durkee*), 1 pkg.	124
w/bacon, precooked, freeze-dried	
(*Mountain House*), 1.05 oz. dry	180
w/bacon bits, freeze-dried	
(*Mountain House*), 1.1 oz. dry	170

Eggs, scrambled, continued
    w/bacon bits, mix** (*Durkee*), 1 pkg. 181
    w/butter, freeze-dried
      (*Mountain House*), 1.1 oz. dry 160

*Prepared according to package directions
**Prepared according to package directions, with water

FROZEN BREAKFASTS, one serving*
*See also "Eggs," "French Toast"
and "Pancakes & Waffles"*

---

                                                calories
French toast, w/sausages (*Swanson*), 6½ oz. 450
omelet, w/cheese sauce and ham (*Swanson*), 7 oz. 400
omelet, Spanish (*Swanson*), 8 oz. 250
omelet, western, in pastry
    (*Pepperidge Farm*), 8¾ oz. 300
pancakes, w/blueberry sauce (*Swanson*), 7 oz. 400
pancakes and sausages (*Swanson*), 6 oz. 460
scrambled eggs:
    Canadian bacon and cheese, in pastry
      (*Pepperidge Farm*), 7¾ oz. 290
    and sausages, w/hash browns
      (*Swanson*), 6¼ oz. 420

*As packaged

FRENCH TOAST, one slice*, except as noted
See also "Frozen Breakfasts"

---

                                                calories
frozen:
    (*Aunt Jemima*) 85
    (*Downyflake*) 135
    cinnamon swirl (*Aunt Jemima*) 97
    raisin (*Downyflake*) 135
freeze-dried (*Mountain House*), ⅓-oz. serving 50

French Toast, continued
mix* (*McCormick/Schilling* Batter Mix) 119

As packaged or prepared
**Prepared according to package directions*

PANCAKES & WAFFLES
See also "Frozen Breakfasts"

---

	calories
pancake, frozen (*Downyflake*), 1 pancake	80
pancake and waffle batter, frozen:	
plain, pancake (*Aunt Jemima*), 4" pancake*	70
plain, pancake (*Mrs. Smith's*), 1 1.3-oz. pancake* . . .	77
plain, waffle (*Mrs. Smith's*), 1 4-oz. waffle*	285
blueberry, pancake (*Aunt Jemima*), 4" pancake*	68
buttermilk, pancake (*Aunt Jemima*), 4" pancake	71
pancake, frozen (*Downyflake*), 1 pancake	80
pancake and waffle mix:	
plain (*Aunt Jemima* Original), ¼ cup	108
plain (*Aunt Jemima* Original), 4" pancake*	73
plain (*Dia-Mel*), 3" pancake*	34
plain (*Hungry Jack* Extra Lights), 4" pancake*	70
plain (*Hungry Jack* Panshakes), 4" pancake*	83
plain (*Martha White Flapstax*), 1 oz.	91
plain, freeze-dried	
(*Mountain House* Old West), 2.62 oz.	280
blueberry (*Hungry Jack*), 4" pancake*	107
buckwheat (*Aunt Jemima*), ¼ cup	107
buckwheat (*Aunt Jemima*), 4" pancake*	67
buttermilk (*Aunt Jemima*), ⅓ cup	175
buttermilk (*Aunt Jemima*), 4" pancake*	100
buttermilk (*Aunt Jemima* Complete), ½ cup	239
buttermilk	
(*Aunt Jemima* Complete), 4" pancake*	80
buttermilk (*Betty Crocker*), ⅓ cup	170
buttermilk (*Betty Crocker*), 4" pancake*	93
buttermilk (*Betty Crocker* Complete), ½ cup	210
buttermilk	
(*Betty Crocker* Complete), 4" pancake*	70

pancake & waffle mix, continued

buttermilk (*Hungry Jack*), 4" pancake* 80
buttermilk
  (*Hungry Jack* Complete), 4" pancake* 63
whole wheat (*Aunt Jemima*), 1/3 cup 142
whole wheat (*Aunt Jemima*), 4" pancake* 83
waffles, frozen:
  plain (*Aunt Jemima* Original Jumbo), 1 waffle 86
  plain (*Downyflake*), 1 waffle 60
  plain (*Downyflake* Hot 'N Buttery), 1 waffle 65
  plain (*Downyflake* Jumbo), 1 waffle 85
  plain (*Eggo* Homestyle), 1 waffle 120
  apple and cinnamon
    (*Aunt Jemima* Jumbo), 1 waffle 86
  apple and cinnamon (*Eggo*), 1 waffle 150
  blueberry (*Aunt Jemima* Jumbo), 1 waffle 86
  blueberry (*Downyflake*), 1 waffle 90
  blueberry (*Eggo*), 1 waffle 120
  blueberry (*Mrs. Smith's*), 1 waffle 130
  buttermilk (*Aunt Jemima* Jumbo), 1 waffle 86
  buttermilk (*Downyflake*—10-oz. pkg.), 1 waffle 50
  buttermilk (*Downyflake*—19-oz. pkg.), 1 waffle 85
  buttermilk (*Eggo*), 1 waffle 110
  buttermilk (*Mrs. Smith's*), 1 waffle 120
  homestyle (*Mrs. Smith's*), 1 waffle 120
  (*Roman Meal*), 1 waffle 110
  strawberry (*Eggo*), 1 waffle 120

*Prepared and/or cooked according to package directions

CEREALS & CORN PRODUCTS, DRY (UNCOOKED)
*See also "Cereals, Cooked," "Cereals, Ready-to-Eat"
and "Flour"*

---

calories

barley, pearled, regular or quick:
  (*Quaker Scotch Brand*), 1/4 cup 172
corn grits or hominy:
  (*Albers*), 1/4 cup 150

corn grits or hominy, continued

(*Quaker* Instant), 1 packet	79
golden (*Van Camp*), 4 oz.	60
golden, w/red and green peppers	
(*Van Camp*), 4 oz.	60
white, regular or quick (*Aunt Jemima*), 3 tbsp.	101
white, regular or quick (*Quaker*), 3 tbsp.	101
white (*Van Camp*), 4 oz.	63
artificial cheese flavor	
(*Quaker* Instant), 1 packet	104
imitation bacon bits (*Quaker* Instant), 1 packet	101
imitation ham bits (*Quaker* Instant), 1 packet	99

corn meal:

white (*Albers*), 1 oz.	100
white (*Aunt Jemima*), 3 tbsp.	102
white (*Quaker*), 3 tbsp.	102
white, bolted, mix (*Aunt Jemima*), 1/6 cup	99
white, self-rising (*Aunt Jemima*), 1/6 cup	98
white, self-rising, bolted (*Aunt Jemima*), 1/6 cup	99
yellow (*Albers*), 1 oz.	100
yellow (*Aunt Jemima*), 3 tbsp.	102

farina:

(*Cream of Wheat*), 1 oz.	100
(*Cream of Wheat* Instant), 1 oz.	100
(*Cream of Wheat* Mix 'n Eat), 1-oz. packet	100
(*Cream of Wheat* Quick), 1 oz.	100
w/baked apple and cinnamon	
(*Cream of Wheat* Mix 'n Eat), 1 1/4-oz. packet	130
w/brown sugar and cinnamon	
(*Cream of Wheat* Mix 'n Eat), 1 packet	130
w/honey graham	
(*Cream of Wheat* Mix 'n Eat), 1 packet	130
w/hot chocolate	
(*Cream of Wheat* Mix 'n Eat), 1 packet	130

oatmeal or oats:

(*Ralston*), 1/4 cup	110
instant (*H-O*—box), 1/2 cup	130
instant (*H-O*—packet), 1 packet	110
instant (*Quaker*), 1 packet	105
instant (*Ralston*), 1/4 cup	90
quick (*H-O*), 1/2 cup	130
quick or old-fashioned (*Quaker*), 1/3 cup	109

Cereals & Corn Products, Dry (Uncooked), oatmeal or oats, continued

quick or old-fashioned
   (*3-Minute Brand*), ⅓ cup 110
w/apple and cinnamon
   (*Harvest* Instant), ⅓ cup 140
w/apple and cinnamon
   (*Quaker* Instant), 1 packet 134
w/bran and raisins (*Quaker* Instant), 1 packet 153
w/cinnamon and spice
   (*Harvest* Instant), ⅓ cup 180
w/cinnamon and spice
   (*Quaker* Instant), 1 packet 170
w/honey and graham (*Quaker* Instant), 1 packet 136
w/maple and brown sugar
   (*Harvest* Instant), ⅓ cup 170
w/maple and brown sugar
   (*H–O* Instant), 1 packet 160
w/maple and brown sugar
   (*Quaker* Instant), 1 packet 163
w/peaches and cream (*Harvest* Instant), ⅓ cup 140
peaches and cream (*Quaker* Instant), 1 packet 140
w/raisins and spice (*Quaker* Instant), 1 packet 159
strawberries and cream
   (*Quaker* Instant), 1 packet 140
masa harina (*Quaker*), ⅓ cup 137
masa trigo (*Quaker*), ⅓ cup 149
wheat, toasted (*Wheatena*), ¼ cup 120
whole wheat (*Quaker Pettijohns*), ⅓ cup 106
whole wheat
   (*Ralston* Instant and Regular), ¼ cup 90

CEREALS, COOKED*, about ¾ cup, except as noted
See also "Cereals & Corn Products, Dry (Uncooked)"
and *"Cereals, Ready-to-Eat"*

calories

barley, pearled, quick (*Quaker Scotch Brand*) 172
barley, pearled, regular (*Quaker Scotch Brand*) 129
farina:
    (*Cream of Wheat*) 100
    (*Cream of Wheat* Instant or Quick) 100
    (*Cream of Wheat* Mix 'n Eat)** 140
    prepared w/water (*Pillsbury*) 90
    w/baked apple flavor and cinnamon
      (*Cream of Wheat* Mix 'n Eat)** 170
oatmeal and oats:
    instant (*H-O*—box) 170
    instant (*H-O*—packet) 150
    quick (*H-O*) 170
    w/brown sugar and cinnamon
      (*Cream of Wheat* Mix 'n Eat) 170
    w/honey graham (*Cream of Wheat* Mix 'n Eat) 170
    w/hot chocolate (*Cream of Wheat* Mix 'n Eat) 170
    w/maple and brown sugar (*H-O* Instant) 200
    peaches and cream (*Quaker* Instant) 210
    strawberries and cream (*Quaker* Instant) 210

***Prepared according to package directions, with 2 oz. whole
milk*

> **CEREALS, READY-TO-EAT,** one ounce
> and/or approximate cup measure*, except as noted
> See also "Cereals & Corn Products, Dry (Uncooked)"
> and "Cereals, Cooked"

calories

bran and high-fiber:
　(*All-Bran*), 1 oz. = 1/3 cup 70
　(*Bran Buds*), 1 oz. = 1/3 cup 70
　(*Bran Chex*), 1 oz. = 2/3 cup 90
　(*Corn Bran*), 1 oz. = 2/3 cup 109
　(*Kellogg's* 40% Bran Flakes), 1 oz. = 2/3 cup 90
　(*Most*), 1 oz. = 1/2 cup 100
　(*Nabisco* 100% Bran), 1 oz. 70
　(*Post* 40% Bran Flakes), 1 oz. 90
　(*Ralston* 40% Bran Flakes), 1 oz. = 3/4 cup 90
　w/apples and cinnamon (*Fruit & Fibre*), 1 oz. 90
　w/dates, raisins and walnuts
　　(*Fruit & Fibre*), 1 oz. 90
　w/fruit (*Kellogg's Fruitful Bran*), 3/4 cup 110
　w/oats
　　(*Kellogg's Cracklin' Oat Bran*), 1 oz. = 1/2 cup 120
　w/raisins
　　(*Kellogg's* Raisin Bran), 1.3 oz. = 3/4 cup 110
　w/raisins (*Post* Honey Nut Crunch), 1 oz. 90
　w/raisins (*Post* Raisin Bran), 1 oz. 90
　w/raisins (*Ralston* Raisin Bran), 1 oz. = 3/4 cup 120
corn:
　(*Cocoa Puffs*), 1 oz. = 1 cup 110
　(*Corn Chex*), 1 oz. = 1 cup 110
　(*Corn Total*), 1 oz. = 1 cup 110
　(*Country Corn Flakes*), 1 oz. = 1 cup 110
　(*Kellogg's Banana Frosted Flakes*),
　　　1 oz. = 2/3 cup 110
　(*Kellogg's Corn Flakes*), 1 oz. = 1 cup 110
　(*Kellogg's Honey & Nut Corn Flakes*),
　1 oz. = 3/4 cup 110
　(*Kellogg's Sugar Frosted Flakes*), 1 oz. = 3/4 cup 110
　(*Kix*), 1 oz. = 1 1/2 cups 110
　(*Nutri•Grain*), 1 oz. = 1/2 cup 110

Cereals, Ready-to-Eat, corn, continued

(*Post* Honeycomb), 1 oz. 110
(*Post Toasties* Corn Flakes), 1 oz. 110
(*Ralston* Corn Flakes), 1 oz. = 1 cup 110
(*Ralston* Sugar Frosted Flakes), 1 oz. = ¾ cup 110
(*Sugar Corn Pops*), 1 oz. = 1 cup 110
(*Trix*), 1 oz. = 1 cup 110
brown sugar and honey flavor
  (*Body Buddies*), 1 oz. = 1 cup 110
chocolate chip flavor
  (*Cookie Crisp*), 1 oz. = 1 cup 110
fruit flavor, natural
  (*Body Buddies*), 1 oz. = 1 cup 110
strawberry flavor
  (*Post* Strawberry Honeycomb), 1 oz. 120
vanilla wafer flavor
  (*Cookie Crisp*), 1 oz. = 1 cup 110
corn bran, *see "bran and high-fiber," above*
granola and "natural" cereals:
  (*Heartland*), 1 oz. = ¼ cup 130
  (*C. W. Post* Hearty), 1 oz. 130
  (*Quaker* 100% Natural), 1 oz. = ¼ cup 138
w/apple and cinnamon
  (*Quaker* 100% Natural), 1 oz. = ¼ cup 135
w/blueberries, freeze-dried
  (*Mountain House*), 2 oz. 290
w/cinnamon and raisins
  (*Nature Valley*), 1 oz. = ⅓ cup 130
w/coconut (*Heartland*), 1 oz. = ¼ cup 130
w/coconut and honey
  (*Nature Valley*), 1 oz. = ⅓ cup 150
w/fruit and nuts
  (*Nature Valley*), 1 oz. = ⅓ cup 130
w/raisins (*C. W. Post* Hearty), 1 oz. 120
w/raisins (*Heartland*), 1 oz. = ¼ cup 130
w/raisins and dates
  (*Quaker* 100% Natural), 1 oz. = ¼ cup 134
w/raisins and milk, freeze-dried
  (*Mountain House*), 2 oz. 280
toasted oat mixture
  (*Nature Valley*), 1 oz. = ⅓ cup 130
granola bars, *see "Breakfast Bars & Beverages," page 32*

Cereals, Ready-to-Eat, continued

granola snacks,
  see "Granola & Similar Snacks," page 282
oats:
  (*Alpha-Bits*), 1 oz. 110
  (*Cheerios*), 1 oz. = 1¼ cups 110
  (Cinnamon *Life*), 1 oz. = ⅔ cup 105
  (*Froot Loops*), 1 oz. = 1 cup 110
  (*Honey-Nut Cheerios*), 1 oz. = ¾ cup 110
  (*Life*), ⅔ cup 105
  (*Lucky Charms*), 1 oz. = 1 cup 110
  (*Post* Fortified Oat Flakes), 1 oz. 100
rice:
  (*Cocoa Krispies*), 1 oz. = ¾ cup 110
  (*Featherweight* Crisp Rice), 1 oz. = 1 cup 110
  (*Kellogg's Frosted Krispies*), 1 oz. = ¾ cup 110
  (*Kellogg's* Frosted Rice), 1 oz. = 1 cup 110
  (*Kellogg's Marshmallow Krispies*),
    1.3 oz. = 1¼ cups 140
  (*Kellogg's Strawberry Krispies*), 1 oz. = ¾ cup 110
  (*Malt-O-Meal* Puffed Rice), 1 oz. = 2 cups 100
  (*Quaker* Puffed Rice), 1 oz. = 2 cups 110
  (*Ralston* Crispy Rice), 1 oz. = 1 cup 110
  (*Rice Chex*), 1 oz. = 1⅛ cup 110
  (*Rice Krinkles*), 1 oz. = ⅞ cup 110
  (*Rice Krispies*), 1 oz. = 1 cup 110
  (*Van Brode* Cocoa Rice), 1 oz. = ¾ cup 110
  (*Van Brode* Crisp Rice), 1 oz. = 1 cup 110
  (*Van Brode* Crisp Rice—Low Sodium),
    1 oz. = 1 cup 110
  (*Van Brode* Sugar Frosted Rice),
    1 oz. = ¾ cup 110
wheat:
  (*Buc Wheats*), 1 oz. = ¾ cup 110
  (*Crispy Wheats 'N Raisins*), 1 oz. = ¾ cup 110
  (*Frosted Mini Wheats* w/apple flavor),
    1 oz. = 4 biscuits 110
  (*Frosted Mini Wheats* w/sugar),
    1 oz. = 4 biscuits 110
  (*Honey Smacks*), 1 oz. = ¾ cup 110
  (*Malt-O-Meal* Puffed Wheat), 1 oz. = 2 cups 100
  (*Nabisco* Shredded Wheat), ⅚-oz. biscuit 90

Cereals, Ready-to-Eat, wheat, continued

(*Nabisco Spoon Size* Shredded Wheat),
   1 oz. = $2/3$ cup 110

(*Nutri•Grain*), 1 oz. = $2/3$ cup 110

(*Pep*), 1 oz. = $3/4$ cup 110

(*Quaker* Puffed Wheat), 1 oz. = 2 cups 108

(*Quaker* Shredded Wheat), 1.3 oz. = 2 biscuits 104

(*Sunshine* Shredded Wheat), 1 biscuit** 85

(Super *Sugar Crisp* Wheat Puffs),
   1 oz. = $7/8$ cup 110

(*Toasted Mini-Wheats*), 1 oz. = 5 biscuits 110

(*Total*), 1 oz. = 1 cup 110

(*Van Brode* Wheat Flakes), 1 oz. = $3/4$ cup 110

(*Wheat Chex*), 1 oz. = $2/3$ cup 100

(*Wheaties*), 1 oz. = 1 cup 110

w/raisins (*Nutri•Grain*), 1.4 oz. = $2/3$ cup 140

w/raisins (*Wheat & Raisin Chex*),
   $1 1/3$ oz. = $3/4$ cup 130

wheat bran, *see "bran and high fiber," above*

wheat germ (*Kretschmer*), 1 oz. = $1/4$ cup 123

wheat germ, w/sugar and honey
   (*Kretschmer*), 1 oz. = $1/4$ cup 123

miscellaneous mixed grains:

(*Apple Jacks*), 1 oz. = 1 cup 110

(*Cap'n Crunch*), 1 oz. = $3/4$ cup 121

(*Cap'n Crunch* Crunchberries), 1 oz. = $3/4$ cup 120

(*Cap'n Crunch* Peanut Butter),
   1 oz. = $3/4$ cup 127

(*Concentrate*), 1 oz. = $1/3$ cup 110

(*Count Chocula*), 1 oz. = 1 cup 110

(*Franken Berry*), 1 oz. = 1 cup 110

(*Grape-Nuts*), 1 oz. 100

(*Grape-Nuts* Flakes), 1 oz. 100

(*Kellogg's C-3PO's*), 1 oz. = $3/4$ cup 110

(*Kellogg's Crispix*), 1 oz. = $3/4$ cup 110

(*King Vitaman*), 1 oz. = $1 1/4$ cups 113

(*Product 19*), 1 oz. = $3/4$ cup 110

(*Quisp*), 1 oz. = $1 1/6$ cups 121

(*Raisins, Rice & Rye*), 1.3 oz. = $3/4$ cup 140

(*Ralston Fruit Rings*), 1 oz. = 1 cup 110

(*Special K*), 1 oz. = 1 cup 110

(*Tasteeos*), 1 oz. = $1 1/4$ cups 110

Cereals, Ready-to-Eat, miscellaneous mixed grains, continued
　(*Team Flakes*), 1 oz. = 1 cup 110

　*Note the variance in cup measurements
**As packaged

BREAKFAST BARS & BEVERAGES

　　　　　　　　　　　　　　　　　　　　　　　calories
bars, clusters and squares:
　(*Nature Valley* Breakfast Squares), 2 bars* 380
　almond (*Nature Valley* Granola Bars), 1 bar* 120
　almond (*Nature Valley* Granola Cluster), 1 roll* 150
　almond crunch
　　(*Carnation* Breakfast Bar), 1.44-oz. bar 200
　apple
　　(*Nature Valley* Granola & Fruit Bars), 1 bar* 150
　apple (*Nature Valley* Granola Bars), 1 bar* 130
　apple cinnamon
　　(*Nature Valley* Granola Cluster), 1 roll* 150
　caramel (*Nature Valley* Granola Cluster), 1 roll* 150
　cherry
　　(*Nature Valley* Granola & Fruit Bars), 1 bar* 150
　chocolate
　　(*Nature Valley* Granola Cluster), 1 roll* 140
　chocolate chip
　　(*Carnation* Breakfast Bar), 1.49-oz. bar 200
　chocolate chip
　　(*Hershey's New Trail* Granola Bars), 1 bar* 200
　chocolate chip
　　(*Nature Valley* Chewy Granola Bars), 1 bar* 150
　chocolate chip
　　(*Nature Valley* Granola Cluster), 1 roll* 160
　chocolate chip, chocolate-dipped
　　(*Quaker Granola Dipps*), 1-oz. bar 140
　chocolate crunch
　　(*Carnation* Breakfast Bar), 1.49-oz. bar 200
　cinnamon (*Nature Valley* Granola Bars), 1 bar* 110
　coconut (*Nature Valley* Granola Bars), 1 bar* 120

Breakfast Bars & Beverages, bars, clusters and squares, continued

date
 (*Nature Valley* Granola & Fruit Bars), 1 bar* 150
honey and oats, chocolate-dipped
 (*Quaker Granola Dipps*), 1-oz. bar 140
oats and honey
 (*Nature Valley* Granola Bars), 1 bar* 110
peanut (*Nature Valley* Granola Bars), 1 bar* 120
peanut butter
 (*Hershey's New Trail* Granola Bars), 1 bar* 200
peanut butter
 (*Nature Valley* Granola Bars), 1 bar* 120
peanut butter
 (*Nature Valley* Chewy Granola Bars), 1 bar* 140
peanut butter crunch
 (*Carnation* Breakfast Bar), 1.51-oz. bar 210
peanut butter and chocolate chips
 (*Crunchola*), 1 bar* 160
raisin
 (*Nature Valley* Chewy Granola Bars), 1 bar* 130
raisin (*Nature Valley* Granola Cluster), 1 roll* 150
raisin and almond, chocolate-dipped
 (*Quaker Granola Dipps*), 1-oz. bar 140
raspberry
 (*Nature Valley* Granola and Fruit Bars), 1 bar* ... 150
rocky road, chocolate-dipped
 (*Quaker Granola Dipps*), 1-oz. bar 130
yogurt and granola, orange (*Crunchola*), 1 bar* 140
yogurt and granola, strawberry
 (*Crunchola*), 1 bar* 140
cereal beverage (Instant *Postum*), 6 fl. oz. 12
cereal beverage, coffee flavor
 (Instant *Postum*), 6 fl. oz. 12
drinks, breakfast, *see "Flavored Milk Beverages," page 57*

*As packaged

Chapter 2

BREADSTUFFS, CRACKERS AND FLOUR PRODUCTS

BREAD, one slice, as packaged*, except as noted
See also "Bread, Mixes," "Sweet Bread, Mixes,"
"Rolls, Biscuits & Muffins" and "Breadsticks"

---

	calories
apple, w/cinnamon (*Pepperidge Farm*)	70
bran and high fiber:	
(*Arnold Bran'nola*)	90
(*Brownberry* Whole Bran)	75
(*Monk's* Hi-Fibre)	50
(*Oroweat Bran'nola*)	93
(*Pepperidge Farm* Honey Bran)	95
brown, canned (*B & M*), 1/2" slice	80
brown, w/raisins, canned (*B & M*), 1/2" slice	80
cinnamon (*Pepperidge Farm*)	80
corn and molasses (*Pepperidge Farm* Thin Sliced)	70
cornbread, see "Sweet Bread, Mixes," page 39	
cracked wheat, see "wheat, cracked," below	
date-nut (*Dromedary*), 1-oz. slice	80
date-nut (*Thomas'*)	90
date-walnut (*Pepperidge Farm*)	75
French:	
(*Francisco*—unsliced), 1-oz. slice	80
(*Pepperidge Farm*), 1-oz. slice	75
(*Pepperidge Farm* Brown & Serve), 1-oz. slice	70
(*Pepperidge Farm* Twin), 1-oz. slice	70
gluten (*Oroweat*)	70

Bread, continued

(*Hillbilly*) 70
Italian
  (*Pepperidge Farm* Brown & Serve), 1-oz. slice 75
multi-grain (*Pepperidge Farm* Very Thin) 40
oat (*Arnold Bran'nola* Country Oat) 110
oatmeal:
  (*Brownberry*) 80
  (*Northridge*) 70
  (*Pepperidge Farm*) 70
  (*Pepperidge Farm* Thin) 70
onion (*Pepperidge Farm* Party), 2 small slices 30
pita or pocket bread, *see "Rolls, Biscuits & Muffins,"*
  page 42
pumpernickel:
  (*Arnold*) 75
  (*Brownberry* Sandwich Dark Bread) 75
  (*Levy*) 85
  (*Oroweat* Bavarian Pumpernickel) 69
  (*Oroweat* Bohemian Pumpernickel) 100
  (*Pepperidge Farm* Family) 80
  (*Pepperidge Farm* Party Pumpernickel),
    2 small slices 35
protein (*Thomas' Protogen*) 47
raisin:
  (*Arnold*) 75
  (*Brownberry* Raisin Cinnamon) 85
  (*Brownberry* Raisin Nut) 95
  (*Monk's*) 70
  (*Northridge* Royal Raisin Nut) 85
  (*Oroweat* Raisin Nugget) 85
  (*Pepperidge Farm*) 75
  (*Thomas'* Cinnamon Raisin Loaf) 60
(*Roman Meal*) 70
rye:
  (*Arnold*) 75
  (*Arnold* Seeded Dill) 75
  (*Arnold* Melba Thin) 50
  (*Arnold* Seeded Rye) 75
  (*Brownberry* Extra Thin) 65
  (*Grossinger's*) 70
  (*Levy*) 80

Bread, rye, continued

(*Levy* Seeded)	80
(*Oroweat* Buffet Rye), 2 small slices	50
(*Oroweat* Dark Rye)	65
(*Oroweat* Dill Rye)	70
(*Oroweat* Hearth Rye)	61
(*Oroweat* Russian Rye)	70
(*Oroweat* Swedish Rye)	51
(*Pepperidge Farm* Family Rye)	85
(*Pepperidge Farm* Jewish Rye)	90
(*Pepperidge Farm* Mustard Rye)	55
(*Pepperidge Farm* Party Rye), 2 small slices	30
(*Pepperidge Farm* Sandwich—1½ lb.)	95
(*Pepperidge Farm* Seedless Rye)	80
(*Pepperidge Farm* Very Thin)	45
(*Weight Watchers* Soft Light)	40
(*Wonder* hearty/mild)	75
rye and wheat (*Monk's*)	60
sourdough (*Di Carlo*)	70
wheat:	
(*Arnold* Sprouted Wheat)	65
(*Arnold* Bran'nola Hearty Wheat)	105
(*Brownberry* Health Nut)	85
(*Brownberry* Natural Wheat)	85
(*Brownberry* Great Grains)	70
(*Fresh Horizons*)	50
(*Fresh & Natural*)	70
(*Home Pride* Butter Top)	75
(*Home Pride* Honey Wheat)	70
(*Home Pride* Honey Wheatberry)	70
(*Northridge*)	70
(*Northridge* Thin Sliced)	45
(*Oroweat* American Granary)	70
(*Oroweat* Honey Wheat Berry)	85
(*Oroweat* Low-Sodium)	70
(*Oroweat* Soya)	67
(*Oroweat* Sprouted Wheat)	65
(*Oroweat* Thin Sliced)	45
(*Oroweat* Wheat Nuggets)	79
(*Pepperidge Farm* Family—2 lb.)	70
(*Pepperidge Farm* Honey Wheatberry)	70
(*Pepperidge Farm* Sandwich)	55

Bread, wheat, continued

    (*Pepperidge Farm* Sprouted Wheat) 70
    (*Pepperidge Farm* Wheat—1½ lb.) 95
    (*Pepperidge Farm* Wheat Germ—Thin Sliced) 65
    (*Taystee*) 80
    (*Wonder* Family Wheat) 75
wheat, bran, *see "bran and high fiber," above*
wheat, cracked:
    (*Northridge*) 70
    (*Pepperidge Farm* Thin Sliced) 70
    (*Taystee*) 80
    (*Weight Watchers* Wholesome) 40
    (*Wonder*) 75
wheat, whole:
    (*Arnold* Brick Oven) 80
    (*Arnold* Brick Oven—16 oz.) 60
    (*Arnold* Brick Oven Small Family) 60
    (*Arnold* Measure Up) 40
    (*Arnold* Stoneground 100%) 55
    (*Home Pride* 100%) 70
    (*Monk's* Stone Ground) 70
    (*Oroweat* 100%) 94
    (*Northridge* 100%) 70
    (*Pepperidge Farm* Thin Sliced) 65
    (*Pepperidge Farm* Very Thin) 45
    (*Thomas'*) 50
    (*Wonder* 100%) 70
white:
    (*Arnold Bran'nola* Old Style) 105
    (*Arnold* Brick Oven White—1 lb.) 65
    (*Arnold* Brick Oven White—2 lb.) 85
    (*Arnold* Country White) 95
    (*Arnold* Hearthstone White—2 lb.) 85
    (*Arnold* Measure Up) 40
    (*Arnold* Small Family White) 65
    (*Brownberry* Extra Thin) 70
    (*Brownberry* Sandwich) 75
    (*D'Agostino*) 75
    (*Fresh Horizons*) 50
    (*Home Pride* Butter Top) 75
    (*Monk's*) 60
    (*Northridge*) 70

Bread, white, continued

    (*Northridge* Honey Egg) 70
    (*Northridge* Low Sodium) 70
    (*Northridge* Soya Nut) 67
    (*Northridge* Thin) 45
    (*Oroweat* Old Style) 75
    (*Pepperidge Farm* — 1½ lb.) 95
    (*Pepperidge Farm* Large Family White—
      Thin Sliced) 75
    (*Pepperidge Farm* Sandwich) 65
    (*Pepperidge Farm* Thin Sliced) 75
    (*Pepperidge Farm* Toasting) 85
    (*Pepperidge Farm* Very Thin) 45
    (*Taystee*) 75
    (*Taystee* Low Sodium) 75
    (*Weight Watchers* Old Fashioned) 40
    (*Wonder*) 70
    (*Wonder* Low Sodium) 70
    w/buttermilk (*Wonder*) 75
    w/cracked wheat (*Pepperidge Farm* — 1½ lb.) 95
Vienna bread (*Francisco*) 80
Vienna bread (*Pepperidge Farm* Thick Sliced) 75

*Be careful about comparing the calories in brands of presliced bread. Bread is packaged in different size slices and, to be accurate, you must be sure you're comparing slices of the same size. (See "What You Should Know About Using This Book," pages 13-17)

BREAD, MIXES*
See also "Bread" and "Sweet Bread, Mixes"

---

                                            calories
rye (*Pillsbury Poppin' Fresh*), ½" slice 110
wheat (*Pillsbury Poppin' Fresh*), ½" slice 110
white (*Pillsbury Poppin' Fresh*), ½" slice 110

*Prepared according to package directions

SWEET BREAD, MIXES*
See also "Bread," "Bread, Mixes"
and "Rolls, Biscuits & Muffins"

calories

applesauce spice (*Pillsbury*), 1/12 of loaf	150
apricot nut (*Pillsbury*), 1/12 of loaf	160
banana (*Pillsbury*), 1/12 of loaf	150
blueberry nut (*Pillsbury*), 1/12 of loaf	150
carrot nut (*Pillsbury*), 1/12 of loaf	150
cherry nut (*Pillsbury*), 1/12 of loaf	170
cornbread:	
(*Ballard*), 1/8 of cornbread	140
(*Dromedary*), 2" × 2" square	130
(*Martha White Mexican*), 1/4 of pkg.	220
cranberry (*Pillsbury*), 1/12 of loaf	160
date (*Pillsbury*), 1/12 of loaf	160
nut (*Pillsbury*), 1/12 of loaf	160

Prepared according to package directions

ROLLS, BISCUITS & MUFFINS, one piece*,
except as noted
See also "Bread" and "Cakes, Cookies, Pies & Pastries"

calories

bagels, frozen:	
plain (*Lender's*)	150
egg (*Lender's*)	160
garlic (*Lender's*)	160
onion (*Lender's*)	160
pizza, see "Pizza, Frozen," page 180	
poppy seed (*Lender's*)	160
pumpernickel (*Lender's*)	160
raisin (*Lender's* Raisin 'n Honey)	200
rye (*Lender's*)	150

Rolls, Biscuits & Muffins, bagels, frozen, continued
  sesame seed (*Lender's*) 160
  wheat and raisin (*Lender's*) 190
biscuits (*Wonder*) 100
biscuits, mix** (*Bisquick*), 2 oz. or ½ cup 240
biscuits, refrigerated:
  (*Ballard Oven Ready*) 50
  (*1869 Brand* Baking Powder) 100
  (*1869 Brand Butter Tastin'*) 100
  (*Hungry Jack Butter Tastin'* Flaky) 90
  (*Hungry Jack* Flaky) 85
  (*Pillsbury* Country Style) 50
  (*Pillsbury Tenderflake*
    Baking Powder Dinner Biscuits) 55
  butter (*Pillsbury*) 50
  butter (*Pillsbury Big Country*) 95
  butter (*Pillsbury* Good 'N Buttery) 95
  buttermilk (*Ballard Oven Ready*) 50
  buttermilk (*1869 Brand*) 100
  buttermilk (*Hungry Jack* Extra Rich) 55
  buttermilk (*Hungry Jack* Flaky) 85
  buttermilk (*Hungry Jack* Fluffy) 90
  buttermilk (*Pillsbury*) 50
  buttermilk (*Pillsbury Big Country*) 100
  buttermilk (*Pillsbury Extra Lights*) 55
  buttermilk
    (*Pillsbury Tenderflake* Dinner Biscuits) 55
  buttermilk, bake and serve
    (*Pillsbury* Big Premium) 140
  buttermilk, bake and serve
    (*Pillsbury* Heat 'N Eat) 85
  buttermilk, bake and serve (*Weight Watchers*) 40
  wheat, bake and serve (*Weight Watchers*) 40
buns, *see "rolls," below*
croissants:
  almond (*Pepperidge Farm*) 210
  apple filled (*Sara Lee*) 240
  butter (*Pepperidge Farm*) 240
  butter (*Pepperidge Farm*—tray) 200
  butter (*Sara Lee*) 170
  butter, small (*Pepperidge Farm* Petite) 130
  cheese (*Sara Lee*) 170

Rolls, Biscuits & Muffins, croissants, continued

 chocolate (*Pepperidge Farm*) 260
 chocolate filled (*Sara Lee*) 290
 cinnamon (*Pepperidge Farm*) 210
 cinnamon-nut-raisin filled (*Sara Lee*) 340
 raisin (*Pepperidge Farm*) 200
 strawberry filled (*Sara Lee*) 240
 walnut (*Pepperidge Farm*) 210
 wheat and honey (*Sara Lee*) 170
muffins:
 (*Arnold* Extra Crisp) 150
 blueberry (*Howard Johnson's Toastee*) 121
 blueberry (*Thomas' Toast-r-Cakes*) 110
 bran (*Arnold Bran'nola*) 160
 bran (*Thomas' Toast-r-Cakes*) 110
 corn (*Howard Johnson's Toastee*) 112
 corn (*Thomas' Toast-r-Cakes*) 120
 English (*Monk's*) 130
 English (*Pepperidge Farm*) 130
 English (*Thomas'*) 130
 English (*Wonder*) 130
 English, apple granola (*Oroweat*) 180
 English, bacon and cheese (*Pepperidge Farm*) 140
 English, cinnamon apple (*Pepperidge Farm*) 140
 English, cinnamon chip (*Pepperidge Farm*) 160
 English, cinnamon-raisin (*Pepperidge Farm*) 150
 English, extra sour (*Oroweat*) 150
 English, high-fiber (*Monk's*) 130
 English, honey-butter (*Oroweat*) 151
 English, honey-wheat
  (*Oroweat* Honey Wheat Berry 152
 English, honey-wheat (*Thomas'*) 129
 English, raisin (*Oroweat*) 163
 English, raisin (*Thomas'*) 153
 English, sourdough (*Oroweat*) 143
 English, sourdough (*Pepperidge Farm*) 140
 English, wheat, stone ground (*Pepperidge Farm*) 130
 oatmeal (*Howard Johnson's Toastee*) 95
 orange (*Howard Johnson's Toastee*) 127
 raisin (*Arnold*) 170
 raisin (*Wonder* Raisin Rounds) 150
 raisin bran (*Howard Johnson's Toastee*) 104

muffins, continued

sourdough (*Wonder*)	130

muffins, mix**:

apple, spicy (*Duncan Hines*), 1 muffin	120
apple cinnamon	
(*Betty Crocker*), 1/12 of pkg.	100
banana nut (*Duncan Hines*), 1 muffin	130
blueberry, wild (*Betty Crocker*), 1/12 of pkg.	100
blueberry, wild (*Duncan Hines*), 1 muffin	110
bran (*Duncan Hines*), 1 muffin	110
bran (*Martha White*), 1 large muffin	165
bran (*Martha White*), 1 medium muffin	110
cherry, tart (*Betty Crocker*), 1/12 of pkg.	100
corn (*Betty Crocker*), 1/12 of pkg.	140
corn (*Dromedary*)	130
corn (*Flako*)	140
corn (*Martha White*), 2-oz. muffin	135
fruit (*Martha White*), 1/6 of pkg.	150
pita or pocket bread, mini (*Sahara*)	80
pita or pocket bread, wheat, mini (*Sahara*)	75
popover, mix** (*Flako*)	170

rolls:

brown and serve (*Wonder* Half & Half)	80
brown and serve (*Wonder* Home Bake)	85
brown and serve (*Taystee*)	83
buttermilk, brown and serve (*Wonder*)	85
club (*Pepperidge Farm*)	120
club, brown and serve (*Pepperidge Farm*)	100
crescent, heat and serve	
(*Pepperidge Farm* Butter Crescent)	130
crescent, refrigerator (*Ballard*)	95
crescent, refrigerator (*Pillsbury*)	100
deli style (*Pepperidge Farm*)	180
dinner (*Arnold* Party Rounds)	55
dinner (*Home Pride*)	90
dinner (*Pepperidge Farm*)	60
dinner (*Pepperidge Farm* Old Fashioned)	50
dinner (*Pepperidge Farm* Party Rolls)	20
dinner (*Wonder*)	85
dinner, w/poppy seeds (*Pepperidge Farm* Party)	45
dinner, brown and serve	
(*Pepperidge Farm* Hearth)	50

rolls, continued

dinner, heat and serve
  (*Pepperidge Farm* Golden Twist) 110
dinner, refrigerator (*Butterflake*) 110
finger, w/poppy seeds (*Pepperidge Farm*) 60
finger, w/sesame seeds (*Pepperidge Farm*) 60
frankfurter or hot dog (*Arnold*) 110
frankfurter or hot dog (*Pepperidge Farm*) 140
frankfurter or hot dog (*Taystee*) 120
frankfurter or hot dog (*Wonder*) 120
frankfurter wrap, refrigerator
  (*Pillsbury* Weiner Wrap) 60
frankfurter wrap, cheese, refrigerator
  (*Pillsbury* Weiner Wrap) 60
French (*Pepperidge Farm* — 4 pack) 240
French (*Pepperidge Farm* — 9 pack) 110
French, sourdough (*Pepperidge Farm*) 100
French, brown and serve (*Francisco*) 90
French, brown and serve
  (*Pepperidge Farm* — large), ½ roll 180
French, brown and serve
  (*Pepperidge Farm* — small), ½ roll 120
French, brown and serve (*Wonder*) 75
gem style, brown and serve (*Wonder*) 85
hamburger (*Arnold*) 110
hamburger (*Pepperidge Farm*) 130
hamburger (*Taystee*) 120
hamburger (*Wonder*) 120
kaiser and hoagie (*Wonder*), ½ roll 230
pan roll (*Wonder*) 100
parkerhouse (*Pepperidge Farm*) 50
parkerhouse (*Pillsbury*) 75
sandwich (*Francisco*) 160
sandwich, cracked wheat (*Pepperidge Farm*) 150
sandwich, Dutch egg (*Arnold*) 130
sandwich, mustard bran (*Pepperidge Farm*) 160
sandwich, onion, w/poppy seeds
  (*Pepperidge Farm*) 150
sandwich, poppy seed (*Pepperidge Farm*) 130
sandwich, sesame seed (*Pepperidge Farm*) 132
sandwich, soft (*Arnold*) 110
sandwich, soft, poppy seed (*Arnold*) 110

rolls, continued

sandwich, soft, sesame seed (*Arnold*) 110
sandwich, wheat (*Oroweat*) 200
sourdough French (*Francisco*) 90
sourdough French, brown and serve (*Francisco*) 90
variety (*Francisco*) 100
wheat (*Pillsbury Pipin' Hot* Loaf), 1" slice 80
white (*Pillsbury Pipin' Hot* Loaf), 1" slice 80
rolls, mix** (*Pillsbury* Hot Rolls) 100

As packaged—note variation in sizes
**Prepared according to package directions*

BREADSTICKS, one piece*, except as noted

---

	calories
plain (*Pepperidge Farm* Snack Sticks)	16
plain (*Stella D'Oro*)	40
plain (*Stella D'Oro* Dietetic—salt free)	43
plain, soft, refrigerator (*Pillsbury Pipin' Hot*)	100
cheese (*Pepperidge Farm* Snack Sticks)	18
onion (*Stella D'Oro*)	40
pumpernickel (*Pepperidge Farm* Snack Sticks)	16
rye (*Pepperidge Farm* Snack Sticks)	16
sesame:	
(*Pepperidge Farm* Snack Sticks)	16
(*Stella D'Oro*)	52
(*Stella D'Oro* Dietetic—salt free)	57
cheese (*Twigs* Snack Sticks)	14
whole wheat (*Stella D'Oro*)	40

As packaged—note variation in sizes

CROUTONS, ¼ cup, except as noted
See also "Crumbs & Meal"
and "Stuffing & Stuffing Mixes"

calories

plain:
   (*Bel-Air*) 30
   (*Brownberry* "Buttery" Toasted) 45
bacon (*Bel-Air*) 40
bacon and cheese (*Pepperidge Farm*), ⅓ oz.* 47
Caesar salad (*Brownberry*) 45
cheese:
   (*Brownberry*) 45
   bleu (*Pepperidge Farm*), ⅓ oz.* 47
   cheddar and Romano
     (*Pepperidge Farm*), ⅓ oz.* 40
   Italian (*Bel-Air*) 50
cheese-garlic (*Bel-Air*) 50
cheese-garlic (*Pepperidge Farm*), ⅓ oz.* 47
Dijon mustard rye and cheese
   (*Pepperidge Farm*), 1.3 oz.* 47
garlic (*Bel-Air*) 40
herb-seasoned (*Croutettes*), .7 oz.** 70
onion-garlic (*Brownberry*) 45
onion-garlic (*Pepperidge Farm*), ⅓ oz.* 47
seasoned:
   (*Bel-Air*) 45
   (*Brownberry*) 45
   (*Pepperidge Farm*), ⅓ oz.* 47
sour cream and chive (*Pepperidge Farm*), ⅓ oz.* 47

  *Approximately ¼ cup
**Approximately ½ cup

CRUMBS & MEAL, one ounce, except as noted
See also "Croutons" and "Stuffing & Stuffing Mixes"

          calories

breadcrumbs:
  (*Colonna*), 2 tbsp. 29
  (*Pepperidge Farm*) 110
  (*Wonder*) 108
  herb-seasoned (*Pepperidge Farm* Premium) 110
  seasoned (*Contadina*), 2 tbsp. 50
  toasted (*Old London*) 105
corn-flake crumbs (*Kellogg's*) 110
corn meal or grits,
  see "Cereals & Corn Products, Dry," page 24
cracker crumbs:
  (*Premium* Saltines) 120
  graham (*Keebler*) 122
  graham (*Sunshine*) 119
matzo meal (*Manischewitz*) 110

STUFFING & STUFFING MIXES
See also "Croutons" and "Crumbs & Meal"

          calories

stuffing, dry:
  chicken, pan style (*Pepperidge Farm*), 1 oz. 110
  cornbread (*Pepperidge Farm*), 1 oz. 110
  cube (*Pepperidge Farm*), 1 oz. 110
  herb (*Pepperidge Farm*), 1 oz. 110
  (*Pepperidge Farm*), 1 oz. 110
  seasoned, pan style (*Pepperidge Farm*), 1 oz. 110
stuffing mixes*:
  beef (*Stove Top*), 1/2 cup 180
  (*Bell's*—6-oz. pkg.), 1/2 cup 220
  (*Bell's*—16-oz. pkg.), 1/2 cup 233
  chicken (*Stove Top*), 1/2 cup 180

stuffing mixes, continued
   cornbread (*Stove Top*), ½ cup 170
   herb-seasoned (*Croutettes*), ½ cup 130
   pork (*Stove Top*), ½ cup 170
   (*Stove Top Americana* New England), ½ cup 180
   (*Stove Top Americana* San Francisco), ½ cup 170
   with rice (*Stove Top*), ½ cup 180

*Prepared according to package directions

SEASONED COATING MIXES,
one envelope, as packaged

---

                                             calories

for chicken:
   (*Shake 'n Bake*) 279
   barbecue style (*Shake 'n Bake*) 366
   crispy country mild (*Shake 'n Bake*) 318
   Italian flavor (*Shake 'n Bake*) 286
for fish (*Shake 'n Bake*) 226
for hamburger (*Shake 'n Bake*) 163
for pork (*Shake 'n Bake*) 260
for pork and ribs, barbecue style (*Shake 'n Bake*) 290

FLOUR, one cup, except as noted
See also "Cereals & Corn Products, Dry (Uncooked),"
"Yeast, Baker's" and "Baking Powder & Cornstarch"

---

                                             calories

all-purpose:
   (*Ballard*) 400
   (*Gold Medal*), 4 oz.* 400
   (*Pillsbury's Best*) 400
   (*White Deer*), 4 oz.* 400
   unbleached (*Pillsbury's Best*) 400
bread (*Pillsbury's Best*) 400
bread, high-protein
   (*Gold Medal Better For Bread*), 4 oz.* 400

Flour, continued

buckwheat (*Elam's* Pure), 4 oz.* 401
cake:
  (*Swans Down*) 400
  self-rising (*Presto*) 400
  self-rising (*Swans Down*) 360
(*Drifted Snow*), 4 oz.* 400
gluten (*Featherweight*) 420
(*King Midas*) 400
(*La Pina*), 4 oz.* 400
(*Red Band*), 4 oz.* 400
rye:
  medium (*Pillsbury's Best*) 400
  wheat (*Pillsbury's Best* Bohemian Style) 400
  whole (*Elam's* Stone Ground 100%), 4 oz.* 405
sauce and gravy (*Pillsbury's Best*), 2 tbsp. 50
self-rising:
  (*Aunt Jemima*) 436
  (*Ballard*) 380
  (*Gold Medal*), 4 oz.* 380
  (*Pillsbury's Best*) 380
  (*Red Band*), 4 oz.* 380
  unbleached (*Ballard*) 380
  unbleached (*Pillsbury's Best*) 380
(*Softasilk*), 4 oz.* 100
soybean (*Featherweight*) 470
unbleached:
  (*Gold Medal*), 4 oz.* 400
  (*Red Band*), 4 oz.* 400
  white, w/wheat germ (*Elam's*), 4 oz.* 414
whole wheat:
  (*Elam's* Stone Ground), 4 oz.* 416
  (*Gold Medal*), 4 oz.* 390
  (*Pillsbury's Best*) 400

*Approximately 1 cup

YEAST, BAKER'S

	calories
active, dry (*Fleischmann's*), ¼-oz. pkg.	20
active, fresh (*Fleischmann's*), 6-oz. pkg.	15
household (*Fleischmann's*), ½ oz.	15

BAKING POWDER & CORNSTARCH

	calories
baking powder (*Calumet*), 1 tsp.	2
baking powder (*Davis*), 1 tsp.	5
cornstarch (*Argo/Kingsford's*), 1 tbsp.	30

CRACKERS, one piece*, except as noted
See also "Chips, Puffs & Similar Snacks"

	calories
(*American Harvest*)	16
animal crackers, *see "Cookies," page 237*	
arrowroot, *see "Cookies," page 238*	
bacon flavor (*Nabisco* Bacon Thins)	10
bacon flavor (*Old London* Bacon Rounds)	12
butter flavor:	
(*Hi-Ho*)	19
(*Keebler* Club)	16
(*Pepperidge Farm* Thins)	20
(*Ritz*)	20
(*Tam-Tams*)	14
(*Sunshine* Banquet Wafers)	14
cheese-filled (*Frito-Lay's*), 1½-oz. pkg.	200
cheese-filled sandwich (*Cheez Waffles*), 1 oz.	140
cheese flavor:	
(*Cheese Nips*)	6
(*Cheez-It*)	6

Crackers, cheese flavor, continued

(*Dixie Belle* Cheese Snacks)	6
(*Old London* Cheese Rounds)	12
(*Pepperidge Farm* Thins)	18
(*Ralston* Cheese Snacks)	6
(*Ritz*)	14
(*Tid Bit*)	4
Cheddar (*Better Cheddars*—thins)	6
Cheddar (*Dixie Belle* Cheddar Snacks)	7
Cheddar (*FFV* Cheddar Thins)	10
Cheddar (*Pepperidge Farm Goldfish*), ¼ oz.	35
Cheddar (*Pepperidge Farm Tiny Goldfish*)	3
Cheddar (*Ralston* Cheddar Snacks)	7
nacho and corn (*Nabisco* Thins)	9
Parmesan (*Pepperidge Farm Tiny Goldfish*)	3
and chive (*Dip In A Chip*)	9
and chive (*Dixie Belle* Cheese and Chive Snacks)	7
and chive (*Ralston* Cheese and Chive Snacks)	7
and ham (*FFV*)	14
cheese sandwich, peanut-butter filled (*Frito-Lay's*), 1.5 oz.	210
cheese sandwich, peanut-butter filled (*Kraft Handi-Snacks*), 1 pkg.	190
(*Chicken In A Biskit*)	10
(*Dixie Belle* Crackers—unsalted tops)	12
(*Dixie Belle* Rich & Crisp)	16
(*Estee*—unsalted)	15
(*FFV* Appetizer Crackers)	14
garlic (*Manischewitz* Garlic *Tams*)	13
garlic (*Old London* Melba Rounds)	10
graham crackers, *see "Cookies," page* •••	
matzo: one sheet or piece:	
(*Manischewitz* American)	115
(*Manischewitz* Egg)	11
(*Manischewitz* Egg 'n Onion)	112
(*Manischewitz* Matzo Cracker)	9
(*Manischewitz* Matzo Thins)	91
(*Manischewitz* Miniatures)	9
(*Manischewitz* Passover Matzo)	129
(*Manischewitz* Passover Egg Matzo)	132
(*Manischewitz* Passover Thin Tea Matzo)	103

Crackers, wheat, continued

(*Keebler* Wheat Toast) 16
(*Manischewitz* Wheat Crackers) 9
(*Manischewitz* Wheat *Tams*) 13
(*Nabisco* Wheat Rounds) 15
(*Nabisco* Wheat Thins) 9
(*Pepperidge Farm* Hearty) 25
(*Pepperidge Farm* Thins) 15
(*Ralston* Snacks) 9
(*Ralston Snackers*) 18
(*Sunshine* Wheat Wafers) 9
(*Triscuit*) 20
cheese and garlic, toasted (*Hain*) 13
cracked (*Pepperidge Farm*) 28
w/onion (*Pepperidge Farm*) 20
onion (*Hain*) 12
pumpernickel (*Hain*) 13
and rye (*Hain*) 11
sesame (*Hain*) 13
sour cream and chive (*Hain*) 12
sourdough (*Hain*) 12
vegetable (*Hain*) 12
whole wheat (*Hain* Rich Crackers) 16
(*Wheatsworth*) 14
whole grain (*Old London* Melba Toast) 20
zweiback toast (*Nabisco*) 30

As packaged—note variation in sizes

Chapter 3

CREAM, MILK AND MILK BEVERAGES

> **MILK,** eight fluid ounces, except as noted
> *See also "Cream" and "Flavored Milk Beverages"*

	calories
buttermilk, .5% fat (*Meadow Gold*)	105
buttermilk, 1.5% fat (*Foremost*)	120
buttermilk, 1.5% fat (*Friendship*)	120
buttermilk, cultured (*Borden*)	90
condensed, canned:	
(*Borden Eagle Brand*), 1/2 cup	480
(*Borden Magnolia Brand*), 1/2 cup	480
dry nonfat, reconstituted* (*Carnation*)	80
evaporated, canned:	
(*Carnation*), 1/2 cup	170
(*Pet*), 1/2 cup	170
filled (*Jerzee*), 1/2 cup	150
low-fat (*Carnation*), 1/2 cup	110
skimmed (*Carnation*), 1/2 cup	100
skimmed (*Pet*), 1/2 cup	100
half and half, *see "Cream," page 55*	
skim or low-fat:	
(*Borden*)	90
(*Borden* Hi-Protein Brand)	140
(*Foremost Profile*)	86
(*Foremost So-Lo*)	140
(*Hood Nuform* Low-fat)	100
(*Hood Silouet* Skim)	80
(*Light n' Lively*)	110
(*Meadow Gold*)	87
(*Weight Watchers*)	90

Milk, skim or low-fat, continued
   fortified (*Borden Skim-Line*) 100
whole:
   (*Hood*) 150
   3.3% fat (*Foremost*) 150
   3.3% fat (*Meadow Gold*) 150
   3.5% fat (*Borden*) 150
   3.5% fat (*Foremost*) 160
   3.7% fat (*Sealtest*) 157

CREAM, one tablespoon
See also "Milk" and "Creamers, Non-Dairy"

---

calories

half and half:
   (*Hood*) 20
   10.5% fat (*Foremost*) 19
   10.5% fat (*Sealtest*) 19
   12% fat (*Meadow Gold*) 30
heavy, whipping*:
   (*Foremost*) 54
   (*Hood*) 50
   36% fat (*Meadow Gold*) 50
   36% fat (*Sealtest*) 52
light, table or coffee:
   (*Hood*) 30
   18% fat (*Sealtest*) 28
medium, whipping* (*Sealtest*) 44
sour, *see "Sour Cream," page 56*
whipped, *see "Dessert Toppings & Syrups," page 258*

Unwhipped (volume is approximately doubled when whipped)

SOUR CREAM, one tablespoon
See also "Cream"

calories

plain or regular:
   (*Foremost*) 29
   (*Hood*) 30
   (*Meadow Gold*) 29
   (*Sealtest*) 30
half and half (*Hood Nuform*) 20

CREAMERS, NON–DAIRY,
one tablespoon, except as noted
See also "Cream"

calories

dry form:
   (*Coffee-mate*) 30
   (*Coffee-mate*), 1 packet 16
   (*Cremora*) 36
liquid form:
   (*Coffee-mate*)* 13
   (*Coffee Rich*) 20
   (*Poly Rich*), 1 fl. oz. 43
   (*Sanna*) 24
   half and half (*Meadow Gold*) 27
whipped, *see "Dessert Toppings," page 258*

*Liquid reconstituted: 2 parts water and 1 part dry form

FLAVORED MILK BEVERAGES,
eight fluid ounces, except as noted
See also "Eggnog, Nonalcoholic" and
"Cocoa & Flavored Mixes, Dry"

---

	calories
banana, canned (*Sego* Very Banana), 10 fl.-oz. can	225
butterscotch, canned (*Slender*), 10 fl.-oz. can	225
chocolate:	
drink, 2% fat, dairy pack (*Meadow Gold*)	185
milk, dairy pack (*Sealtest*)	200
milk, 1% fat (*Borden* Dutch Brand)	160
milk, 3.3% fat, dairy pack (*Foremost*)	218
milk, 3.3% fat, dairy pack (*Meadow Gold*)	200
milk, low-fat, dairy pack (*Hood*)	150
canned (*Borden* Dutch Chocolate Drink)	210
canned (*Slender*), 10 fl.-oz. can	225
canned (*Sego*), 10 fl.-oz. can	225
canned (*Sego Lite*), 10 fl.-oz. can	150
canned (*Sego* Dutch and Very Chocolate), 10 fl.-oz. can	225
canned (*Sego Lite* Dutch Chocolate), 10 fl.-oz. can	150
mix* (*Carnation* Instant Breakfast)	280
mix* (*Milk Maker*)	140
mix* (*Pillsbury* Instant Breakfast)	290
mix* (*Slender*), 6 fl. oz.	225
chocolate fudge:	
canned (*Slender*), 10 fl.-oz. can	225
chocolate malt:	
canned (*Slender*), 10 fl.-oz. can	225
canned (*Sego* Very Chocolate), 10 fl.-oz. can	225
mix* (*Carnation* Instant Breakfast)	280
mix* (*Pillsbury* Instant Breakfast)	290
mix* (*Slender*), 6 fl. -oz.	225
chocolate marshmallow, canned (*Slender*), 10 fl.-oz. can	225
cocoa, *see* "Cocoa & Flavored Mixes, Dry," page 283	
coffee:	
mix* (*Carnation* Instant Breakfast)	280

Flavored Milk Beverages, coffee, continued

    mix* (*Slender*), 6 fl. oz. 225
strawberry:
    canned (*Sego* Very Strawberry), 10 fl.-oz. can 225
    mix* (*Carnation* Instant Breakfast) 280
    mix* (*Pillsbury* Instant Breakfast) 290
vanilla:
    canned (*Slender*), 10 fl.-oz. can 225
    canned (*Sego Lite*), 10 fl.-oz. can 150
    canned (*Sego* Very Vanilla), 10 fl.-oz. can 225
    mix* (*Carnation* Instant Breakfast) 280
    mix* (*Pillsbury* Instant Breakfast) 290
    mix* (*Slender*), 6 fl. -oz. 225

*Prepared according to package directions, with whole milk

EGGNOG, NONALCOHOLIC, four fluid ounces

---

                                           calories
dairy pack, 6% fat (*Foremost*) 206
dairy pack, 6% fat (*Meadow Gold*) 164
dairy pack, 6% fat (*Sealtest*) 174

Chapter 4

YOGURT

> **YOGURT,** one serving*
> See also "Frozen Yogurt"

	calories
plain:	
(*Borden Lite Line*), 8 oz.	180
(*Breyers*), 6 oz.	130
(*Colombo*), 8 oz.	150
(*Colombo Lite*), 8 oz.	110
(*Dannon*), 8 oz.	150
(*Friendship*), 8 oz.	170
(*Hood Nuform*), 8 oz.	140
(*Weight Watchers*), 8 fl. oz.	90
(*Yami*), 8 fl. oz.	140
(*Yoplait*), 6 oz.	130
apple:	
cinnamon (*Yoplait Breakfast Yogurt*), 6 oz.	240
crisp (*New Country*), 8 oz.	210
Dutch (*Dannon*), 8 oz.	260
Dutch (*Sweet 'N Low*), 8 oz.	150
spiced (*Colombo*), 8 oz.	240
spiced (*Hood* Swiss Style), 8 oz.	230
apricot (*Dannon*), 8 oz.	260
apricot (*Yami*), 8 fl. oz.	240
banana:	
(*Dannon*), 8 oz.	260
(*Sweet 'N Low*), 8 oz.	150
(*Yoplait Custard Style*), 6 oz.	190
banana-strawberry (*Colombo*), 8 oz.	235
berries (*Yoplait Breakfast Yogurt*), 6 oz.	230

Yogurt, continued

berries, mixed (*New Country*), 8 oz. 210
berries, mixed (*Yoplait*), 6 oz. 190
blackberry (*Yami*), 8 fl. oz. 240
blueberry:
    (*Breyers*), 6 oz. 210
    (*Colombo*), 8 oz. 250
    (*Dannon*), 8 oz. 260
    (*Friendship*), 8 oz. 230
    (*Hood* Swiss Style), 8 oz. 230
    (*Light n' Lively*), 5 oz. 150
    (*Light n' Lively*), 6 oz. 180
    (*Meadow Gold* Swiss Style), 8 oz. 245
    (*Meadow Gold* Western Style), 8 oz. 249
    (*Sweet 'N Low*), 8 oz. 150
    (*Weight Watchers*), 8 fl. oz. 150
    (*Yami*), 8 fl. oz. 240
    (*Yoplait*), 6 oz. 190
    (*Yoplait Custard Style*), 6 oz. 190
    supreme (*New Country*), 8 oz. 210
boysenberry:
    (*Dannon*), 8 oz. 260
    (*Meadow Gold* Swiss Style), 8 oz. 245
    (*Sweet 'N Low*), 8 oz. 150
    (*Yoplait*), 6 oz. 190
cherry:
    (*Dannon*), 8 oz. 260
    (*Friendship*), 8 oz. 230
    (*Hood* Swiss Style), 8 oz. 230
    (*Sweet 'N Low*), 8 oz. 150
    (*Yami*), 8 fl. oz. 240
    (*Yoplait*), 6 oz. 190
    black (*Breyers*), 6 oz. 210
    black (*Colombo*), 8 oz. 230
    black (*Light n' Lively*), 5 oz. 150
    black (*Light n' Lively*), 6 oz. 180
cherry-vanilla (*Borden* Natural), 8 oz. 270
cherry-vanilla (*Colombo*), 8 oz. 250
coffee:
    (*Colombo*), 8 oz. 200
    (*Dannon*), 8 oz. 200
    (*Friendship*), 8 oz. 210

Yogurt, coffee, continued

(*Yoplait Custard Style*), 6 oz. 180
fruit, citrus (*Yoplait Breakfast Yogurt*), 6 oz. 250
fruit crunch (*New Country*), 8 oz. 210
fruit, orchard (*Yoplait Breakfast Yogurt*), 6 oz. 240
fruit, tropical (*Sweet 'N Low*), 8 oz. 150
fruit, tropical (*Yoplait Breakfast Yogurt*), 6 oz. 250
granola-strawberry (*Colombo*), 8 oz. 240
Hawaiian salad (*New Country*), 8 oz. 210
w/honey (*Yoplait Custard Style*), 6 oz. 160
lemon:
  (*Borden* Natural), 8 oz. 320
  (*Colombo*), 8 oz. 220
  (*Dannon*), 8 oz. 200
  (*Hood* Swiss Style), 8 oz. 230
  (*Sweet 'N Low*), 8 oz. 150
  (*Yami*), 8 fl. oz. 240
  (*Yoplait*), 6 oz. 190
  (*Yoplait Custard Style*), 6 oz. 190
  supreme (*New Country*), 8 oz. 210
orange:
  (*Meadow Gold* Western Style), 8 oz. 249
  (*Yoplait*), 6 oz. 190
  Mandarin (*Yami*), 8 fl. oz. 240
  supreme (*New Country*), 8 oz. 210
peach:
  (*Breyers*), 6 oz. 210
  (*Dannon*), 8 oz. 260
  (*Friendship*), 8 oz. 230
  (*Hood* Swiss Style), 8 oz. 230
  (*Light n' Lively*), 5 oz. 150
  (*Light n' Lively*), 6 oz. 180
  (*Meadow Gold* Western Style), 8 oz. 249
  (*Sweet 'N Low*), 8 oz. 150
  (*Yoplait*), 6 oz. 190
  and cream (*New Country*), 8 oz. 210
  melba (*Colombo*), 8 oz. 230
piña colada:
  (*Colombo*), 8 oz. 240
  (*Dannon*), 8 oz. 260
  (*Friendship*), 8 oz. 230
  (*Yoplait*), 6 oz. 190

Yogurt, continued

pineapple:
  (*Borden* Natural), 8 oz. 260
  (*Breyers*), 6 oz. 190
  (*Light n' Lively*), 6 oz. 180
  (*Meadow Gold* Western Style), 8 oz. 249
  (*Yoplait*), 6 oz. 190
pineapple-orange (*Dannon*), 8 oz. 260
raspberry:
  (*Breyers* Red Raspberry), 6 oz. 210
  (*Colombo*), 8 oz. 250
  (*Dannon* Red Raspberry), 8 oz. 260
  (*Friendship*), 8 oz. 230
  (*Hood* Swiss Style), 8 oz. 230
  (*Light n' Lively* Red Raspberry), 5 oz. 140
  (*Light n' Lively* Red Raspberry), 6 oz. 170
  (*Meadow Gold* Swiss Style), 8 oz. 245
  (*Meadow Gold* Western Style), 8 oz. 249
  (*Sweet 'N Low*), 8 oz. 150
  (*Weight Watchers*), 8 fl. oz. 150
  (*Yoplait*), 6 oz. 190
  (*Yoplait Custard Style*), 6 oz. 190
  supreme (*New Country*), 8 oz. 210
strawberry:
  (*Borden* Natural), 8 oz. 230
  (*Breyers*), 6 oz. 210
  (*Colombo*), 8 oz. 230
  (*Dannon*), 8 oz. 260
  (*Friendship*), 8 oz. 230
  (*Light n' Lively*), 5 oz. 150
  (*Light n' Lively*), 6 oz. 180
  (*Meadow Gold* Swiss Style), 8 oz. 245
  (*Meadow Gold* Western Style), 8 oz. 249
  (*Sweet 'N Low*), 8 oz. 150
  (*Weight Watchers*), 8 fl. oz. 150
  (*Yami*), 8 fl. oz. 240
  (*Yoplait*), 6 oz. 190
  (*Yoplait Custard Style*), 6 oz. 190
  supreme (*New Country*), 8 oz. 210
strawberry-banana:
  (*Light n' Lively*), 5 oz. 160
  (*Light n' Lively*), 6 oz. 200

Yogurt, strawberry-banana, continued

(*Yoplait*), 6 oz. 190
strawberry fruit cup (*Light n' Lively*), 5 oz. 150
strawberry fruit cup (*Light n' Lively*), 6 oz. 180
strawberry-vanilla (*Colombo*), 8 oz. 260
strawberry-walnut (*Breyers*), 6 oz. 180
vanilla:
  (*Dannon*), 8 oz. 200
  (*Friendship*), 8 oz. 210
  (*Yoplait Custard Style*), 6 oz. 180
  bean (*Breyers*), 6 oz. 180
  French (*Colombo*), 8 oz. 210
  French (*New Country*), 8 oz. 210
vanilla-honey (*Colombo*), 8 oz. 220

*Note variations in sizes

FROZEN YOGURT, one serving*
See also "Yogurt & Yogurt Drinks"
and "Ice Cream & Frozen Confections"

---

                                             calories

banana (*Colombo*), 3½ oz. 130
blueberry (*Colombo*), 3½ oz. 130
blueberry (*Danny*), 8 oz. 210
boysenberry, bar, carob-coated
  (*Danny* Frozen Yogurt Bar), 2½ fl.-oz. bar 140
cherry (*Yami Pushups*), 3 fl. oz. 90
cherry vanilla (*Colombo*), 3½ oz. 130
chocolate:
  (*Colombo*), 3½ oz. 130
  (*Danny*), 8 oz. 190
  bar (*Danny* Frozen Yogurt Bar), 2½ fl.-oz. bar 60
  bar, chocolate coated
    (*Danny* Frozen Yogurt Bar), 2½-oz. bar 130
coffee (*Colombo*), 3½ oz. 130
honey almond (*Colombo*), 3½ oz. 130
lemon (*Colombo*), 3½ oz. 130
lemon-lime (*Yami Pushups*), 3 fl. oz. 90

Frozen Yogurt, continued

mint chocolate (*Colombo*), 3½ oz. 130
orange (*Yami Pushups*), 3 fl. oz. 90
peach (*Colombo*), 3½ oz. 130
peanut butter (*Colombo*), 3½ oz. 130
piña colada:
  (*Colombo*), 3½ oz. 130
  (*Danny*), 8 oz. 230
  (*Danny* Frozen Yogurt Bar), 2½ fl.-oz. bar 70
pistachio (*Colombo*), 3½ oz. 130
raspberry:
  (*Colombo*), 3½ oz. 130
  (*Yami Pushups*), 3 fl. oz. 80
  (*Danny*), 8 oz. 210
  bar, chocolate-coated
    (*Danny* Frozen Yogurt Bar), 2½ fl.-oz. bar 130
  red (*Sealtest* Frozen Yogurt Stick), 4 fl. oz. 80
strawberry:
  (*Colombo*), 3½ oz. 130
  (*Danny*), 8 oz. 210
  (*Sealtest* Frozen Yogurt Stick), 4 fl. oz. 80
  (*Yami Pushups*), 3 fl. oz. 80
  bar, chocolate-coated
    (*Danny* Frozen Yogurt Bar), 2½ fl.-oz. bar 130
tangerine (*Colombo*), 3½ oz. 130
vanilla:
  (*Colombo*), 3½ oz. 130
  (*Danny*), 8 fl. oz. 180
  (*Sealtest* Frozen Yogurt Stick), 4 fl. oz. 80
  bar (*Danny* Frozen Yogurt Bar), 2½ fl.-oz. bar 60
  bar, chocolate-coated
    (*Danny* Frozen Yogurt Bar), 2½ fl.-oz. bar 130

*Note variations in sizes

Chapter 5

CHEESE AND CHEESE PRODUCTS

> **CHEESE,** one ounce, except as noted
> *See also "Cheese Food," "Cheese Spreads,"*
> *"Cottage Cheese" and "Cheese Entrees, Frozen"*

	calories
American:	
(*Borden*)	110
(*Dorman's*)	106
(*Hood*)	110
(*Kraft*)	105
(*Kraft Deluxe*—loaf or slices)	110
(*Kraft Old English*)	110
(*Land O Lakes*)	110
(*Pauly*)	106
(*Saffola*—loaf)	93
(*Saffola*—slices)	96
(*Vera Sharp*)	104
hot pepper (*Sargento*)	106
asiago (*Frigo*)	113
blue:	
(*Borden Blufort*), 1¼-oz. portion	131
(*Borden* Danish)	105
(*Borden Flora Danica*)	105
(*Dorman's* Danish)	100
(*Frigo*)	99
(*Kraft* Natural)	100
(*Pauly* Danish)	100
(*Sargento*)	100
(*Bonbel*—round)	94

Cheese; Colby, continued

    reduced calorie (*Sargento* Longhorn Style)   89
cottage, *see "Cottage Cheese," page 74*
cream:
    (*Kraft Philadelphia Brand*)   100
    w/chives (*Kraft Philadelphia Brand*)   100
    w/pimentos (*Kraft Philadelphia Brand*)   100
    soft (*Friendship*)   103
    soft (*Kraft Philadelphia Brand*)   100
    soft, w/chives and onion
      (*Kraft Philadelphia Brand*)   100
    soft, w/olives and pimento
      (*Kraft Philadelphia Brand*)   90
    soft, w/pineapple (*Kraft Philadelphia Brand*)   90
    soft, w/strawberries (*Kraft Philadelphia Brand*)   100
    soft, w/toasted onion
      (*Kraft Philadelphia Brand*)   90
    whipped (*Kraft Philadelphia Brand*)   100
    whipped, w/bacon and horseraddish
      (*Kraft Philadelphia Brand*)   90
    whipped, w/blue cheese
      (*Kraft Philadelphia Brand*)   100
    whipped, w/chives (*Kraft Philadelphia Brand*)   90
    whipped, w/onions (*Kraft Philadelphia Brand*)   90
    whipped, w/pimentos
      (*Kraft Philadelphia Brand*)   90
    whipped, w/smoked salmon
      (*Kraft Philadelphia Brand*)   100
    imitation (*King Smoothee*)   65
    imitation
      (*Weight Watchers*), 1/3 cup   60
Edam:
    (*Dorman's*)   101
    (*House of Gold*)   105
    (*Kraft* Natural)   100
    (*Pauly*)   101
    (*Sargento*)   101
farmer:
    (*Friendship*)   40
    (*Sargento*)   72
    (*Wispride*)   100
feta (*Sargento*)   75

Cheese, continued

Mozzarella:
  (*Borden*) 96
  (*Dorman's* — part skim) 72
  (*Frigo*) 79
  (*Kraft*) 79
  (*Kraft* Natural — part skim) 80
  (*Pauly* — part skim) 80
  (*Sargento*) 80
  (*Sargento* — part skim) 79
  imitation (*Sargento*) 90
  pizza (*Sargento*) 79
  w/pizza spices (*Sargento*) 79
Muenster:
  (*Borden* — natural) 85
  (*Dorman's*) 104
  (*Kraft* Natural) 100
  (*Kraft* Processed) 102
  (*Pauly*) 104
  (*Sargento* Red Rind) 104
Neufchâtel:
  plain (*Borden*) 73
  plain (*Kraft* Natural) 80
  flavored, *see "Cheese Spreads," page 74*
nuworld (*Kraft*) 104
Parmesan:
  (*Dorman's*) 111
  (*Frigo*) 107
  (*Kraft* Natural) 110
  (*Pauly*) 111
  grated (*Colonna*), 1/2 oz. 52
  grated (*Frigo*), 1/2 oz. 65
  grated (*Kraft*) 130
  imitation (*Sargento*) 115
Parmesan and Romano (*Sargento*) 110
(*Pauly Slim Line*) 60
pepato (*Frigo*) 110
pimento:
  (*Borden* American) 104
  (*Kraft* American) 104
  (*Kraft* Deluxe*) 110

Cheese, continued

pizza:
  (*Borden*) 85
  (*Frigo*) 73
  (*Kraft*) 73
Port du Salut:
  (*Dorman's*) 100
  (*Kraft*) 100
  (*Pauly*) 100
primost (*Kraft*) 134
primost (*Sargento*) 132
pot cheese (*Sargento*) 30
Provolone:
  (*Borden*) 93
  (*Dorman's*) 100
  (*Frigo*) 99
  (*Kraft* Natural) 90
  (*Pauly*) 100
  (*Sargento*) 100
Quese de Papa (*Sargento*) 105
Queso Blanco (*Sargento*) 104
ricotta:
  (*Brunetto*—whole milk) 48
  (*Frigo*—part skim) 45
  (*Polly-O*—whole milk) 50
  (*Sargento*—whole milk) 54
  (*Sargento*—part skim) 43
  w/honey (*Sargento*—whole milk) 28
Romano:
  (*Borden Romano Pecorina*) 114
  (*Dorman's*) 110
  (*Frigo*) 110
  (*Kraft Casino Brand*) 100
  (*Pauly*) 110
  (*Sargento*) 110
  (*Sargento Pecorino*) 110
  grated (*Kraft*) 130
Roquefort:
  (*Borden Napoleon Brand*) 107
  (*Dorman's*) 105
  (*Kraft*) 105
  (*Pauly*) 105

Cheese, continued

sap sago (*Kraft*) 76
Sardo Romano (*Kraft*) 110
(*Sargento Nibblin' Curds*) 105
Scamorze (*Frigo*) 79
Scamorze (*Kraft* Natural—part skim) 80
Skandor (*Pauly* Swedish) 100
string (*Sargento*) 79
Swiss:
  (*Borden* Processed) 100
  (*Borden* Finland Imported) 104
  (*Borden* Switzerland Imported) 104
  (*Dorman's* Natural) 107
  (*Dorman's* Processed) 95
  (*Kraft*—aged) 100
  (*Kraft* Natural—chunk or slices) 110
  (*Kraft* Processed—slices) 90
  (*Pauly* Natural) 107
  (*Pauly* Processed) 95
  (*Pauly* Iceland Baby Swiss) 100
  (*Sargento*) 107
  (*Sargento*—low sodium) 100
taco (*Sargento*) 105
Tilsiter:
  (*Dorman's*) 96
  (*Pauly*) 96
  (*Sargento*) 96
Tybo (*Sargento* Red Wax) 98
washed curd (*Kraft*) 108

*Note: Unless otherwise noted, the figure listed for any cheese above applies to all of the forms in which it may be packaged— slices, loaves, wedges, etc. Be careful not to confuse "real" cheese with a "cheese spread" or "cheese food" that bears the same or a similar name. Generally, it isn't hard to differentiate between cheese and cheese spreads, but cheese foods sometimes pose a problem (especially when they're packaged in slices). Check the label if you're confused about a product; if it is a cheese food, the label will say so.

CHEESE FOOD, one ounce
See also "Cheese" and "Cheese Spreads"

                                             calories

American:
- (*Borden*) 90
- (*Borden Lite Line*) 50
- (*Borden Lite Line*—sliced) 90
- (*Clearfield*) 90
- (*Golden Image*) 90
- (*Harvest Moon Brand*) 70
- (*Kraft* Singles) 90
- (*Light n' Lively*) 70
- (*Pauly*) 90
- grated (*Kraft*) 130

bacon (*Kraft Cheez 'n Bacon* Singles) 100

Cheddar:
- (*Wispride*) 90
- bacon (*Kraft*) 90
- garlic (*Kraft*) 90
- port wine (*Kraft*) 90
- sharp (*Borden Lite Line*—sliced) 50
- sharp (*Cracker Barrel*) 90
- sharp (*Light n' Lively*) 70
- smoked (*Cracker Barrel*) 90
- tangy (*Cracker Barrel*) 90

Colby (*Borden Lite Line*—sliced) 50
hickory smoke flavor (*Kraft Smokelle*) 93
jalapeño (*Kraft* Singles) 90
(*Kraft Munst-ett*) 101
(*Kraft Superblend*) 92
Monterey Jack (*Borden Lite Line*—sliced) 50
Monterey Jack (*Kraft* Singles) 90
Muenster (*Borden Lite Line*—sliced) 50
(*Pauly Sweet Munchee*) 100

pimento:
- (*Borden*) 91
- (*Kraft* Singles) 90
- (*Pauly*) 90

Cheese Food, continued

pizza (*Kraft Pizzalone*) 90
port wine (*Wispride*) 100
salami (*Kraft*) 94
sharp (*Kraft Singles*) 100
smoked (*Wispride*) 90
Swiss:
   (*Borden Lite Line*—sliced) 50
   (*Kraft Singles*) 90
   (*Pauly*) 90
   (*Wispride*) 100
(*Weight Watchers*) 50
w/crackers (*Kraft Handi Snacks*), 1 pkg. 120

CHEESE SPREADS, one ounce, except as noted
See also "Cheese," "Cheese Food"
and "Dips, Ready to Serve"

---

calories

American:
   (*Hood*) 80
   (*Kraft*) 80
   (*Snack Mate*) 80
blue (*Roka Brand*) 70
Cheddar:
   (*Snack Mate*) 80
   freeze-dried (*Mountain House*) 180
   sharp (*Snack Mate*) 80
   sharp (*Wispride*) 80
cheese and bacon:
   (*Kraft*) 80
   (*Kraft Squeez-a-Snak*) 90
   (*Oscar Mayer*) 70
   (*Snack Mate*) 80
cheese and salami (*Oscar Mayer*) 65
(*Cheez Whiz*) 80
chive and green onion (*Snack Mate*) 80
garlic (*Kraft*) 80

Cheese Spreads, continued

garlic (*Kraft Squeez-a-Snak*) 90
Gruyère (*Dorman's*) 90
Gruyère (*Pauly*) 90
hickory smoke (*Kraft Squeez-a-Snak*) 80
jalapeño pepper (*Cheez Whiz*) 80
jalapeño pepper (*Kraft*) 80
(*Land O Lakes Golden Velvet*) 80
(*Laughing Cow*) 74
Limburger (*Mohawk Valley*) 70
Neufchâtel cheese:
  w/bacon and horseradish (*Kraft Party Snack*) 74
  w/chipped beef (*Kraft Party Snack*) 67
  w/chives (*Kraft Party Snack*) 69
  w/clams (*Kraft Party Snack*) 67
  w/onion (*Kraft Party Snack*) 66
  w/relish (*Kraft Party Snack*) 72
olive and pimento (*Kraft*) 60
pimento:
  (*Cheez Whiz*) 80
  (*Kraft*) 70
  (*Kraft Squeez-a-Snak*) 90
  (*Snack Mate*), 4 tsp. 60
  (*Velveeta*) 80
pineapple (*Kraft*) 70
relish (*Kraft*) 70
sharp:
  (*Kraft Sharpie*) 90
  (*Kraft Squeez-a-Snak*) 80
  (*Old English*) 90
(*Velveeta*) 80
(*Velveeta*—sliced) 90

COTTAGE CHEESE, four ounces, except as noted
See also "Cheese"

---

calories

creamed:
  (*Borden*) 120
  (*Friendship* California Style) 120
  (*Hood*) 120

Cottage Cheese, creamed, continued

    (*Hood* Country Style) 120
    (*Kraft*), 1/2 cup 107
    (*Meadow Gold*), 1/2 cup 117
    (*Sealtest*) 120
    w/chives (*Hood* Chivier Cottage Cheese) 120
    w/peach-pineapple (*Sealtest*), 1/2 cup 115
    w/pineapple (*Friendship*) 140
creamed partially:
    (*Meadow Gold*), 1/2 cup 102
uncreamed or low-fat:
    (*Borden Lite Line*) 90
    (*Friendship* Low Fat) 90
    (*Friendship* Pot Style) 100
    (*Friendship*—salt-free) 90
    (*Hood Nuform*) 90
    (*Sealtest*) 90
    (*Weight Watchers*) 1/3 cup 60

CHEESE ENTREES, FROZEN,
one whole package*, except as noted

---

calories

cheese burritos, enchilladas, *see*
   "Mexican & Mexican-Style Foods," page 172
cheese blintzes (*Golden*), 1 piece** 213
cheese soufflé (*Stouffer's*), 12-oz. pkg. 710
Welsh rarebit (*Stouffer's*), 10-oz. pkg. 710

*Note variation in size
**As packaged

Chapter 6

FRUIT AND FRUIT PRODUCTS

FRUIT, CANNED OR IN JARS,
1/2 cup, except as noted
See also "Fruit, Dried (Uncooked)," "Fruit, Frozen"
and "Fruit Juices"

---

	calories
apple rings, spiced (*Comstock*), 1 ring	20
apples, sliced (*Comstock*), 4 oz.	35
applesauce:	
(*Comstock*)	100
(*Del Monte*)	90
(*Mott's*), 4 oz.	115
(*Musselman's*)	97
(*Seneca*)	90
(*Seneca* Cinnamon)	90
(*Seneca* Golden Delicious)	90
(*Seneca* McIntosh)	90
natural (*Comstock*)	45
natural (*Del Monte*)	50
natural (*Diet Delight*)	50
natural (*Featherweight*)	50
natural (*Mott's* Natural Style), 4 oz.	50
natural (*Musselman's*)	50
natural (*S & W Nutradiet*)	55
natural (*Seneca* Natural)	50
apricots, solids and liquid:	
in juice (*Diet Delight*)	60
in juice (*Featherweight*)	50

Fruit, Canned or in Jars, apricots, solids and liquid, continued

in juice, halves (*Libby's Lite*) 60
in juice, halves (*S & W Nutradiet*) 35
in juice, halves (*Tri/Valley*) 60
in juice, whole (*S & W Nutradiet*) 28
in light syrup, whole, halves, slices or pieces
   (*Tri/Valley*) 80
in syrup, halves, unpeeled (*Del Monte*) 100
in syrup, whole, peeled (*Del Monte*) 100
in heavy syrup, halves, unpeeled (*Libby's*) 110
in heavy syrup, halves or slices (*Tri/Valley*) 110
in heavy syrup, whole (*Tri/Valley*) 100
in water (*Diet Delight*) 35
in water (*Featherweight*) 35
in water, halves, unpeeled (*Del Monte*) 60
in water, halves (*Libby's*) 35
in water, halves (*S & W Nutradiet*) 35
in water, halves or slices (*Tri/Valley*) 35
in water, whole (*Tri/Valley*) 30
cherries, solids and liquid:
in juice (*Diet Delight*) 60
in syrup, dark sweet, w/pits (*Del Monte*) 90
in syrup, dark sweet, pitted (*Del Monte*) 90
in syrup, light sweet, w/pits (*Del Monte*) 100
in water, dark sweet (*Featherweight*) 60
cranberries, fresh-pack (*Ocean Spray*) 25
cranberry sauce, jellied (*Ocean Spray*), 2 oz. 90
cranberry sauce, whole (*Ocean Spray*), 2 oz. 90
cranberry-orange relish (*Ocean Spray*), 2 oz. 100
cranberry-raspberry sauce, jellied
   (*Ocean Spray Cran-Raspberry*), 2 oz. 90
figs, in syrup, whole (*Del Monte*) 100
fruit cocktail, solids and liquid:
   (*Del Monte*) 50
in juice (*Diet Delight*) 50
in juice (*Featherweight*) 50
in juice (*Libby's Lite*) 50
in juice (*S & W Nutradiet*) 40
in juice (*Tri/Valley*) 50
in juice (*Weight Watchers*) 60
in syrup (*Del Monte*) 80
in light syrup (*Tri/Valley*) 70

Fruit, Canned or in Jars, fruit cocktail, solids and liquid, continued

in heavy syrup (*Libby's*) 90
in heavy syrup (*Tri/Valley*) 90
in water (*Diet Delight*) 40
in water (*Featherweight*) 40
in water (*Libby's*) 40
in water (*S & W Nutradiet*) 40
in water (*Tri/Valley*) 40
fruit for salad, solids and liquid:
  in juice (*Diet Delight*) 60
  in juice (*Featherweight*) 50
  in juice (*S & W Nutradiet*) 50
  in juice, quartered (*Tri/Valley*) 60
  in syrup (*Del Monte*) 90
  in heavy syrup (*Libby's*) 100
  in heavy syrup, quartered (*Tri/Valley*) 100
  in extra heavy syrup, sliced, w/grapes
    (*Tri/Valley*) 110
  in water (*Featherweight*) 35
  in water (*S & W Nutradiet*) 35
  in water, quartered, w/grapes (*Tri/Valley*) 35
fruit, mixed:
  chunky (*Del Monte*) 80
  (*Del Monte Fruit Cup*), 5 oz. 100
  in juice (*Tri/Valley*) 50
  in juice, chunky (*Libby's Lite*) 50
  in juice, chunky (*Tri/Valley*) 50
  in light syrup (*Tri/Valley*) 70
  in light syrup, chopped (*Tri/Valley*) 80
  in light syrup, chunky (*Tri/Valley*) 70
  in heavy syrup (*Tri/Valley*) 90
  in heavy syrup, chunky (*Libby's*) 90
  in heavy syrup, chunky (*Tri/Valley*) 90
  in water (*Tri/Valley*) 40
fruit salad, in juice (*Kraft*) 50
fruit salad, tropical, in syrup (*Del Monte*) 90
grapefruit sections, solids and liquid:
  in juice (*Featherweight*) 40
  in juice (*Kraft*) 50
  in water (*S & W Nutradiet*) 40
grapes:
  in light syrup, light seedless (*Tri/Valley*) 80

Fruit, Canned or in Jars, grapes, continued

in heavy syrup, light seedless (*Tri/Valley*) 100
in heavy syrup, Thompson seedless (*Tri/Valley*) 110
in water, light seedless (*Tri/Valley*) 50

oranges, Mandarin, solids and liquid:

in syrup (*Del Monte*), 5½ oz. 100
in light syrup (*Dole*) 76
in water (*Featherweight*) 35
in water (*S & W Nutradiet*) 28

peaches, solids and liquid:

in juice (*Weight Watchers*) 60
in juice, cling or freestone, halves or slices
   (*Diet Delight*) 50
in juice, cling or freestone, halves or slices
   (*Featherweight*) 50
in juice, cling or freestone, halves or slices
   (*S & W Nutradiet*) 30
in juice, freestone (*Del Monte*) 60
in juice, freestone, halves or slices (*Tri/Valley*) 50
in juice, yellow cling, halves or slices
   (*Del Monte*) 50
in juice, yellow cling, halves or slices
   (*Libby's Lite*) 50
in juice, yellow cling, halves or slices
   (*Tri/Valley*) 50
in juice, yellow cling, chunks
   (*Tri/Valley* Naturals) 50
in syrup, freestone, halves or slices (*Del Monte*) 90
in syrup, yellow cling, halves or slices
   (*Del Monte*) 80
in syrup, yellow cling, diced
   (*Del Monte Fruit Cup*), 5 oz. 110
in light syrup, clingstone, halves or slices
   (*Tri/Valley*) 70
in light syrup, yellow cling, quartered or diced
   (*Tri/Valley*) 70
in light syrup, yellow freestone, halves or slices
   (*Tri/Valley*) 70
in heavy syrup, halves or slices (*Libby's*) 100
in heavy syrup, clingstone, halves or slices
   (*Tri/Valley*) 100

Fruit, Canned or in Jars, peaches, solids and liquid, continued

in heavy syrup, freestone, halves or slices
(*Tri/Valley*) 100
in heavy syrup, yellow cling, quartered or diced
(*Tri/Valley*) 100
in heavy syrup, yellow cling, spiced, whole or halves
(*Tri/Valley*) 90
in water, cling, halves (*Diet Delight*) 30
in water, cling, halves or slices (*Featherweight*) 30
in water, cling, halves or slices
(*S & W Nutradiet*) 30
in water, cling, slices (*Diet Delight*) 30
in water, clingstone, halves or slices (*Libby's*) 30
in water, clingstone, halves or slices (*Tri/Valley*) 30
in water, freestone, halves or slices (*Tri/Valley*) 30
pears, Bartlett, solids and liquid:
halves or slices (*Del Monte*) 50
in juice (*Diet Delight*) 60
in juice (*S & W Nutradiet*) 35
in juice (*Weight Watchers*) 60
in juice, halves (*Featherweight*) 60
in juice, halves or quarters (*Libby's Lite*) 60
in juice, halves, slices or quarters (*Tri/Valley*) 60
in syrup, halves or slices (*Del Monte*) 80
in light syrup, halves, slices or diced (*Tri/Valley*) 70
in heavy syrup (*Libby's*) 90
in heavy syrup, halves, slices or diced
(*Tri/Valley*) 90
in water (*Diet Delight*) 35
in water (*Libby's*) 35
in water (*S & W Nutradiet*) 35
in water, halves (*Featherweight*) 40
in water, halves (*Tri/Valley*) 35
pineapple, solids and liquid:
spears (*Del Monte*), 2 spears 50
in juice (*Featherweight*) 70
in juice, chunks, crushed or slices (*Del Monte*) 70
in juice, chunks or crushed (*Dole*) 70
in syrup, chunks, crushed or slices (*Del Monte*) 90
in syrup, chunks, crushed or slices (*Dole*) 95
in water, slices (*Featherweight*) 60
in water, slices (*S & W Nutradiet*) 60

Fruit, Canned or in Jars, continued

plums, purple, solids and liquid:
  in juice (*Featherweight*) 80
  in juice (*S & W Nutradiet*) 52
prunes, stewed, in water (*Featherweight*) 130

FRUIT, DRIED (UNCOOKED),
one ounce, except as noted
See also "Fruit, Canned or in Jars" and "Fruit, Frozen"

---

                                               calories

apple fruit roll:
  (*Betty Crocker Fruit Corners*), 1 roll* 50
  (*Flavor Tree*), 1 roll* 90
apples:
  (*Weight Watchers* Snacks), 1/2-oz. pkg. 50
  evaporated (*Del Monte*) 70
  freeze-dried (*Mountain House*) 100
applesauce, freeze-dried (*Mountain House*) 100
apricot fruit roll:
  (*Betty Crocker Fruit Corners*), 1 roll* 50
  (*Flavor Tree*), 1-oz. roll 100
apricots (*Del Monte*) 70
apricots (*Sunsweet*), 1/2 cup 224
banana chips (*Mountain House*) 155
bananas
  (*Weight Watchers* Tropical Snacks),
    1/2-oz. pkg. 50
blueberries, freeze-dried (*Mountain House*) 134
cherry fruit bar
  (*Betty Crocker Fruit Corners*), 1 bar* 90
cherry fruit roll:
  (*Betty Crocker Fruit Corners*), 1 roll* 50
  (*Flavor Tree*), 1 roll* 90
  (*Sunkist*), 1 roll* 45
coconut, *see "Sweet Baking Ingredients," page 261*
currants, zante:
  (*Del Monte*), 1/2 cup 200
  (*Sun•Maid*) 83
  (*Sun•Maid*), 1/2 cup 206

Fruit, Dried (Uncooked), continued

dates:
  chopped (*Dromedary*) 99
  diced (*Bordo*) 82
  pitted (*Bordo*) 83
  pitted (*Dromedary*) 100
fruit mixed:
  (*Carnation* All Fruit), .9-oz. pouch 80
  (*Del Monte*) 65
  freeze-dried (*Mountain House*), .66 oz. 70
  tropical, w/nuts (*Carnation*), .9-oz. pouch 100
fruit punch fruit roll (*Flavor Tree*), 1 roll* 90
grape fruit bar
  (*Betty Crocker Fruit Corners*), 1 bar* 90
grape fruit roll:
  (*Betty Crocker Fruit Corners*), 1 roll* 50
  (*Flavor Tree*), 1-oz. roll 90
  (*Sunkist*), 1 roll 45
orange fruit roll (*Flavor Tree*), 1 roll* 90
orange fruit roll (*Sunkist*), 1/2-oz. roll* 45
orange-pineapple fruit bar
  (*Betty Crocker Fruit Corners*), 1 bar* 90
oranges
  (*Weight Watchers* Tropical Snacks),
  1/2-oz. pkg. 50
peach fruit roll (*Flavor Tree*), 1 roll* 90
peaches:
  (*Del Monte*) 70
  (*Sunsweet*), 1/2 cup 216
  (*Weight Watchers* Snacks), 1/2-oz. pkg. 50
  freeze-dried (*Mountain House*) 100
pink grapefruit
  (*Weight Watchers* Tropical Snacks),
  1/2-oz. pkg. 50
plum fruit roll (*Flavor Tree*), 1-oz. roll 90
plums, freeze-dried (*Mountain House*) 100
prunes:
  w/pits (*Del Monte*) 60
  w/pits (*Del Monte* Moist-Pak) 60
  pitted (*Del Monte*) 70
raisins:
  golden seedless (*Del Monte*) 87

Fruit, Dried (Uncooked), raisins, continued

golden seedless (*Sun•Maid*) 83
golden seedless (*Sun•Maid*), ½ cup 250
seedless (*Del Monte*) 83
seedless (*Sun•Maid*) 83
seedless (*Sun•Maid*), ½ cup 250
freeze-dried (*Mountain House*), .82 oz. 80
raspberry fruit roll (*Flavor Tree*), 1 roll* 90
strawberries
  (*Weight Watchers* Snacks), ½-oz. pkg. 50
strawberries, freeze-dried (*Mountain House*) 90
strawberry fruit bar
  (*Betty Crocker Fruit Corners*), 1 bar* 90
strawberry fruit roll:
  (*Betty Crocker Fruit Corners*), 1 roll* 50
  (*Flavor Tree*), 1 roll* 90
  (*Sunkist*), 1 roll* 45

As packaged.

FRUIT, FROZEN, five ounces, except as noted
See also "Fruit, Canned or in Jars,"
"Fruit, Dried (Uncooked)"
and "Fruit Juice Bars, Frozen"

---

calories

apples, escalloped (*Stouffer's*), 4 oz. 140
fruit, mixed (*Birds Eye* Quick Thaw) 100
red raspberries (*Birds Eye* Quick Thaw) 100
strawberries, in syrup, halves
  (*Birds Eye* Quick Thaw) 120
strawberries, in lite syrup, halves
  (*Birds Eye* Quick Thaw) 60

FRUIT JUICE BARS, FROZEN, one serving
See also "Frozen Yogurt"
and "Ice Cream & Frozen Confections"

---

	calories
lemonade (*Sunkist*), 3 fl.-oz. bar	80
orange	
(*Dole Fruit 'N Juice Bars*), 2½-oz. bar	70
orange (*Sunkist*), 3 fl.-oz. bar	70
pineapple	
(*Dole Fruit 'N Juice Bars*), 2½ fl.-oz. bar	70
strawberry	
(*Dole Fruit 'N Juice Bars*), 2½ fl.-oz. bar	70

FRUIT JUICES, six fluid ounces, except as noted
See also "Fruit & Fruit-Flavored Drinks"
and "Vegetable Juices"

---

	calories
apple:	
bottled (*Ocean Spray*)	90
bottled (*Red Cheek*)	80
bottled (*Seneca*)	90
canned or bottled (*Mott's*)	80
canned or bottled (*Mott's* Natural Style)	80
canned (*Musselman's*)	80
canned (*Tree Top*)	75
canned (*Weight Watchers*), ⅓ cup	45
frozen* (*Seneca*)	90
frozen* (*Seneca* Natural)	90
frozen* (*Tree Top*)	75
apple-grape, frozen, reconstituted 1 + 3	
(*Welch's* Orchard)	90
fruit, mixed, canned	
(*Weight Watchers* Medley), ⅓ cup	45
grape:	
bottled (*Seneca*)	115

Fruit Juices, grape, continued

bottled (*Welch's*)	120
canned (*Weight Watchers*), ⅓ cup	45
frozen* (*Minute Maid*)	99
frozen* (*Seneca*)	100
frozen* (*Seneca* Natural)	115
frozen, reconstituted 1 + 3 (*Welch's*)	100
frozen, reconstituted 1 + 3 (*Welch's* Orchard)	120
red, bottled (*Welch's*)	120
white, bottled (*Welch's*)	120
sparkling, red, bottled (*Welch's*)	120
sparkling, white, bottled (*Welch's*)	120

grapefruit:

bottled (*Ocean Spray*)	70
canned (*Del Monte*)	70
canned (*Libby's*)	75
dairy pack (*Kraft*)	70
dairy pack (*Tropicana*)	75
frozen* (*Minute Maid*)	75
pink, canned (*Texsun*)	77

juice blend, frozen, reconstituted 1 + 3
(*Welch's* Orchard Frozen Harvest) 90

lemon:

fresh (*Sunkist*), 2 tbsp.	8
bottled (*ReaLemon*), 2 tbsp.	6
bottled (*Seneca*), 2 tbsp.	6
frozen, full-strength (*Minute Maid*), 2 tbsp.	7

lime, bottled (*ReaLime*), 2 tbsp. 4
lime, bottled, sweetened (*Rose's*), 2 tbsp. 49

orange:

canned (*Del Monte*)	80
canned (*Libby's*)	90
canned, sweetened (*Libby's*)	100
canned (*Texsun*)	83
dairy pack (*Kraft*)	80
dairy pack (*Sunkist*)	80
dairy pack (*Tropicana*)	83
frozen* (*Minute Maid*)	90
frozen* (*Snow Crop*)	90
frozen*, from concentrate (*Minute Maid*)	83
frozen*, from concentrate (*Sunkist*)	80

Fruit Juices, continued

orange-grapefruit:
  canned (*Libby's*) 80
  dairy pack (*Kraft*) 80
  frozen* (*Minute Maid*) 76
orange-pineapple, canned (*Texsun*) 89
orange-pineapple, dairy pack (*Kraft*) 80
pear apple (*Tree Top*) 75
pear grape (*Tree Top*) 83
pineapple:
  canned (*Del Monte*) 100
  canned (*Dole*) 103
  canned (*Texsun*) 97
  frozen* (*Minute Maid*) 92
pineapple-grapefruit, canned (*Texsun*) 91
pineapple-orange, frozen* (*Minute Maid*) 94
prune:
  bottled or canned (*Mott's* Super) 120
  bottled or canned (*Sunsweet*) 120
  canned (*Del Monte*) 120
tangerine, sweetened, frozen* (*Minute Maid*) 85

*Reconstituted according to package directions

FRUIT & FRUIT-FLAVORED DRINKS,
six fluid ounces, except as noted
See also "Fruit Juices" and "Soft Drinks & Mixers"

---

                                         calories

apple:
  canned (*Hawaiian Punch*) 90
  canned (*Hi-C*) 90
  mix* (*Kool-Aid*) 75
  mix* (*Wyler's* Crystals) 68
  soft pack (*Capri Sun*), 6¾ fl. oz. 90
apple-cherry, canned
    (*Musselman's* Breakfast Cocktail) 83
apple, grape, canned
    (*Musselman's* Breakfast Cocktail) 83

Fruit & Fruit-Flavored Drinks, continued

apricot nectar:
  canned (*Del Monte*) 100
  canned (*Heart's Delight*) 100
  canned (*Libby's*) 110
  canned (*Sunsweet*) 105
  canned (*Tri/Valley*) 100
apricot-pineapple nectar, unsweetened,
    canned (*S & W Nutradiet*) 35
banana nectar, canned (*Libby's*) 60
berry, wild, canned (*Hi-C*) 90
cherry:
  canned (*Hawaiian Punch*) 90
  canned (*Hi-C*) 100
  mix* (*Kool-Aid*) 68
  mix*, sugar-free (*Kool-Aid*) 3
  black, mix* (*Wyler's*) 75
  wild, mix* (*Wyler's*) 68
citrus, canned (*Hi-C* Citrus Cooler) 100
cranberry juice cocktail, bottled (*Ocean Spray*) 110
cranberry juice cocktail, low-calorie, bottled
    (*Ocean Spray*) 35
cranberry-apple, bottled (*Ocean Spray Cranapple*) 130
cranberry-apple, low-calorie, bottled
    (*Ocean Spray Cranapple*) 30
cranberry-apple, frozen, reconstituted 1 + 3
    (*Welch's*) 120
cranberry-apricot, bottled
    (*Ocean Spray Cranicot*) 120
cranberry-grape, frozen, reconstituted 1 + 3
    (*Welch's*) 110
cranberry-raspberry, bottled
    (*Ocean Spray Cran-Raspberry*) 110
grape:
  bottled (*Welch's*) 110
  bottled (*Welchade*) 90
  bottled (*Welch's* Concord Juice Cocktail) 110
  dairy pack (*Tropicana*) 70
  canned (*Hawaiian Punch*) 90
  canned (*Hi-C*) 100
  soft pack (*Capri Sun*), 6¾ fl. oz. 104
  frozen, reconstituted 1 + 3 (*Welchade*) 90

Fruit & Fruit-Flavored Drinks, grape, continued

mix* (*Kool-Aid*) 68
mix* (*Tang*) 90
mix* (*Wyler's*) 68
grape-cranberry, bottled
  (*Ocean Spray Cran-Grape*) 110
grapefruit:
  dairy pack (*Tropicana*) 70
  mix* (*Tang*) 90
  pink, bottled
    (*Ocean Spray* Pink Grapefruit Juice Cocktail) 80
grapefruit-orange, canned
  (*Musselman's* Breakfast Cocktail) 68
guava nectar, canned (*Libby's*) 70
lemonade:
  canned (*Country Time*) 68
  soft pack (*Capri Sun*), 6¾ fl. oz. 92
  freeze-dried (*Mountain House*), 1 serving 80
  frozen* (*Country Time*) 68
  frozen* (*Minute Maid*) 74
  frozen* from concentrate (*Sunkist*) 110
  mix* (*Country Time*) 68
  mix* (*Kool-Aid*) 68
  mix* (*Minute Maid* Crystals) 80
  mix* (*Wyler's*) 68
  pink, frozen* (*Country Time*) 68
  pink, frozen* from concentrate (*Sunkist*) 110
  pink, mix* (*Country Time*) 68
  pink, mix* (*Kool-Aid*) 68
  pink, mix* (*Minute Maid* Crystals) 80
lemon-lime, mix* (*Country Time*) 68
lemon-lime, mix* (*Gatorade*) 45
lemon-limeade, frozen* (*Minute Maid*) 75
lemon flavor tea, *see "Tea," page 287*
limeade, frozen* (*Minute Maid*) 75
mango nectar, canned (*Libby's*) 60
mixed flavors, bottled (*Ocean Spray Crantastic*) 110
orange and orange flavor:
  canned (*Bama*) 90
  canned (*Hawaiian Punch*) 100
  canned (*Hi-C*) 100
  dairy pack (*Tropicana*) 70

Fruit & Fruit-Flavored Drinks, orange and orange flavor, continued

soft pack (*Capri Sun*), 6¾ fl. oz. 103
mix* (*Borden* Instant Breakfast Drink) 90
mix* (*Gatorade*) . . . . : . . . 45
mix* (*Kool-Aid*) 68
mix* (*Tang*) 90
mix* (*Wyler's*) 75
imitation juice, frozen* (*Birds Eye Awake*) 80
imitation juice, frozen* (*Birds Eye Orange Plus*) 100
orange-apricot, canned
    (*Musselman's* Breakfast Cocktail) 75
orange-pineapple, canned
    (*Musselman's* Breakfast Cocktail) 75
orangeade, freeze-dried
    (*Mountain House*), .87 oz. 90
peach, canned (*Hi-C*) 100
peach nectar, canned:
    (*Heart's Delight*) 100
    (*Libby's*) 90
    (*Tri/Valley*) 90
pear nectar, canned:
    (*Heart's Delight*) 100
    (*Libby's*) 100
    (*Tri/Valley*) 100
pear-passion fruit nectar, canned (*Libby's*) 60
pineapple-grapefruit, canned (*Del Monte*) 90
pineapple-grapefruit, dairy pack (*Tropicana*) 70
pineapple-orange, canned (*Del Monte*) 90
pineapple-pink grapefruit, canned (*Del Monte*) 90
pineapple-pink grapefruit, canned (*Dole*) 101
punch:
    all flavors, canned (*Hawaiian Punch*) 90
    all flavors, frozen* (*Hawaiian Punch*) 90
    fruit, canned (*Bama*) 90
    fruit, canned (*Hi-C*) 100
    fruit, dairy pack (*Tropicana*) 70
    fruit, soft pack (*Capri Sun*), 6¾ fl. oz. 102
    fruit, tropical, mix* (*Kool-Aid*) 75
    fruit, tropical, mix* (*Wyler's*) 68
    rainbow, mix* (*Kool-Aid*) 75
    sunshine, mix* (*Kool-Aid*) 75
raspberry, mix* (*Kool-Aid*) 68

Prepared or reconstituted according to package directions

Chapter 7

VEGETABLES AND VEGETABLE PRODUCTS

VEGETABLES, CANNED OR IN JARS,
1/2 cup, except as noted
*See also "Vegetables, Dried & Mixes"
and "Vegetables, Frozen"*

---

            calories

asparagus:
(*Joan of Arc Pride*), 4 oz.*	24
(*S & W Nutradiet*)	17
spears and tips (*Del Monte*)	20
spears (*Le Sueur*)	30
cuts (*Green Giant*)	20
puree (*Cellu*)	25
bamboo shoots (*Chun King*), 4¼ oz.	20
bamboo shoots (*La Choy*), 4 oz.* drained	12

bean salad:
three-bean (*Green Giant*)	80
three-bean (*Joan of Arc*), 3½ oz.	80
four-bean (*Joan of Arc*), 3½ oz.	93
bean sprouts (*Chun King*), 4 oz.*	20
bean sprouts (*La Choy*), ⅔ cup, drained	8
beans, baked, *see "Beans, Baked & Baked-Style," page 111*	
beans, black turtle (*Progresso*)	103

beans, butter:
(*Joan of Arc*)	100
(*Van Camp*)	80
speckled, seasoned w/pork (*Luck's*), 7½ oz.	230
beans, cannellini or white kidney (*Progresso*)	95

Vegetables, Canned or in Jars, continued

beans, chili:
  (*Comstock*) 140
  (*Hunt-Wesson*), 4 oz.* 100
  (*Joan of Arc*) 110
  (*Van Camp* Mexican Style) 120
  in chili gravy (*Dennison's*), 7½ oz. 180
  hot, in chili gravy (*Luck's*), 7½ oz. 200
  in sauce (*Hormel*), 4 oz.* 104
beans, fava (*Progresso*) 90
beans, great Northern, seasoned w/pork
  (*Luck's*), 7¼ oz. 220
beans, green:
  (*Comstock*) 25
  whole (*Del Monte*) 20
  whole (*Seneca*) 20
  cut (*Del Monte*) 20
  cut (*Green Giant*) 20
  cut (*Seneca*) 20
  cut (*S & W Nutradiet*) 20
  cut, kitchen style (*Green Giant*) 20
  cut, and shelled beans, seasoned w/pork
    (*Luck's*), 8 oz. 200
  French style (*Del Monte*) 20
  French style (*Green Giant*) 18
  French style (*Seneca*) 20
  Italian style (*Del Monte*) 25
  seasoned, French style (*Del Monte*) 20
beans, kidney:
  (*S & W Nutradiet*) 90
  (*Van Camp* New Orleans Style), 8 oz. 180
  red (*Comstock*) 120
  red (*Hunt's*), 4 oz.* 120
  red (*Luck's* Special Cook), 7½ oz. 190
  red (*Progresso*) 93
  red, dark (*Joan of Arc*) 115
  red, dark (*Van Camp*) 90
  red, light (*Joan of Arc*) 110
  red, light (*Van Camp*) 90
  red, seasoned w/pork (*Luck's*), 7½ oz. 220
  salad, *see "bean salad," above*
  white, *see, "beans, cannellini or white kidney," above*

Vegetables, Canned or in Jars, continued

beans, lima:
   (*Comstock*) 110
   (*Del Monte*) 70
   (*Seneca*) 80
   butter (*Comstock*) 100
   green (*Featherweight*) 80
   w/ham (*Dennison's*), 7½ oz. 250
   seasoned w/pork (*Luck's*), 7½ oz. 230
   small, green, seasoned w/pork (*Luck's*), 7½ oz. 220
beans, mixed pinto and great northern, seasoned w/pork
   (*Luck's*), 7¼ oz. 200
beans, Navy, seasoned w/pork (*Luck's*), 7½ oz. 230
beans, October, seasoned w/pork
   (*Luck's*), 7¼ oz. 230
beans, pinto:
   (*Joan of Arc*) 110
   (*Progresso*) 83
   w/onions, seasoned w/pork (*Luck's*), 7½ oz. 230
   seasoned w/pork (*Luck's*), 7¼ oz. 220
beans, red (*Joan of Arc* Fancy) 115
beans, red (*Van Camp*) 95
beans, refried:
   (*Old El Paso*) 120
   w/green chiles (*Old El Paso*) 50
   w/sausage (*Old El Paso*) 234
beans, wax:
   (*Comstock*) 20
   cut (*Del Monte*) 20
   cut (*Featherweight*) 25
   cut (*Seneca*) 20
   French style (*Del Monte*) 20
beans, western (*Van Camp*), 8 oz. 210
beans, yellow-eye, seasoned w/pork
   (*Luck's*), 7½ oz. 220
beets:
   (*Comstock*—water pack) 40
   whole, cut or sliced (*Del Monte*) 35
   whole (*Seneca*—in jars) 35
   whole, cut, sliced or diced (*Seneca*) ... 35
   shoestring (*Seneca*) 25
   sliced (*Featherweight*) 45

Vegetables, Canned or in Jars, beets, continued

sliced (*Seneca*—in jars)	35
sliced (*S & W Nutradiet*)	35
Harvard (*Comstock*)	100
Harvard (*Seneca*)	80
pickled (*Comstock*)	90
pickled, whole (*Seneca*—in jars)	80
pickled, crinkle-cut (*Del Monte*)	80
pickled, sliced (*Seneca*)	80
pickled, w/onion, whole (*Seneca*—in jars)	80
puree (*Cellu*)	50

blackeye peas:
(*Joan of Arc*), 3½ oz.	71
(*Progresso*)	83
and corn, seasoned w/pork (*Luck's*), 7½ oz.	220
seasoned w/pork (*Luck's*), 7¼ oz.	210

cabbage:
red, sweet and sour (*Greenwood*)	60

sauerkraut, *see "sauerkraut," below*

carrots:
(*Comstock*)	35
whole, sliced or diced (*Del Monte*)	30
diced (*Seneca*)	20
sliced (*Featherweight*)	30
sliced (*S & W Nutradiet*)	30
sliced (*Seneca*)	20
puree (*Cellu*)	35

chickpeas or garbanzos:
(*Joan of Arc* Ceci Beans)	125
(*Old El Paso*)	77
(*Progresso*)	98
(*S & W Nutradiet*)	105

collard greens, chopped, seasoned w/pork
(*Luck's*), 7½ oz.	100

corn:
whole kernel (*Comstock*)	90
whole kernel (*Del Monte*)	70
whole kernel (*Del Monte*—vacuum pack)	90
whole kernel (*Featherweight*)	80
whole kernel (*Green Giant*)	80
whole kernel (*Green Giant*—vacuum pack)	90
whole kernel (*Green Giant* Golden Shoepeg)	90

Vegetables, Canned or in Jars, corn, continued

    whole kernel
      (*Joan of Arc* Golden Corn), 3½ oz. 68
    whole kernel (*Le Sueur*) 80
    whole kernel (*S & W Nutradiet*) 80
    whole kernel (*Seneca*) 80
    cream style (*Comstock*) 100
    cream style (*Del Monte*) 80
    cream style (*Green Giant*) 100
    cream style (*S & W Nutradiet*) 100
    cream style (*Seneca*) 80
    white, whole kernel (*Del Monte*) 70
    white, whole kernel
      (*Green Giant*—vacuum pack) 90
    white, cream style (*Del Monte*) 90
    white, cream style (*Joan of Arc*), 3½ oz. 95
corn and peppers (*Green Giant Mexicorn*) 80
garbanzo beans, *see "chickpeas or garbanzos," above*
mushrooms:
    (*Green Giant*), 2-oz. can 14
    (*Seneca*) 70
    in butter sauce (*Green Giant*), 2 oz. 30
onions:
    boiled (*O & C*), 1 oz. 8
    French fried (*O & C*), 1 oz. 175
    in cream sauce (*O & C*), 1 oz. 143
    sweet (*Heinz*), 1 oz. 40
peas:
    (*Comstock*) 70
    (*Seneca*) 60
    early, June (*Le Sueur*) 60
    early, small (*April Showers*) 60
    sweet (*Del Monte*) 60
    sweet (*Green Giant*) 60
    sweet (*Joan of Arc*), 3½ oz. 55
    sweet (*S & W Nutradiet*) 40
    sweet, small (*Del Monte*) 50
    sweet, small (*Green Giant Sweetlets*) 50
    sweet, small (*Le Sueur*) 60
    seasoned (*Del Monte*) 60
    puree (*Cellu*) 70
peas, early, w/onions (*Green Giant*) 60

Vegetables, Canned or in Jars, continued

peas, sweet, w/onions (*Green Giant*)	60
peas and carrots:	
(*Comstock*)	60
(*Del Monte*)	50
(*S & W Nutradiet*)	35
(*Seneca*)	50
peas, crowder, seasoned w/pork (*Luck's*), 7½ oz.	200
peas, field w/snaps, seasoned w/pork	
(*Luck's*), 7½ oz.	200
peas, white acre w/snaps, seasoned w/pork	
(*Luck's*), 7½ oz.	200
pepperoncini, mild Greek (*Vlasic*), 1 oz.	4
peppers:	
banana, hot (*Heinz*), 1 oz.	6
banana rings, hot (*Vlasic*), 1 oz.	4
cherry, hot (*Heinz*), 1 oz.	8
cherry, mild (*Vlasic*), 1 oz.	8
cherry, sweet mild (*Heinz*), 1 oz.	8
chili, whole, strips or diced (*Ortega*), 1 oz.	6
chili, green, whole or diced (*Del Monte*)	20
chili, green, whole (*Old El Paso*), 1 chili	7
chili, green, chopped (*Old El Paso*), 2 tbsp.	8
chili, hot, whole or diced (*Ortega*), 1 oz.	8
chili, jalapeño, whole or diced (*Del Monte*)	30
chili, jalapeño, whole (*Old El Paso*), 2 peppers	13
chili, Mexican jalapeño (*Vlasic*), 1 oz.	8
rings, hot (*Heinz*), 1 oz.	4
rings, sweet mild (*Heinz*), 1 oz.	4
slices, hot (*Heinz*), 1 oz.	4
slices, sweet mild (*Heinz*), 1 oz.	4
potato salad, German	
(*Hormel* Short Order), 7½-oz. can	220
potato salad, German (*Read*), 4 oz.*	115
potatoes, white:	
whole or sliced (*Del Monte*)	45
sliced, w/beef	
(*Hormel* Short Order), 7½-oz. can	250
potatoes au gratin, w/bacon	
(*Hormel* Short Order), 7½-oz. can	240
potatoes, scalloped, w/ham	
(*Hormel* Short Order), 7½-oz. can	260

Vegetables, Canned or in Jars, continued

pumpkin:
  (*Del Monte*) 35
  (*Joan of Arc*), 4 oz.* 46
  (*Libby's*) 40
  pie filling, *see "Pie Fillings, Canned," page 251*
salad, garden (*Joan of Arc*), 3½ oz. 60
salad greens, seasoned w/pork (*Luck's*), 7½ oz. 100
sauerkraut:
  (*Claussen*) 17
  (*Comstock*) 30
  (*Del Monte*) 25
  (*Vlasic* Old Fashioned) 16
spinach:
  (*Del Monte*) 25
  (*Featherweight*) 35
  (*Seneca*) 25
  (*Tri/Valley*) 25
  puree (*Cellu*) 50
squash, puree (*Cellu*) 50
succotash:
  whole kernel (*Comstock*) 80
  whole kernel (*Seneca*) 80
  cream style (*Comstock*) 110
tomatoes:
  (*Claussen* Kosher), 3.5 oz. 18
  whole (*Del Monte*) 25
  whole (*Diet Delight*) 25
  whole (*Featherweight*) 20
  whole (*Hunt's*), 4 oz.* 20
  whole (*S & W Nutradiet*) 25
  whole, pear, in juice w/basil (*Tri/Valley*) 25
  whole, round (*Libby's*) 25
  whole, round (*Tri/Valley*) 25
  whole, round or pear, in tomato juice
    (*Tri/Valley*) 25
  whole, round or pear, in puree (*Tri/Valley*) ... 30
  crushed, round or pear, in puree (*Tri/Valley*) .. 40
  stewed (*Del Monte*) 35
  stewed (*Hunt's*), 4 oz.* 35
  stewed (*Libby's*) 35
  stewed (*S & W Nutradiet*) 30

Vegetables, Canned or in jars, tomatoes, continued

stewed, sliced (*Tri/Valley*)	35
w/green chiles (*Old El Paso*)	26
w/jalapeños (*Ortega*), 4 oz.*	28
tomato paste, *see "Tomato Paste & Puree," page 112*	
tomato puree, *see "Tomato Paste & Puree," page 112*	
tomato sauce, *see "Sauces," page 206*	
turnip greens w/diced turnips, seasoned w/pork (*Luck's*), 7½ oz.	90
vegetables, chop suey (*La Choy*), 1 cup, drained	20
vegetables, mixed:	
(*Del Monte*)	40
(*Featherweight*)	40
(*Seneca*)	40
Chinese (*La Choy*), 1 cup, drained	24
vegetable stew (*Dinty Moore*), 7½-oz. can	162
water chestnuts (*Ch un King*), 8½-oz can	70
water chestnuts (*La Choy*)	32
yams:	
whole, in heavy syrup (*Royal Prince*), 4 oz.*	147
cut, in light syrup (*Princella*), 4 oz.*	105
cut and pieces, in syrup (*Tri/Valley*)	105
in orange-pineapple sauce (*Royal Prince*), 4 oz.*	180
zucchini, in tomato sauce (*Del Monte*)	30

*Approximately ½ cup

VEGETABLES, DRIED & MIXES
See also "Vegetables, Canned or in Jars"
and "Vegetables, Frozen"

---

	calories
beans, chili, dried (*Hain Naturals*), ½ cup	110
beans, green, freeze-dried (*Mountain House*), ⅓ oz. dry	40
carrots, freeze-dried (*Mountain House*), ⅓ oz. dry	35
corn, freeze-dried (*Mountain House*), ¾ oz. dry	90

Vegetables, Dried & Mixes, continued

mushrooms, freeze-dried
   (*Mountain House*), ⅓ oz. dry 25
onions, dehydrated (*Mountain House*), .71 oz. 80
onions, salad, dehydrated (*French's*), 1 tbsp. 15
peas, green, freeze-dried
   (*Mountain House*), ¾ oz. dry 90
potato pancakes, mix* (*Tato Mix*), 2¾-oz. serving 132
potatoes, hash brown, freeze-dried
   (*Mountain House*), 1½ oz. dry 150
potatoes, mashed
   (*Borden Country Store*), ⅓ cup flakes 70
potatoes, mashed, freeze-dried
   (*Mountain House*), .63 oz. dry 70
potatoes and beef, freeze-dried
   (*Mountain House*), 2 oz. dry 290
potatoes, mix*:
   au gratin (*Betty Crocker*), ½ cup 150
   au gratin, tangy (*French's* Casserole), ½ cup 150
   cheese, hickory smoked (*Betty Crocker*), ½ cup 150
   chicken and herb (*Betty Crocker*), ½ cup 120
   creamed (*Betty Crocker*—oven method), ½ cup 170
   creamed
      (*Betty Crocker*—saucepan method), ½ cup 180
   dinner mix *see "Dinner & Side Dish Mixes," page 192*
   hash browns, w/onions
      (*Betty Crocker*), ½ cup 150
   julienne (*Betty Crocker*), ½ cup 130
   mashed (*Betty Crocker* Potato Buds), ½ cup 130
   mashed (*French's Big Tate*), ½ cup 140
   mashed (*French's* Idaho), ½ cup 120
   mashed (*Hungry Jack* Flakes), ½ cup 140
   scalloped (*Betty Crocker*), ½ cup 140
   scalloped
      (*French's* Crispy Top Casserole), ½ cup 160
   scalloped, cheese (*French's* Casserole), ½ cup 160
   w/sour cream and chives
      (*Betty Crocker*), ½ cup 160
   w/sour cream and chives
      (*French's* Casserole), ½ cup 170
soup greens (*Durkee*), 2½-oz. jar 216
soy beans, dried (*Hain*), 7.5 oz. 190

Vegetables, Dried & Mixes, continued

spinach, freeze-dried
  (*Mountain House*), 1/4 oz. dry 35
squash, freeze-dried (*Mountain House*), 1/4 oz. dry 40
tomato powder (*Tri/Valley*), 1 oz. 90
vegetable flakes, dehydrated (*French's*), 1 tbsp. 12

*Prepared according to package directions

VEGETABLES, FROZEN
See also "Vegetable Entrees, Frozen,"
"Vegetables, Canned or in jars"
and "Vegetables, Dried & Mixes"

---

	calories
artichoke hearts (*Birds Eye* Deluxe), 3 oz.	30
artichoke hearts (*Seabrook Farms*), 3 oz.	30
asparagus:	
spears or cut spears (*Birds Eye*), 3.3 oz.	25
spears or cut spears (*Seabrook Farms*), 3.3 oz.	25
cut spears in butter sauce (*Green Giant*), 1/2 cup	70
beans, butter:	
speckled (*Green Giant*), 1/2 cup	140
speckled (*Seabrook Farms*), 3.3 oz.	120
speckled (*Southland*), 3.3 oz.	120
beans, golden, whole (*Hanover*), 3.3 oz.	32
beans, golden, cut (*Hanover*), 3.3 oz.	30
beans, green:	
(*Comstock*), 3.5 oz.	35
(*Green Giant*), 1/2 cup	20
whole (*Birds Eye* Deluxe), 3 oz.	25
whole (*Hanover* Blue Lake), 3.3 oz.	30
whole (*Seabrook Farms*), 3 oz.	25
cut (*Birds Eye*), 3 oz.	25
cut (*Green Giant Harvest Fresh*), 1/2 cup	25
cut (*Hanover* Blue Lake), 3.3 oz.	32
cut (*Seabrook Farms*), 3 oz.	25
cut (*Southland*), 3 oz.	25
French style (*Birds Eye*), 3 oz.	25

Vegetables, Frozen, beans, green, continued

French style (*Hanover*), 3.3 oz. 29
French style (*Seabrook Farms*), 3 oz. 25
French style (*Southland*), 3 oz. 25
Italian style (*Birds Eye*), 3 oz. 30
Italian style (*Hanover*), 3.3 oz. 41
Italian style (*Seabrook Farms*), 3 oz. 30
cut or French style, in butter sauce
(*Green Giant*), 1/2 cup 40
beans, green, French style, w/toasted almonds
(*Birds Eye* Combination), 3 oz. 50
beans, green, French style, w/cauliflower and carrots
(*Birds Eye* Farm Fresh), 3.2 oz. 25
beans, green, w/corn, carrots and pearl onions
(*Birds Eye* Farm Fresh), 3.2 oz. 45
beans, green, w/mushrooms in cream sauce
(*Green Giant*), 1/2 cup 80
beans, green, and spaetzle
(*Birds Eye* Bavarian Style), 3.3 oz. 110
beans, lima:
(*Green Giant Harvest Fresh*), 1/2 cup 110
(*Green Giant*), 1/2 cup 100
baby (*Birds Eye*), 3.3 oz. 130
baby (*Comstock*), 3.5 oz. 160
baby (*Hanover*), 3.3 oz. 126
baby (*Seabrook Farms*), 3.3 oz. 130
baby butter (*Seabrook Farms*), 3.3 oz. 140
Fordhook (*Birds Eye*), 3.3 oz. 100
Fordhook (*Hanover*), 3.3 oz. 108
Fordhook (*Seabrook Farms*), 3.3 oz. 100
tiny (*Birds Eye* Deluxe), 3.3 oz. 110
tiny (*Seabrook Farms*), 3.3 oz. 110
tiny (*Southland*), 3.2 oz. 130
in butter sauce (*Green Giant*), 1/2 cup 120
beans, pinto (*Seabrook Farms*), 3.2 oz. 160
beans, refried (*Patio*), 4 oz. 63
beans, Romano (*Comstock*), 3.5 oz. 35
beans, wax (*Comstock*), 3.5 oz. 35
beans, wax, cut (*Seabrook Farms*), 3 oz. 25
blackeye peas (*Seabrook Farms*), 3.3 oz. 130
blackeye peas (*Southland*), 3.3 oz. 130

Vegetables, Frozen, continued

broccoli:

florets (*Birds Eye* Deluxe), 3.3 oz.	25
spears (*Birds Eye*), 3.3 oz.	25
spears (*Green Giant Harvest Fresh*), 1/2 cup	30
spears (*Seabrook Farms*), 3.3 oz.	25
spears, baby (*Birds Eye* Deluxe), 3.3 oz.	30
spears, mini 　(*Green Giant Harvest Get Togethers*), 1/2 cup	16
cut (*Green Giant*), 1/2 cup	16
cut (*Green Giant Harvest Fresh*), 1/2 cup	30
cut (*Hanover*), 3.3 oz.	30
cut (*Seabrook Farms*), 3.3 oz.	25
chopped (*Birds Eye*), 3.3 oz.	25
chopped (*Seabrook Farms*), 3.3 oz.	25
fanfare 　(*Green Giant Harvest Get Togethers*), 1/2 cup	80
w/butter sauce, spears (*Green Giant*), 1/2 cup	40
w/cheddar cheese sauce (*Stouffer's*), 41/2 oz.	130
w/cheese sauce (*Birds Eye*), 5 oz.	120
w/cheese sauce (*Green Giant*), 1/2 cup	70
w/white cheddar cheese sauce 　(*Green Giant*), 1/2 cup	70

broccoli w/almonds

(*Birds Eye* Combination), 3.3 oz.	50

broccoli and carrots

(*Green Giant* Fanfare), 1/2 cup	25

broccoli, carrots and pasta twists

(*Birds Eye* Blue Ribbon), 3.3 oz.	90

broccoli, carrots and water chestnuts

(*Birds Eye* Farm Fresh), 3.2 oz.	30

broccoli and cauliflower:

(*Green Giant* Medley), 1/2 cup	60
(*Green Giant* Supreme), 1/2 cup	20
cut (*Hanover*), 3.3 oz.	18

broccoli, cauliflower and carrots

(*Birds Eye* Farm Fresh), 3.2 oz.	25

broccoli, cauliflower and carrots, w/cheese sauce

(*Birds Eye*), 5 oz.	100

broccoli, cauliflower and carrots, w/cheese sauce

(*Green Giant*), 1/2 cup	60

Vegetables, Frozen, continued

broccoli, cauliflower and red peppers
(*Birds Eye* Deluxe), 3.3 oz. 25

broccoli, corn and red peppers
(*Birds Eye* Farm Fresh), 3.2 oz. 50

broccoli, green beans, pearl onions and red peppers
(*Birds Eye* Farm Fresh), 3.2 oz. 25

broccoli and water chestnuts
(*Birds Eye* Combination), 3.3 oz. 30

Brussels sprouts:
(*Birds Eye*), 3.3 oz. 35
(*Green Giant*), 1/2 cup 30
(*Seabrook Farms*), 3.3 oz. 35
(*Hanover*), 3.3 oz. 49
baby (*Birds Eye* Deluxe), 3.3 oz. 40
baby (*Seabrook Farms*), 3.3 oz. 40
w/butter sauce (*Green Giant*), 1/2 cup 50
w/cheese sauce (*Green Giant*), 1/2 cup 80
baby, w/cheese sauce (*Birds Eye*), 4.5 oz. 120

Brussels sprouts, cauliflower and carrots
(*Birds Eye* Farm Fresh), 3.2 oz. 30

carrots:
(*Comstock*), 3.5 oz. 40
whole (*Seabrook Farms*), 3.3 oz. 40
whole, baby (*Birds Eye* Deluxe), 3.3 oz. 40
sliced (*Hanover*), 3.3 oz. 39
crinkle cut, w/butter sauce
(*Green Giant*), 1/2 cup 80

carrots, baby, w/sweet peas and pearl onions
(*Birds Eye* Deluxe), 3.3 oz. 50

cauliflower:
(*Birds Eye*), 3.3 oz. 25
(*Seabrook Farms*), 3.3 oz. 25
cut (*Green Giant*), 1/2 cup 16
cut (*Hanover*), 3.3 oz. 25
florets (*Birds Eye* Deluxe), 3.3 oz. 25
florets (*Hanover*), 3.3 oz. 23
w/cheese sauce (*Birds Eye*), 5 oz. 120
w/cheese sauce (*Green Giant*), 1/2 cup 60
w/white cheddar cheese sauce
(*Green Giant*), 1/2 cup 70

Vegetables, Frozen, continued

cauliflower w/almonds
   (*Birds Eye* Combination), 3.3 oz. 40
cauliflower and carrots
   (*Green Giant* Bonanza), 1/2 cup 60
cauliflower and green beans
   (*Green Giant* Festival), 1/2 cup 16
cauliflower, green beans and corn
   (*Birds Eye* Farm Fresh), 3.2 oz. 35
collard greens, chopped (*Seabrook Farms*), 3.3 oz. 25
collard greens, chopped (*Southland*), 3.3 oz. 25
corn:
   on cob (*Birds Eye*), 1 ear 120
   on cob (*Birds Eye Big Ears*), 1 ear 160
   on cob (*Comstock*), 3.5 oz. 120
   on cob
      (*Green Giant Niblet Ears*—4 ears), 5 1/2" ear 140
   on cob (*Ore-Ida*), 6" ear 150
   on cob (*Seabrook Farms*), 5" ear 120
   on cob, small (*Birds Eye Little Ears*), 2 ears 130
   on cob, small (*Green Giant Nibblers*), 2 ears 160
   whole kernel (*Birds Eye*), 3.3 oz. 80
   whole kernel (*Comstock*), 3.5 oz. 110
   whole kernel (*Green Giant*), 1/2 cup 65
   whole kernel (*Green Giant Niblets*), 1/2 cup 100
   whole kernel (*Hanover*), 3.3 oz. 93
   whole kernel (*Seabrook Farms*), 3.3 oz. 80
   cream style (*Green Giant*), 1/2 cup 120
   sweet (*Birds Eye* Deluxe Tendertreat), 3.3 oz. 80
   white, whole kernel (*Seabrook Farms*), 3.3 oz. 80
   w/butter sauce (*Green Giant Niblets*), 1/2 cup 100
   w/cream sauce (*Green Giant Niblets*), 1/2 cup 130
   white, w/butter sauce
      (*Green Giant* Shoepeg), 1/2 cup 100
corn and broccoli (*Green Giant* Bounty), 1/2 cup 60
corn, green beans and pasta curls
   (*Birds Eye* Combination), 3.3 oz. 110
corn fritters (*Mrs. Paul's*), 2 oz. or 1 fritter 125
eggplant, fried sticks (*Mrs. Paul's*), 3.5 oz. 260
eggplant Parmesan (*Mrs. Paul's*), 5.5 oz. 270
eggplant Parmigiana, *see "Vegetable Entrees, Frozen,"*
   page 111

Vegetables, Frozen, continued

kale:
  leaf (*Southland*), 3.3 oz. 25
  chopped (*Seabrook Farms*), 3.3 oz. 25
  chopped (*Southland*), 3.3 oz. 25
mixed vegetables, *see "vegetables, mixed," below*
mushrooms w/butter sauce
  (*Green Giant*), ½ cup 70
mushrooms, cocktail, *see "Appetizers, Hors d'Oeuvres &*
  Snacks, Canned, Dried or in Jars," page 131
mustard greens, chopped
  (*Seabrook Farms*), 3.3 oz. 20
mustard greens, chopped (*Southland*), 3.3 oz. 20
okra:
  whole (*Birds Eye*), 3.3 oz. 30
  whole (*Hanover*), 3.3 oz. 37
  whole (*Seabrook Farms*), 3.3 oz. 30
  whole (*Southland*), 3.3 oz. 30
  cut (*Birds Eye*), 3.3 oz. 25
  cut (*Hanover*), 3.3 oz. 26
  cut (*Seabrook Farms*), 3.3 oz. 25
  cut (*Southland*), 3.3 oz. 25
onions:
  whole, small (*Birds Eye*), 4 oz. 40
  whole, small (*Seabrook Farms*), 3.3 oz. 35
  chopped (*Ore-Ida*), 2 oz. 20
  chopped (*Seabrook Farms*), 3 oz. 24
  chopped (*Southland*), 2 oz. 15
  pearl (*Birds Eye* Deluxe), 3.3 oz. 35
  small, w/cheese sauce (*Green Giant*), ½ cup 90
  small, w/cream sauce (*Birds Eye*), 3 oz. 110
  fried rings (*Mrs. Paul's*), 2.5 oz. 150
  fried rings (*Ore-Ida* Onion Ringers), 2 oz. 150
pea pods, Chinese, *see "snow peas," below*
peas, blackeye, *see "blackeye peas," above*
peas, crowder (*Seabrook Farms*), 3.2 oz. 130
peas, crowder (*Southland*), 3.3 oz. 135
peas, field, w/snap peas (*Southland*), 3.3 oz. 130
peas, green:
  (*Birds Eye*), 3.3 oz. 80
  (*Comstock*), 3.5 oz. 90
  (*Seabrook Farms*), 3.3 oz. 80

Vegetables, Frozen, peas, green, continued

early, June (*Green Giant*), 1/2 cup 60
small (*Birds Eye* Tender Tiny Peas), 3.3 oz. 60
sweet (*Green Giant*), 1/2 cup 60
sweet (*Green Giant Harvest Fresh*), 1/2 cup 80
sweet (*Hanover*), 3.3 oz. 80
tiny (*Seabrook Farms*), 3.3 oz. 60
w/cream sauce (*Birds Eye*), 2.6 oz. 130
w/cream sauce (*Green Giant*), 1/2 cup 100
early, sweet w/butter sauce
    (*Green Giant*), 1/2 cup 90
peas and carrots:
    (*Comstock*), 3.5 oz. 70
    (*Seabrook Farms*), 3.3 oz. 60
peas, carrots and pearl onions
    (*Birds Eye* Farm Fresh), 3.2 oz. 60
peas, sweet and cauliflower
    (*Green Giant* Medley), 1/2 cup 40
peas and pearl onions
    (*Birds Eye* Combination), 3.3 oz. 70
peas and onions (*Seabrook Farms*), 3.3 oz. 70
peas, onions and carrots in butter sauce
    (*Le Sueur*), 1/2 cup 90
peas and pearl onions w/cheese sauce
    (*Birds Eye*), 5 oz. 140
peas, pea pods and water chestnuts in butter sauce
    (*Green Giant*), 1/2 cup 80
peas and potatoes in cream sauce
    (*Birds Eye* Combination), 2.6 oz. 140
peas w/rice and mushrooms
    (*Birds Eye* Combination), 2.3 oz. 110
peas, purple hull (*Southland*), 3.3 oz. 130
peppers, sweet:
    green (*Seabrook Farms*), 3 oz. 18
    green (*Southland*), 2 oz. 15
    green, diced (*Southland*), 2 oz. 10
    red (*Seabrook Farms*), 3 oz. 24
peppers and onions (*Southland*), 2 oz. 15
potato pancakes (*Golden*), 1 5/8-oz. pancake 85
potato pirogen (*Golden*), 1 3/4-oz. pirogen 61
potato and cheese pierogies
    (*Mrs. Paul's*), 3 pierogies 280

Vegetables, Frozen, continued

potatoes:

whole, boiled (*Seabrook Farms*), 3.2 oz. 60

whole, peeled (*Birds Eye*), 3.2 oz. 60

whole, small, peeled (*Ore-Ida*), 3 oz. 80

au gratin (*Stouffer's*), 3¹³/16 oz. 135

bites (*Birds Eye Tiny Taters*), 3.2 oz. 200

in butter sauce, sliced (*Green Giant*), ¹/2 cup 80

diced and hash shredded
(*Seabrook Farms*), 4 oz. 80

fried (*Heinz* Self-Sizzling Fries), 17 pieces 156

fried
(*Ore-Ida* Country Style Dinner Fries), 3 oz. 120

fried (*Ore-Ida* Crispers), 3 oz. 240

fried (*Ore-Ida* Golden Fries), 16 pieces 130

fried, cottage fries (*Birds Eye*), 2.8 oz. 120

fried, cottage fries (*Ore-Ida*), 3 oz. 140

fried, cottage fries (*Seabrook Farms*), 2.8 oz. 110

fried, crinkle cut (*Birds Eye*), 3 oz. 110

fried, crinkle cut
(*Ore-Ida* Golden Crinkles), 12 pieces 120

fried, crinkle cut
(*Ore-Ida* Pixie Crinkles), 3 oz. 160

fried, crinkle cut (*Seabrook Farms*), 3 oz. 120

fried, French (*Birds Eye*), 3 oz. 110

fried, French (*Birds Eye Tasti Fries*), 2.5 oz. 140

fried, French (*Seabrook Farms*), 3 oz. 120

fried, morsels (*Ore-Ida Crispy Crowns*), 3 oz. 150

fried, planks (*Ore-Ida* Home Style), 3 oz. 110

fried, shoestring (*Birds Eye*), 3.3 oz. 140

fried, shoestring (*Ore-Ida*), 3 oz. 160

fried, shoestring (*Seabrook Farms*), 3 oz. 140

fried, slices (*Ore-Ida* Home Style), 3 oz. 110

fried, steak fries (*Birds Eye*), 3 oz. 110

fried, thins (*Ore-Ida* Home Style), 3 oz. 130

fried, wedges (*Ore-Ida* Home Style), 3 oz. 100

fried, w/onions, morsels
(*Ore-Ida Crispy Crowns*), 3 oz. 170

hash brown (*Birds Eye*), 4 oz. 70

hash brown (*Ore-Ida* Southern Style), 3 oz. 70

hash brown O'Brien (*Ore-Ida*), 3 oz. 80

hash brown, shredded (*Birds Eye*), 3 oz. 60

Vegetables, Frozen, potatoes, continued

hash brown, shredded (*Ore-Ida*), 1 patty 130
patties (*Ore-Ida* Golden Patties), 2.5 oz. 130
puffs (*Birds Eye Tasti Puffs*), 2.5 oz. 190
puffs (*Ore-Ida Tater Tots*), 9 pieces 160
puffs, bacon flavor
  (*Ore-Ida Tater Tots*), 9 pieces 160
puffs, onion flavor
  (*Ore-Ida Tater Tots*), 9 pieces 160
scalloped (*Stouffer's*), 4 oz. 125
wedges (*Birds Eye* Farm Style), 3 oz. 110
potatoes and sweet peas, w/bacon cream sauce
  (*Green Giant*), 1/2 cup 110
potatoes, stuffed, w/cheese flavor topping
  (*Green Giant* Entree), 5 oz. 200
potatoes, stuffed, w/sour cream and chives
  (*Green Giant* Entree), 5 oz. 230
potatoes, sweet (yams):
  w/apples (*Stouffer's*), 5 oz. 160
  candied, orange or yellow (*Mrs. Paul's*), 4 oz. 181
  candied, w/apples (*Mrs. Paul's*), 4 oz. 150
rutabagas (*Southland*), 4 oz. 50
snow peas:
  (*Hanover*), 3.3 oz. 37
  (*La Choy* Pea Pods), 3 oz. 35
  (*Seabrook Farms*), 2 oz. 20
spinach:
  (*Green Giant Harvest Fresh*), 1/2 cup 30
  leaf or chopped (*Birds Eye*), 3.3 oz. 20
  leaf or chopped (*Seabrook Farms*), 3.3 oz. 20
  in butter sauce (*Green Giant*), 1/2 cup 50
  w/cream sauce (*Green Giant*), 1/2 cup 70
  creamed (*Birds Eye*), 3 oz. 60
  creamed (*Stouffer's*), 4 1/2 oz. 190
spinach soufflé, *see "Vegetable Entrees, Frozen," page 111*
spinach and water chestnuts
  (*Birds Eye* Combination), 3.3 oz. 25
squash:
  (*Southland*), 3.6 oz. 80
  butternut (*Southland*), 4 oz. 45
  crookneck (*Seabrook Farms*), 3.3 oz. 18
  crookneck (*Southland*), 3.3 oz. 20

Vegetables, Frozen, squash, continued

winter, cooked (*Seabrook Farms*), 4 oz.   45
zucchini, *see "zucchini," below*

succotash:
(*Seabrook Farms*), 3.3 oz.   100
w/baby lima beans (*Comstock*), 3.5 oz.   140
w/Fordhook lima beans (*Hanover*), 3.3 oz.   94

stew vegetables, *see "vegetables, mixed," below*

turnip greens, chopped (*Seabrook Farms*), 3.3 oz.   20

turnip greens, w/diced turnips
(*Seabrook Farms*), 3.3 oz.   20

turnips:
(*Southland*), 3.3 oz.   20
mashed (*Southland*), 3.6 oz.   95
w/roots (*Southland*), 3.3 oz.   20

vegetables, mixed:
(*Birds Eye*), 3.3 oz.   60
(*Birds Eye International* New England Style),
3.3 oz.   70
(*Birds Eye International* San Francisco Style),
3.3 oz.   100
(*Comstock*), 3.5 oz.   80
(*Comstock* California Blend), 3.5 oz.   35
(*Comstock* Winter Mix), 3.5 oz.   35
(*Green Giant*), 1/2 cup   50
(*Green Giant Harvest Fresh*), 1/2 cup   60
(*Hanover* Autumn Blend), 3.3 oz.   25
(*Hanover* Country Mix Blend), 3.3 oz.   79
(*Hanover* 5-Way), 3.3 oz.   59
(*Hanover* Harvest Blend), 3.3 oz.   76
(*Hanover* Summer Vegetables), 3.3 oz.   38
(*Seabrook Farms*), 3.3 oz.   65
gumbo (*Southland*), 3.2 oz.   45
soup (*Hanover* 10-Way), 3.3 oz.   74
soup (*Southland*), 3.2 oz.   60
stew (*Ore-Ida*), 3 oz.   60
stew (*Southland*), 4 oz.   60
in butter sauce (*Green Giant*), 1/2 cup   80
w/onion sauce (*Birds Eye* Combination), 2.6 oz.   100

vegetables, mixed, international:
Caribbean blend (*Hanover*), 3.3 oz.   25
Chinese style (*Birds Eye International*), 3.3 oz.   80

vegetables, mixed, international, continued

Chinese style (*Birds Eye* Stir Fry), 3.3 oz. 30
Chinese style
  (*Green Giant Harvest Get Togethers*), ½ cup 60
Chinese style (*La Choy*), ½ cup 25
Continental blend (*Hanover*), 3.3 oz. 33
Far Eastern style
  (*Birds Eye International*), 3.3 oz. 80
Italian style (*Birds Eye International*), 3.3 oz. 110
Italian style (*Comstock*), 3.5 oz. 40
Japanese style (*Birds Eye International*), 3.3 oz. 100
Japanese style (*Birds Eye* Stir Fry), 3.3 oz. 30
Japanese style
  (*Green Giant Harvest Get Togethers*), ½ cup 45
Mexicana style
  (*Birds Eye International*), 3.3 oz. 120
Oriental blend (*Hanover*), 3.3 oz. 27
Oriental style (*Comstock*), 3.5 oz. 35
Romano blend (*Hanover*), 3.3 oz. 29
yams, *see "potatoes, sweet," above*
zucchini:
  (*Seabrook Farms*), 3.3 oz. 16
  sliced (*Southland*), 3.2 oz. 15
  sliced, baby (*Birds Eye*), 3.3 oz. 16
  sticks, light batter-fried (*Mrs. Paul's*), 3 oz. 180

VEGETABLE ENTREES, FROZEN, one whole package*
See also "Vegetables, Frozen"

---

calories

asparagus w/mornay sauce, in pastry
  (*Pepperidge Farm*), 7¼-oz. pkg. 250
beans, green and mushroom casserole
  (*Stouffer's*), 4¾-oz. pkg. 150
beans, green w/mushroom sauce, in pastry
  (*Pepperidge Farm*), 7¼-oz. pkg. 270
broccoli w/cheese, in pastry
  (*Pepperidge Farm*), 7¼-oz. pkg. 250
cabbage, stuffed w/meat in tomato sauce
  (*Stouffer's Lean Cuisine*), 1 pkg. 210

Vegetable Entrees, Frozen, continued

cauliflower and cheese sauce, in pastry
  (*Pepperidge Farm*), 7¼-oz. pkg. 220
corn soufflé (*Stouffer's*), 12-oz. pkg. 465
eggplant Parmigiana (*Buitoni*), 12-oz. pkg. 430
green pepper, stuffed:
  (*Green Giant* Baked Entree), 1 pkg. 400
  w/beef, in tomato sauce
    (*Stouffer's*), 15½-oz. pkg. 450
  in tomato sauce
    (*Weight Watchers*), 11¾-oz. pkg. 240
Mexican style picante, in pastry
  (*Pepperidge Farm*), 7¼-oz. pkg. 220
mushrooms Dijon, in pastry
  (*Pepperidge Farm*), 7¼-oz. pkg. 230
Oriental garden w/Szechwan spices, in pastry
  (*Pepperidge Farm*), 7¼-oz. pkg. 230
ratatouille (*Stouffer's*), 5-oz. pkg. 60
ratatouille w/cheese, in pastry
  (*Pepperidge Farm*), 7¼-oz. pkg. 230
spinach almondine, in pastry
  (*Pepperidge Farm*), 7¼-oz. pkg. 260
spinach soufflé (*Stouffer's*), 12-oz. pkg. 405
zucchini Provençale, in pastry
  (*Pepperidge Farm*), 7¼-oz. pkg. 210

*Pay attention to package sizes

BEANS, BAKED & BAKED STYLE,
eight ounces, except as noted

---

                                                    calories
(*Campbell's* Home Style) 270
(*Howard Johnson's*), 1 cup 340
(*Van Camp*) 260
(*Van Camp Beanee Weenee*) 300
w/bacon (*Hormel* Short Order), 7½-oz. can 330
barbecue (*Campbell's*), 7⅞ oz. 250
in brown sugar sauce:
  (*Van Camp*) 290

Beans, Baked & Baked Style, in brown sugar sauce, continued
pea bean (*B & M*)	330
red kidney beans (*B & M*)	330
yellow-eye (*B & M*)	330

w/frankfurters
(*Hormel* Beans 'n Wieners), 7½-oz. can	280

w/frankfurters, freeze-dried
(*Mountain House*), 2.65 oz.	360

w/ham (*Hormel* Short Order), 7½-oz. can	360

in molasses sauce w/brown sugar
(*Campbell's* Old Fashioned)	270

w/pork:
(*Van Camp*)	273
in tomato sauce (*Campbell's*)	250
in tomato sauce (*Joan of Arc*), 1 cup	280

vegetarian:
(*Heinz*)	230
(*Van Camp*)	210

TOMATO PASTE & PUREE, six ounces, except as noted
See also "Sauces"

---

calories

tomato paste:
(*Contadina*)	150
(*Del Monte*)	150
(*Featherweight*)	150
(*Hunt's*)	135
(*Tri/Valley*)	150
Italian style (*Hunt's*)	150

tomato puree:
(*Cellu*), 1 cup	80
(*Featherweight*), 1 cup	90
(*Hunt's*), 4 oz.	45
light (*Tri/Valley*), 1 cup	90
medium (*Tri/Valley*), 1 cup	100
heavy (*Contadina*)	75
heavy (*Tri/Valley*), 1 cup	120
extra heavy (*Tri/Valley*), 1 cup	140

PICKLES & RELISH
See also "Olives" and "Condiments & Seasonings"

	calories
garden mix, hot and spice (*Vlasic*), 1 oz.	4
onions, cocktail, spiced (*Vlasic*), 1 oz.	4
onions, spiced (*Heinz*), 1 oz.	2
pickles, dill and sour:	
whole (*Bond's* Flavor-Pack Dills), 1 pickle*	1
whole (*Bond's* Fresh-Pack Dills), 1 pickle*	2
whole (*Bond's* Fresh-Pack Kosher Dills), 1 pickle*	2
whole (*Claussen* Kosher), 1 piece*	7
whole (*Vlasic* Kosher Crunchy Dills), 1 oz.	4
whole (*Vlasic* Kosher Deli Dills), 1 oz.	4
whole (*Vlasic* Original Dills), 1 oz.	2
whole, baby (*Vlasic* Kosher Baby Dills), 1 oz.	4
whole, no garlic (*Vlasic* Dills), 1 oz.	4
whole, gherkins (*Vlasic* Kosher Dills), 1 oz.	4
whole, unsalted (*Featherweight* Dills), 1 pickle*	4
whole, unsalted (*Featherweight* Kosher Dills), 1 pickle*	4
spears (*Bond's* Fresh-Pack Dills), 1 piece*	2
spears (*Bond's* Fresh-Pack Kosher Dills), 1 piece*	2
spears (*Vlasic* Kosher Dills), 1 oz.	4
slices, unsalted (*Featherweight*), 1 oz.	12
chips, reduced-salt (*Vlasic* Hamburger Dills), 1 oz.	2
pickles, sweet:	
whole (*Bond's* Gherkins), 1 pickle*	19
whole (*Heinz* Gherkins), 1 oz.	35
whole (*Heinz* Midget Gherkins), 1 oz.	35
whole (*Heinz* Sweet Pickles), 1 oz.	35
pieces (*Heinz* Mixed), 1 oz.	40
slices (*Heinz* Sweet Cucumber Slices), 1 oz.	20
slices (*Heinz* Sweet Pickle Slices), 1 oz.	35
sticks (*Heinz* Sweet Cucumber Stix), 1 oz.	25
bread and butter, chunks (*Vlasic* Deli), 1 oz.	25

pickles, sweet, continued

bread and butter, chunks (*Vlasic* Old Fashioned), 1 oz.	25
bread and butter, slices (*Heinz* Cucumber Slices), 1 oz.	25
bread and butter, sticks (*Vlasic* Sweet Stix), 1 oz.	18
sweet and sour, slices (*Claussen*), 3 pieces*	9
relishes:	
barbecue (*Crosse & Blackwell*), 1 tbsp.	22
corn (*Crosse & Blackwell*), 1 tbsp.	15
dill (*Vlasic*), 1 oz.	2
hamburger (*Crosse & Blackwell*), 1 tbsp.	20
hamburger (*Heinz*), 1 oz.	30
hamburger (*Vlasic*), 1 oz.	40
hot dog (*Crosse & Blackwell*), 1 tbsp.	22
hot dog (*Heinz*), 1 oz.	35
hot dog (*Vlasic*), 1 oz.	40
hot pepper (*Crosse & Blackwell*), 1 tbsp.	22
India (*Heinz*), 1 oz.	35
Indian (*Crosse & Blackwell*), 1 tbsp.	26
mustard (*Crosse & Blackwell* Chow Chow), 1 tbsp.	6
piccalilli (*Crosse & Blackwell*), 1 tbsp.	26
piccalilli, green tomato (*Heinz*), 1 oz.	30
sweet (*Crosse & Blackwell*), 1 tbsp.	26
sweet (*Heinz*), 1 oz.	25
sweet (*Vlasic*), 1 oz.	30
salad cubes, sweet (*Heinz*), 1 oz.	30
watermelon rind, pickled (*Crosse & Blackwell*), 1 tbsp.	38

Average-size piece, as packaged

OLIVES, one piece*

---

calories

green:
  Manzanilla (*Grandee*), 1 medium 4
  Manzanilla, pimento-stuffed
    (*Grandee*), 1 queen size 14
ripe:
  (*Lindsay*), 1 large 5
  (*Lindsay*), 1 extra large 5
  (*Lindsay*), 1 giant 8
  (*Lindsay*), 1 jumbo 10
  (*Lindsay*), 1 colossal 13
  (*Lindsay*), 1 super-colossal 16
  (*Lindsay*), 1 super-supreme 18

As packaged; note variations in size

VEGETABLE JUICES, six fluid ounces, except as noted
See also "Fruit Juices"

---

calories

clam- and tomato-flavored cocktail
  (*Mott's Clamato*) 82
tomato juice:
  (*Campbell's*) 35
  (*Del Monte*) 35
  (*Diet Delight*) 35
  (*Hunt's*) 30
  (*Libby's*) 35
  (*S & W Nutradiet*) 35
  (*Sacramento*) 35
  (*Tri/Valley*) 35
  (*Welch's*) 35
tomato cocktail (*Snap-E-Tom*) 40
tomato-flavor cocktail w/beef broth
  (*Mott's Beefamato*) 70

Vegetable Juices, continued

tomato-chile cocktail (*Del Monte*) 40
vegetable-juice cocktail:
  (*Featherweight*) 35
  (*S & W Nutradiet*) 35
  (*Tri/Valley*) 35
  (*"V-8"*) 35
  no salt (*"V-8"*) 40
  spicy hot (*"V-8"*) 35

Chapter 8

VEGETARIAN PROTEIN FOODS AND MEATLESS "MEATS"

VEGETARIAN FOODS, CANNED & DRY
See also "Vegetarian Foods, Frozen"

---

 calories

"beef," sliced (*Worthington*), 2 oz. or 2 slices 110
bits (*Loma Linda Tender Bits*), 4 pieces 80
bits (*Worthington Veja-Bits*), approximately ½ cup ... 70
burgers and burger granules:
  (*Loma Linda Redi Burger*), ½" slice 130
  (*Loma Linda VegeBurger*), ½ cup 79
  (*Loma Linda VegeBurger* NSA), ½ cup 140
  (*Worthington Vegetarian Burger*), ⅓ cup 130
  granules (*Loma Linda VitaBurger*), 3 tbsp. 70
  granules (*Worthington Granburger*), 3 tbsp. 65
"chicken":
  (*Loma Linda Chicken Supreme*), ¼ cup 50
  diced (*Worthington Soyameat*), ¼ cup 120
  fried (*Worthington Fri Chik Soyameat*), 2 pieces 190
  fried (*Loma Linda*), 2 pieces 140
  sliced (*Worthington Soyameat*), 2 slices 130
chili (*Worthington*), ½ cup 190
chops (*Worthington Choplets*), 2 slices 100
cold cuts:
  (*Loma Linda Nuteena*), ½" slice 160
  (*Loma Linda Proteena*), ½" slice 140
  (*Loma Linda Vegelona*), ½" slice 100
  (*Worthington Numete*), ½" slice 160
  (*Worthington Protose*), ½" slice 190

cutlets (*Worthington Cutlets*), 1 1/2" slice 94
"fish" (*Loma Linda Ocean Platter*), 1/4 cup 50
franks (*Loma Linda Big Franks*), 1 frank 100
franks (*Loma Linda Sizzle Franks*), 2 franks 170
links:
  (*Loma Linda Linketts*), 2 links 150
  (*Loma Linda Little Links*), 2 links 80
  (*Worthington Saucettes*), 2 links 130
  (*Worthington Super Links*), 1 link 120
  (*Worthington Veja-Links*), 2 links 140
(*Loma Linda Dinner Cuts*), 2 cuts 110
(*Loma Linda Savory Dinner Loaf*), 1/4 cup 50
(*Loma Linda Tastee Cuts*), 2 cuts 70
"meat" balls
  (*Loma Linda Tender Rounds*), 3 pieces 60
"meat" balls
  (*Worthington Non-Meat Balls*), 3 pieces 120
patties (*Loma Linda Pattie Mix*), 1/4 cup 50
sandwich spread (*Loma Linda*), 3 tbsp. 70
sandwich spread (*Worthington*), 2 1/2 oz. 120
"scallops" (*Loma Linda Vege-Scallops*), 6 pieces 70
"scallops" (*Worthington Vegetable Skallops*),
  1/2 cup drained 70
soy "milk," dry:
  (*Worthington Soyamel*—Regular), 1 oz. 140
  (*Worthington Soyamel*—Fortified), 1 oz. 140
  (*Worthington Soyamel*—Low-fat), 1 oz. 110
"steak" (*Loma Linda Swiss Steak*), 1 steak 140
stew (*Loma Linda Stew Pac*), 2 oz. 70
"turkey" (*Worthington 209*), 2 slices 150

VEGETARIAN FOODS, FROZEN
See also "Vegetarian Foods, Canned & Dry"

calories
"bacon" strips (*Worthington Stripples*), 4 pieces 100
"beef":
  corned, *see "corned beef, roll" or "slices," below*
  roll (*Worthington*), 2 1/2-oz. slice 140

Vegetarian Foods, Frozen, "beef", continued

slices (*Worthington Luncheon Slices*), 2 slices 120
smoked, roll (*Worthington*), 2½ oz. 170
smoked, slices
   (*Worthington Luncheon Slices*), 6 slices 130
"beef" pot pie (*Worthington*), 8-oz. pie 470
"bologna" (*Loma Linda 008*), 2 slices 150
"bologna" (*Loma Linda 012*), 2 slices 380
burger (*Loma Linda Sizzle Burger*), 1 piece 210
burger (*Worthington FriPats*), 1 piece 180
"chicken":
  (*Worthington Chic-Ketts*), ½ cup 180
  fried (*Loma Linda*), 1 piece 180
  roll (*Worthington*), 2½ oz. 170
  slices (*Worthington*), 2 slices 140
"chicken" pot pie (*Worthington*), 8-oz. pie 450
corn dogs (*Loma Linda*), 1 corn dog 200
corned "beef," roll (*Worthington*), 2½ oz. 190
corned "beef," slices
  (*Worthington Luncheon Slices*), 4 slices 160
croquettes (*Worthington Croquettes*), 2 pieces 150
"fish" fillets (*Loma Linda Ocean Fillet*), 1 piece 160
"fish" fillets
  (*Worthington Vegetarian Fillets*), 2 pieces 215
"ham," roll (*Worthington Wham*), 2½ oz. 140
"ham," slices (*Worthington Wham*), 3 slices 140
"meat" balls, Swedish (*Loma Linda*), 4 pieces 95
"salami" (*Worthington*), 2 slices 100
"sausage," breakfast style:
  links (*Worthington Prosage*), 3 links 180
  patties (*Worthington Prosage*), 2 pieces 200
  roll (*Worthington Prosage*), ⅜" slice 90
"steak" (*Loma Linda Griddle Steak*), 1 piece 190
"steak" (*Worthington Stakelets*), 1 piece 180
"tuna" (*Worthington Tuno*), 2 oz. 90
"tuna" pot pie (*Worthington*), 8-oz. pie 460
"turkey":
  smoked, roll (*Worthington*), 2½ oz. 180
  smoked, slices
    (*Worthington Luncheon Slices*), 4 slices 200

Chapter 9

SOUPS, BROTHS AND CHOWDERS

SOUPS, CANNED

See also "Soups, Frozen" and "Soups, Mixes"

Soups are listed below either by the full can, a half can, or an average serving of one cup (eight fluid ounces). Note the variations in size. Also, if "condensed" (cond.) or "semicondensed" (semicond.) is not indicated, this means that the soup is ready to eat.

---

	calories
asparagus, cream of, cond.* (*Campbell's*), 8 oz.	90
bean:	
w/bacon, cond.* (*Campbell's*), 8 oz.	150
w/ham, old-fashioned	
(*Campbell's* Chunky), 9½ oz.	260
w/ham, old-fashioned	
(*Campbell's* Chunky—Individual), 11-oz. can	290
w/ham, old-fashioned, semicond.***	
(*Campbell's* Soup for One), 11 oz.	210
w/ham, old-fashioned	
(*Luck's* Country Soups), 8½ oz.	190
w/ham and onions	
(*Luck's* Country Soups), 8½ oz.	170
w/sausage (*Luck's* Country Soups), 8½ oz.	170
bean, black, cond.* (*Campbell's*), 8 oz.	110
bean, black, w/sherry	
(*Crosse & Blackwell*), 13-oz. can	160
bean, pinto chowder	
(*Luck's* Country Soups), 8½ oz.	210
beef:	
(*Campbell's* Chunky), 9½ oz.	170

Soups, Canned, beef, continued

(*Campbell's* Chunky—Individual), 10¾-oz. can 190
cond.* (*Campbell's*), 8 oz. 80
broth or bouillon, cond.* (*Campbell's*), 8 oz. 15
broth (*College Inn*), 1 cup 18
broth (*Swanson*), 7¼ oz. 20
cabbage (*Manischewitz*), 8 oz. 62
consommé, cond.* (*Campbell's*), 8 oz. 45
and mushroom
    (*Campbell's* Chunky—Individual), 10¾ oz. 210
noodle, cond.* (*Campbell's*), 8 oz. 70
noodle, cond.* (*Campbell's* Homestyle), 8 oz. 90
beef Stroganoff
    (*Campbell's* Chunky—Individual), 10¾ oz. 300
borscht:
    (*Manischewitz*), 8 oz. 90
    low-calorie (*Manischewitz*), 8 oz. 20
cannelloni, mini beef w/vegetables
    (*Chef Boy•ar•dee* Soup di Pasta), 8¼ oz. 210
celery, cream of, cond.* (*Campbell's*), 8 oz. 100
Cheddar cheese, cond.* (*Campbell's*), 8 oz. 130
chicken:
    (*Campbell's* Chunky), 9½ oz. 150
    (*Campbell's* Chunky—Individual), 10¾-oz. can 170
    (*Progresso* Chickarina), 1 cup 100
    (*Progresso* Home Style), 8 oz. 70
    alphabet, cond.* (*Campbell's*), 8 oz. 80
    barley (*Manischewitz*), 8 oz. 83
    broth
        (*Campbell's* Ready to Serve—low-sodium),
        10½ oz. 40
    broth (*College Inn*), 1 cup 35
    broth (*Swanson*), 7¼ oz. 30
    broth, cond.* (*Campbell's*), 8 oz. 35
    broth and noodles, cond.* (*Campbell's*), 8 oz. 60
    broth and rice, cond.* (*Campbell's*), 8 oz. 50
    cream of, cond.* (*Campbell's*), 8 oz. 110
    and dumplings, cond.* (*Campbell's*), 8 oz. 80
    gumbo, cond.* (*Campbell's*), 8 oz. 60
    golden, and noodles, semicond.***
        (*Campbell's* Soup for One), 11 oz. 120
    mushroom, creamy, cond.* (*Campbell's*), 8 oz. 110

Soups, Canned, chicken, continued

noodle (*Dia Mel*), 8 oz.	50
noodle (*Campbell's*—low-sodium), 10½ oz.	170
noodle (*Campbell's* Chunky), 9½ oz.	180
noodle (*Campbell's* Chunky—Individual),	
10¾-oz. can	200
noodle (*Manischewitz*), 8 oz.	46
noodle, cond.* (*Campbell's*), 8 oz.	70
noodle, cond.* (*Campbell's* Homestyle), 8 oz.	70
noodle, O-shape, cond.*	
(*Campbell's* NoodleO's), 8 oz.	70
noodle stars, cond.* (*Campbell's*), 8 oz.	60
w/pasta and meatballs	
(*Chef Boy•ar•dee* Soup de Pasta), 8 oz.	110
rice (*Campbell's* Chunky), 9½ oz.	140
rice (*Manischewitz*), 8 oz.	47
rice, cond.* (*Campbell's*), 8 oz.	60
vegetable (*Campbell's*—low-sodium), 10¾ oz.	240
vegetable (*Campbell's* Chunky), 9½ oz.	170
vegetable (*Hain Naturals* Home-Style), 4¾ oz.	130
vegetable	
(*Hain Naturals* Home-Style—no salt added),	
4¾ oz.	130
vegetable (*Manischewitz*), 8 oz.	55
vegetable, cond.* (*Campbell's*), 8 oz.	70
vegetable, semicond.*** (*Campbell's*), 11 oz.	120
chili beef:	
(*Campbell's* Chunky), 9¾ oz.	260
(*Campbell's* Chunky—Individual), 11-oz. can	290
cond.* (*Campbell's*), 8 oz.	130
clam chowder:	
(*Howard Johnson's*), 1 cup	177
Manhattan (*Campbell's* Chunky), 9½ oz.	150
Manhattan (*Campbell's* Chunky—Individual),	
10¾-oz. can	160
Manhattan (*Crosse & Blackwell*), 13-oz. can	100
Manhattan, cond.* (*Campbell's*), 8 oz.	70
Manhattan, cond.* (*Doxsee*), 6 oz.	50
Manhattan, cond.* (*Snow's*), 7½ oz.	70
New England (*Campbell's* Chunky), 9½ oz.	250
New England (*Campbell's* Chunky—Individual),	
10¾-oz. can	290

Soups, Canned, clam chowder, continued

New England (*Crosse & Blackwell*), 13-oz. can 180
New England (*Doxsee*), 6 oz. 90
New England, cond.* (*Campbell's*), 8 oz. 80
New England, cond.** (*Campbell's*), 8 oz. 150
New England, cond.** (*Snow's*), 7½ oz. 140
New England, semicond.***
   (*Campbell's* Soup for One), 11 oz. 130
New England, semicond.†
   (*Campbell's* Soup for One), 11 oz. 200
corn chowder, New England, cond.**
   (*Snow's*), 7½ oz. 150
crab, à la Maryland
   (*Crosse & Blackwell*), 13-oz. can 100
escarole, in chicken broth (*Progresso*), 1 cup 125
fish chowder, New England, cond.**
   (*Snow's*), 7½ oz. 130
gazpacho (*Crosse & Blackwell*), 13-oz. can 60
green pea, *see "pea," below*
ham and butter bean
   (*Campbell's* Chunky—Individual), 10¾ oz. 280
lentil:
   (*Hain Naturals* Hearty Home-Style),
    4¾ oz. 190
   (*Hain Naturals* Hearty Home-Style—no salt added),
    4¾ oz. 190
   (*Progresso*), 1 cup 150
   w/ham (*Crosse & Blackwell*), 13-oz. can 160
macaroni and bean (*Progresso*), 8 oz. 170
Madrilene consommé, clear
   (*Crosse & Blackwell*), 13-oz. can 160
Madrilene consommé, red
   (*Crosse & Blackwell*), 13-oz. can 60
meatball alphabet, cond.* (*Campbell's*), 8 oz. 100
minestrone:
   (*Campbell's* Chunky), 9½ oz. 140
   (*Crosse & Blackwell*), 13-oz. can 180
   (*Hain Naturals* Hearty Home-Style), 4¾ oz. 190
   (*Hain Naturals* Hearty Home-Style—no salt added),
    4¾ oz. 190
   (*Progresso*), 8 oz. 130
   cond.* (*Campbell's*), 8 oz. 80

w/meatballs and pasta
  (*Chef Boy•ar•dee* Soup di Pasta), 8¼ oz. 140
mushroom:
  barley (*Manischewitz*), 8 oz. 72
  beefy, cond.* (*Campbell's*), 8 oz. 60
  cream of
    (*Campbell's*—low-sodium), 10½-oz. can 190
  cream of, bisque
    (*Crosse & Blackwell*), 13-oz. can 180
  cream of, cond.* (*Campbell's*), 8 oz. 100
  cream of, semicond.***
    (*Campbell's* Soup for One), 11 oz. 180
  cream of, low-calorie, cond.* (*Dia-Mel*), 8 oz. 85
  golden, cond.* (*Campbell's*), 8 oz. 80
noodles and ground beef, cond.*
  (*Campbell's*), 8 oz. 90
onion:
  cream of, cond.* (*Campbell's*), 8 oz. 100
  cream of, cond.†† (*Campbell's*), 8 oz. 140
  French (*Campbell's*—low-sodium), 10½ oz. 80
  French, cond.* (*Campbell's*), 8 oz. 70
oyster stew, cond.* (*Campbell's*), 8 oz. 70
oyster stew, cond.** (*Campbell's*), 8 oz. 150
pea:
  green (*Campbell's*—low-sodium), 7½-oz. can 150
  green (*Progresso*), 8 oz. 180
  green, cond.* (*Campbell's*), 8 oz. 150
  split
    (*Hain Naturals* Hearty Home-Style), 4¾ oz. 210
  split
    (*Hain Naturals* Hearty Home-Style—no salt added)
    4¾ oz. 220
  split (*Manischewitz*), 8 oz. 133
  split, w/ham (*Campbell's* Chunky), 9½ oz. 200
  split, w/ham
    (*Campbell's* Chunky—Individual), 10¾-oz. can ... 230
  split, w/ham and bacon, cond.*
    (*Campbell's*), 8 oz. 170
pepperpot, cond.* (*Campbell's*), 8 oz. 90
potato, cream of, cond.* (*Campbell's*), 8 oz. 70
potato, cream of, cond.†† (*Campbell's*), 8 oz. 110

Soups, Canned, continued

ravioli, beef w/vegetables
   (*Chef Boy•ar•dee* Soup di Pasta), 8¼ oz. 190
ravioli, chicken
   (*Chef Boy•ar•dee* Soup di Pasta), 8¼ oz. 130
shav (*Manischewitz*), 8 oz. 11
Scotch broth, cond.* (*Campbell's*), 8 oz. 80
seafood chowder, New England, cond.**
   (*Snow's*), 7½ oz. 130
shrimp, cream of:
   (*Crosse & Blackwell*), 13-oz. can 180
   cond.* (*Campbell's*), 8 oz. 90
   cond.** (*Campbell's*), 8 oz. 160
sirloin burger (*Campbell's* Chunky), 9½ oz. 200
sirloin burger
   (*Campbell's* Chunky—Individual), 10¾-oz. can 220
steak and potato
   (*Campbell's* Chunky), 9½ oz. 170
steak and potato
   (*Campbell's* Chunky—Individual), 10¾-oz. can 200
tomato:
   (*Campbell's*—low-sodium), 7¼-oz. can 130
   (*Hain Naturals* Hearty Home-Style), 4¾ oz. 150
   (*Hain Naturals* Hearty Home-Style—no salt added),
     4¾ oz. 160
   (*Manischewitz*), 8-oz. can 60
   (*Progresso*), 1 cup 110
   cond.* (*Campbell's*), 8 oz. 90
   cond.** (*Campbell's*), 8 oz. 160
   semicond.***
     (*Campbell's* Royale Soup for One), 11 oz. 180
   bisque, cond.* (*Campbell's*), 8 oz. 120
   creamy, w/meatballs and pasta
     (*Chef Boy•ar•dee* Soup di Pasta), 8¼ oz. 200
   low-calorie, cond.* (*Dia Mel*), 8 oz. 50
   rice, old-fashioned, cond.* (*Campbell's*), 8 oz. 110
turkey:
   noodle, cond.* (*Campbell's*), 8 oz. 60
   vegetable (*Campbell's* Chunky), 9½ oz. 130
   vegetable, cond.* (*Campbell's*), 8 oz. 70
turtle, mock (*Stegner's*), 10½-oz. can 212
turtle, mock (*Stegner's*), 15-oz. can 302

Soups, Canned, continued

vegetable:

(*Campbell's* Chunky), 9½ oz. 130

(*Campbell's* Chunky—Individual), 10¾-oz. can 140

(*Luck's* Country Soups), 8½ oz. 100

(*Manischewitz*), 8 oz. 63

cond.* (*Campbell's*), 8 oz. 80

semicond.***

(*Campbell's* Old World Soup for One), 11 oz. 130

beef (*Campbell's*—low-sodium), 10¾-oz. can 170

beef, cond.* (*Campbell's*), 8 oz. 70

beef, low-calorie, cond.* (*Dia Mel*), 8 oz. 70

beef, old-fashioned

(*Campbell's* Chunky—Individual),

10¾-oz. can 180

beef, w/bacon, burly, semicond.***

(*Campbell's* Soup for One), 11 oz. 150

chunky, w/beef

(*Chef Boy•ar•dee* Soup di Pasta), 8¼ oz. 120

country

(*Chef Boy•ar•dee* Soup di Pasta), 8¼ oz. 110

Italian (*Chef Boy•ar•dee* Soup di Pasta), 8¼ oz. 120

Mediterranean (*Campbell's* Chunky), 9½ oz. 160

old-fashioned (*Campbell's* Chunky), 9½ oz. 160

vegetarian

(*Hain Naturals* Hearty Home-Style), 4¾ oz. 180

vegetarian

(*Hain Naturals* Hearty Home-Style—no salt added),

4¾ oz. 160

vegetarian, cond.* (*Campbell's*), 8 oz. 70

vichyssoise, cream of

(*Crosse & Blackwell*), 13-oz. can 140

won ton, cond.* (*Campbell's*), 8 oz. 40

*Prepared with 4 oz. soup and 4 oz. water
**Prepared with 4 oz. soup and 4 oz. whole milk
***Prepared with 7¾ oz. soup and 3¼ oz. water
†Prepared with 7¾ oz. soup and 3¼ oz. whole milk
††Prepared with 4 oz. soup, 2 oz. water and 2 oz. whole milk

SOUPS, MIXES*, six-ounce cup, except as noted
See also "Soups, Canned" and "Soups, Frozen"

calories

alphabet (*Golden Grain*), 8-oz. cup	55
asparagus (*Knorr*)	45
beef and beef flavor:	
(*Lipton Cup-a-Soup* Trim)	10
barley (*Knorr*)	45
bouillon, *see "bouillon," below*	
broth, *see "broth," below*	
mushroom (*Lipton*), 8-oz. cup	40
noodle (*Knorr* Swiss)	25
noodle (*Lipton Cup-a-Soup*)	45
noodle	
(*Lipton Cup-a-Soup Lots-a-Noodles*), 7-oz. cup	120
noodle, freeze-dried	
(*Mountain House*), .37 oz.**	25
noodle, beef flavor, *see "noodle," below*	
vegetable, w/noodles (*Lipton* Hearty), 8-oz. cup	80
bouillon:	
beef (*Herb-Ox*), 1 cube	7
beef (*Maggi*), 1 cube	6
beef (*Steero*), 1 cube or 1 tsp.	7
beef (*Wyler's*), 1 tsp.	6
chicken (*Herb-Ox*), 1 cube	7
chicken (*Maggi*), 1 cube	7
chicken (*Steero*), 1 cube or 1 tsp.	7
chicken (*Wyler's*), 1 cube	8
onion (*Wyler's*), 1 tsp.	10
vegetable (*Herb-Ox*), 1 cube	7
vegetable (*Steero*), 1 cube or 1 tsp.	7
broth:	
beef (*Maggi* Broth & Seasoning), 1 tsp.	27
beef (*MBT*)	14
brown seasoning and broth	
(*G. Washington's*), .14 oz.	6
brown seasoning and broth	
(*G. Washington's* Kosher), .14 oz.	6

Soups, Mixes, broth, continued

chicken (*Lipton Cup-a-Broth*) 25
chicken (*Maggi* Broth & Seasoning), 1 tsp. 29
chicken (*MBT*) 12
onion (*Maggi* Broth & Seasoning), 1 tsp. 28
onion (*MBT*) 16
onion seasoning and broth
  (*G. Washington's*), .18 oz. 12
onion seasoning and broth
  (*G. Washington's* Kosher), .18 oz. 12
vegetable (*Maggi* Broth & Seasoning), 1 tsp. 27
vegetable (*MBT*) 12
chicken flavor:
(*Lipton Cup-a-Soup* Trim) 10
(*Quick 'n Tender*), 4 1/2-oz. pkg.* 600
(*Stir 'n Ready*), 1.4-oz. pkg. dry 190
bouillon, *see "bouillon," above*
broth, *see "broth," above*
cream of (*Estee*) 50
cream of (*Knorr* Swiss) 80
cream of (*Lipton Cup-a-Soup*) 80
cream of
  (*Lipton Cup-a-Soup Lots-a-Noodles*), 7-oz. cup 150
hearty (*Lipton Cup-a-Soup* Country Style) 70
noodle (*Golden Grain*) 34
noodle (*Knorr*) 45
noodle (*Knorr* Swiss) 20
noodle (*Lipton*), 8-oz. cup 70
noodle (*Lipton Cup-a-Soup*) 45
noodle
  (*Lipton Cup-a-Soup Lots-a-Noodles*), 7-oz. cup 120
noodle, freeze-dried
  (*Mountain House*), .37 oz.** 25
noodle, chicken flavor, *see "noodle," below*
rice (*Lipton Cup-a-Soup*) 45
supreme (*Lipton Cup-a-Soup* Country Style) 100
vegetable (*Lipton Cup-a-Soup*) 40
green pea, *see "pea," below*
leek (*Knorr*) 50
minestrone (*Golden Grain*), 8-oz. cup 66
minestrone (*Manischewitz*) 50
mushroom, cream of (*Estee*) 50

Soups, Mixes, continued

mushroom, golden, w/chicken broth
  (*Lipton*), 8-oz. cup 60
Napoli (*Knorr*) 40
noodle:
  beef (*Cup O' Noodles*), 2½-oz. packet** 290
  chicken
    (*Cup O' Noodles*), 2½-oz. packet** 300
  chicken
    (*Cup O' Noodles* Hearty), 2½-oz. packet** 330
  chicken
    (*Cup O' Noodles* Twin Pack), 1.2-oz. packet** 150
  w/chicken broth (*Lipton*), 8-oz. cup 70
  w/real chicken broth
    (*Lipton* Giggle Noodle), 8-oz. cup 80
  rings (*Lipton Cup-a-Soup*) 50
  rings (*Lipton* Ring-O), 8-oz. cup 60
  shrimp (*Cup O' Noodles*), 2½-oz. packet** 300
  w/vegetables and chicken broth
    (*Lipton* Hearty), 8-oz. cup 80
onion:
  (*Golden Grain*), 8-oz. cup 33
  (*Knorr* Soup Dip) 30
  (*Knorr* Swiss) 45
  (*Lipton Cup-a-Soup*) 30
  (*Lipton*), 8-oz. cup 35
  beefy (*Lipton*), 8-oz. cup 35
  broth, *see "broth," above*
  mushroom (*Lipton*), 8-oz. cup 45
  golden, w/chicken broth (*Lipton*), 8-oz. cup 60
  tomato (*Lipton*), 8-oz. cup 70
oxtail (*Knorr*) 50
pea:
  green (*Knorr*) 55
  green (*Knorr* Swiss) 65
  split (*Manischewitz*) 45
  Virginia style
    (*Lipton Cup-a-Soup* Country Style) 140
potato (*Knorr*) 70
tomato:
  (*Knorr* Swiss) 70
  (*Lipton Cup-a-Soup*) 80

Soups, Mixes, tomato, continued

    beefy (*Lipton Cup-a-Soup* Trim) 10
    cream of (*Estee*) 60
    vegetable (*Estee*) 60
    vegetable, w/noodles
      (*Lipton* Hearty), 8-oz. cup 80
vegetable:
    (*Knorr*) 25
    (*Knorr* Swiss) 75
    (*Lipton Cup-a-Soup Lots-a-Noodles*), 7-oz. cup 110
    (*Manischewitz*) 50
    beef (*Lipton Cup-a-Soup*) 50
    w/beef stock (*Lipton*), 8-oz. cup 50
    bouillon, *see "bouillon," above*
    broth, *see "broth," above*
    country (*Lipton*), 8-oz. cup 80
    cream of (*Estee*) 60
    garden
      (*Lipton Cup-a-Soup Lots-a-Noodles*), 7-oz. cup 130
    harvest (*Lipton Cup-a-Soup* Country Style) 90
    herbed (*Lipton Cup-a-Soup* Trim) 10
    spring vegetable (*Lipton Cup-a-Soup*) 40

  **Prepared according to package directions, except as noted*
***Unprepared dry mix*

SOUPS, FROZEN
See also "Soups, Canned" and "Soups, Mixes*"

---

                                      calories
clam chowder, New England (*Stouffer's*), 8 oz. 200
pea (*Tabatchnick*), 7.5 oz. 186
pea, split, w/ham (*Stouffer's*), 8¼ oz. 190
potato (*Tabatchnick*), 7.5 oz. 95
spinach, cream of (*Stouffer's*), 8 oz. 230
vegetable (*Tabatchnick*), 7.5 oz. 97
won ton (*La Choy*), 7.5 oz. 50

Chapter 10

DIPS, APPETIZERS AND HORS D'OEUVRES

APPETIZERS, HORS D'OEUVRES & SNACKS, CANNED, DRIED OR IN JARS
See also "Appetizers, Hors D'Oeuvres & Snacks, Frozen," "Fish, Smoked"
and "Meat, Fish & Poultry Spreads"

---

	calories
anchovies, flat (*Reese*), 2-oz. can	100
caviar:	
black sturgeon (*Northland Queen*), 1 oz.	74
black sturgeon (*Romanoff*), 1 oz.	74
red salmon (*Romanoff*), 1 oz.	68
red salmon (*Romar Brand*), 1 oz.	68
chicken livers, chopped (*Reese*), 1 oz.	47
clam cocktail, w/sauce (*Sau-Sea*), 4-oz. jar	99
crab cocktail, w/sauce (*Sau-Sea*), 4-oz. jar	107
fish balls (*King Oscar*), 14-oz. can	137
frankfurters, cocktail (*Vienna*), 1 oz.	88
gefilte fish balls, cocktail (*Manischewitz Fishlets*), 1 oz.	31
herring snacks, kippered (*King Oscar* Kippered Snacks), 3¾-oz. can	205
herring, pickled, kippered or salad, see "Fish & Shellfish, Canned or in Jars," see page 164	
mushrooms, cocktail (*Reese* Buttons), 4-oz. jar, drained	25
pâté:	
liver (*Hormel*), 1 tbsp.	33

Appetizers, Hors d'Oeuvres & Snacks, Canned or in Jars, pâté, continued

liver (*Sell's*), 1 tbsp. 45
liver, w/herbs (*Le Parfait*), 1 oz. 73
liver, w/truffles (*Le Parfait*), 1 oz. 73
salami, Danish, cocktail (*Reese* Sticks), 1 oz. 128
sardines, *see Fish & Shellfish, Canned or in Jars," page 165*
sausage rolls, dried:
  (*Cow-Boy Jo's* Beef Jerky), 1/4-oz. pkg. 24
  (*Cow-Boy Jo's* Beef Sausage), 5/8-oz. pkg. 81
  (*Cow-Boy Jo's Smok-O-Roni* Beef Sausage),
    1/2-oz. pkg. 42
  (*Frito-Lay* Beef Jerky), .23 oz. 25
  (*Frito-Lay* Hot Sausage), 1 oz. 80
  (*Frito-Lay* Smoked Beef Polish Sausage),
    1-oz. pkg. 70
  (*Frito-Lay* Smoked Beef Sticks), .5 oz. 80
  (*Frito-Lay* Summer Sausage), .7 oz. 110
  (*Lowrey's* Pickled Hot Sausage), 1 1/4-oz. pkg. 110
  (*Lowrey's* Pickled Polish Sausage), 5/8-oz. pkg. 50
sausage rolls, freeze-dried
  (*Mountain House*), 1 oz. 110
sausages, cocktail, smoked
  (*Kahn's* Cocktail Smokies), 2 links* 171
sausages, Vienna:
  (*Armour Star*), 3 sausages* 150
  (*Wilson's Certified*), 3 sausages* 144
  barbecue (*Libby's*), 3 sausages* 154
  beef broth (*Libby's*), 3 sausages* 137
  chicken (*Hormel*), 1 sausage* 45
shrimp cocktail, w/sauce (*Sau-Sea*), 4-oz. jar 112
shrimp cocktail, w/sauce (*Sau-Sea*), 6-oz. jar 121

*As packaged

APPETIZERS, HORS D'OEUVRES & SNACKS, FROZEN,
one piece*, except as noted
*See also "Appetizers, Hors d'Oeuvres & Snacks,
Canned, Dried or in Jars"*

	calories
cheese straws (*Durkee*), 1 piece	29
dim sum:	
turkey-vegetable	
(*Royal Dragon Potsticker*), 1-oz. piece	45
turkey-shrimp-vegetable	
(*Royal Dragon Shaomai*), .6-oz.	27
shrimp-bamboo shoot	
(*Royal Dragon Hargow*), 1/2-oz. piece	27
egg rolls:	
Cantonese	
(*Van de Kamp's* Chinese Classics),	
101/2-oz. pkg.	550
chicken (*Chun King*), 1/2-oz. roll	90
chicken (*La Choy*), .45-oz. roll	30
chicken and mushroom (*Mow Sang*), 1-oz. roll	69
lobster (*Choy*), .45-oz. roll	27
meat and shrimp (*Chun King*), 1/2-oz. roll	100
meat and shrimp	
(*Chun King*), 21/2-oz. roll	130
meat and shrimp (*La Choy*), .45-oz. roll	27
meat and shrimp (*La Choy*), 1/4-oz. roll	17
pork, barbecue (*Mow Sang*), 1-oz. roll	74
shrimp (*Chun King*), 1/2-oz. roll	90
shrimp (*La Choy*), .45-oz. roll	27
shrimp (*La Choy*), 3-oz. roll	80
shrimp (*Mow Sang*), 1-oz. roll	64
vegetable (*Mow Sang*), 1-oz. roll	66
franks in pastry	
(*Durkee Franks-N-Blankets*), 1 piece	45
spring roll (*Royal Dragon*), 11/2-oz. roll	106
spring roll, cocktail (*Royal Dragon*), 1/2-oz. roll	40
wontons (*Royal Dragon*), 1/3-oz. piece	30

*As packaged; note variations in size

DIPS, READY TO SERVE
See also "Dip Mixes" and "Cheese Spreads"

	calories
avocado (*Kraft*), 2 tbsp.	50
bacon and horseradish (*Kraft*), 2 tbsp.	60
bacon and horseradish (*Kraft* Premium), 1 oz.	50
bean, hot (*Hain*), 2 tbsp.	50
bean, onion (*Hain*), 2 tbsp.	45
blue cheese (*Kraft* Premium), 1 oz.	50
buttermilk (*Kraft*), 2 tbsp.	80
buttermilk (*Kraft* Premium), 1 oz.	80
buttermilk and bacon (*Kraft* Premium), 1 oz.	80
buttermilk and onion (*Kraft* Premium), 1 oz.	70
clam (*Kraft*), 2 tbsp.	60
clam (*Kraft* Premium), 1 oz.	50
cucumber, creamy (*Kraft* Premium), 1 oz.	50
enchilada (*Fritos*), 3¹/8-oz. serving	120
garlic (*Kraft*), 2 tbsp.	60
jalapeño bean (*Fritos*), 3¹/8-oz. serving	100
jalapeño bean (*Hain*), 2 tbsp.	50
jalapeño pepper (*Kraft*), 2 tbsp.	50
jalapeño pepper (*Kraft* Premium), 1 oz.	60
onion:	
creamy (*Kraft* Premium), 1 oz.	50
French (*Kraft* Premium), 1 oz.	50
French (*Kraft*), 2 tbsp.	60
green (*Kraft*), 2 tbsp.	50
taco (*Hain* Taco Dip & Sauce), ¼ cup	20

DIP MIXES, one packet
See also "Dips, Ready to Serve"

---

calories

garlic and onion (*McCormick/Schiller*), 1¼ oz. 158
horseradish w/imitation bacon bits
   (*McCormick/Schiller*), 1¼ oz. 153
onion, toasted (*McCormick/Schiller*), 1¼ oz. 103
onion soup and dip mix, *see "Soup Mixes," page 128*

Chapter 11

FROZEN DINNERS AND POT PIES

FROZEN DINNERS, one complete dinner*
See also "Frozen Pot Pies,"
"Meat & Poultry Entrees, Frozen"
and "Fish & Shellfish, Frozen"

---

                                                                    calories
beans and franks:
  (*Banquet American Favorite's*), 10¼-oz. pkg. 500
  (*Morton*), 10¾-oz. pkg. 530
  (*Swanson*), 12½-oz. pkg. 550
beef:
  (*Banquet Extra Helping*), 16-oz. pkg. 864
  (*Morton*), 10-oz. pkg. 260
  (*Swanson*), 11½-oz. pkg. 320
  chopped
    (*Banquet American Favorite's*), 11-oz. pkg. 434
  chopped
    (*Banquet Extra Helping*), 18-oz. pkg. 1028
  chopped, beefsteak
    (*Swanson Hungry-Man*), 17¼-oz. pkg. 620
  chopped sirloin (*Le Menu*), 12¼-oz. pkg. 420
  chopped sirloin
    (*Morton Steak House*), 9½-oz. pkg. 760
  chopped sirloin (*Swanson*), 11½-oz. pkg. 370
  w/gravy
    (*Banquet American Favorite's*), 10-oz. pkg. 345
  pepper, Oriental (*Chun King*), 1 dinner** 310
  pepper, Oriental (*La Choy*), 12-oz. pkg. 250

Frozen Dinners, beef, continued

rib eye (*Morton Steak House*), 9-oz. pkg. 820
Salisbury steak, *see "Salisbury steak," below*
short ribs, boneless, in barbecue sauce
    (*Armour Dinner Classics*), 10½-oz. pkg. 460
sliced (*Morton Country Table*), 14-oz. pkg. 510
sliced, w/broccoli
    (*Armour Classic Lites*), 10¼-oz. pkg. 280
sliced (*Swanson Hungry-Man*), 16-oz. pkg. 490
sirloin strip (*Morton Steak House*), 9½-oz. pkg. 760
sirloin tips
    (*Armour Dinner Classics*), 11-oz. pkg. 380
sirloin tips (*Le Menu*), 11½-oz. pkg. 390
steak, teriyaki, *see "steak," below*
Swiss steak, *see "Swiss steak," below*
tenderloin (*Morton Steak House*), 9½-oz. pkg. 890
beef burgundy
    (*Armour Dinner Classics*), 10½-oz. pkg. 330
beef Stroganoff
    (*Armour Dinner Classics*), 11¼-oz. pkg. 370
burrito, bean and beef (*Swanson*), 15¼-oz. pkg. 720
chicken:
    à la king (*Le Menu*), 10¼-oz. pkg. 320
    boneless (*Morton*), 10-oz. pkg. 230
    boneless (*Morton* King Size), 17-oz. pkg. 530
    boneless
        (*Swanson Hungry-Man*), 17½-oz. pkg. 790
Parmigiana, *see "chicken Parmigiana," below*
chicken chow mein, *see "chicken chow mein," below*
and dressing
    (*Banquet Extra Helping*), 19-oz. pkg. 808
and dumplings
    (*Banquet Extra Helping*), 19-oz. pkg. 883
fried (*Banquet American Favorite's*), 11-oz. pkg. 359
fried (*Banquet Extra Helping*), 17-oz. dinner 744
fried (*Morton*), 11-oz. pkg. 460
fried (*Morton Country Table*), 15-oz. pkg. 710
fried (*Morton* King Size), 17-oz. pkg. 860
fried, barbecue flavor (*Swanson*), 9¼ oz.*** 520
fried, breast (*Swanson*), 10¾ oz.*** 650
fried, breast (*Swanson Hungry-Man*), 14 oz.*** 890
fried, dark meat (*Swanson*), 10¼ oz.*** 600

  fried, dark meat
    (*Swanson Hungry-Man*), 14 oz.*** 890
  sweet and sour (*Le Menu*), 11½-oz. pkg. 460
chicken burgundy
    (*Armour Classic Lites*), 11¼-oz. pkg. 230
chicken chow mein:
    (*Chun King*), 1 dinner** 320
    (*La Choy*), 12-oz. pkg. 260
  and sweet and sour pork
    (*Chun King*), 1 dinner** 390
chicken fricassee
    (*Armour Dinner Classics*), 11¾-oz. pkg. 330
chicken Parmigiana
    (*Swanson Hungry-Man*), 20-oz. pkg. 820
chicken Parmigiana, breast
    (*Le Menu*), 11½-oz. pkg. 400
chicken, teriyaki
    (*Armour Dinner Classics*), 10½-oz. pkg. 340
clams, fried (*Taste O' Sea Platter*), 6½-oz. pkg. 540
cod almondine
    (*Armour Dinner Classics*), 12-oz. pkg. 360
cod, batter-fried
    (*Taste O' Sea Batter Dipt*), 8¾-oz. pkg. 500
cod fillet, Divan
    (*Armour Classic Lites*), 13¾-oz. pkg. 280
enchilada:
  beef
    (*Banquet International Favorite's*), 12-oz. pkg. 497
  beef (*Morton*), 11-oz. pkg. 280
  beef (*Patio*), 13-oz. pkg. 550
  beef (*Swanson*), 15-oz. pkg. 510
  beef (*Van de Kamp's*), 12-oz. pkg. 390
  beef, w/chili and beans (*Patio*), 16-oz. pkg. 850
  beef and cheese, w/chili and beans
    (*Patio*), 16-oz. pkg. 820
  cheese
    (*Banquet Extra Helpings*), 21¼-oz. dinner 777
  cheese
    (*Banquet International Favorite's*), 12-oz. pkg. 543
  cheese (*Patio*), 12¾-oz. pkg. 470
  cheese (*Van de Kamp's*), 12-oz. pkg. 450

Frozen Dinners, continued

fish:

   (*Banquet American Favorite's*), 8¾-oz. pkg. 553

   (*Morton*), 9-oz. pkg. 260

   (*Taste O' Sea*), 9-oz. pkg. 390

   and chips

      (*Banquet Extra Helpings*), 14-oz. dinner 769

   and chips (*Swanson*), 10½-oz. pkg. 590

   and chips

      (*Swanson Hungry-Man*), 14¾-oz. pkg. 850

   English style (*Taste O' Sea*), 9-oz. pkg. 510

   Italian style (*Taste O' Sea*), 9-oz. pkg. 510

   New England style (*Taste O' Sea*), 9-oz. pkg. 500

fish cake (*Taste O' Sea*), 8-oz. pkg. 380

fish fillet (*Van de Kamp's*), 12-oz. pkg. 300

flounder, fried (*Taste O' Sea*), 9-oz. pkg. 350

haddock, fried (*Taste O' Sea*), 9-oz. pkg. 380

ham (*Banquet American Favorite's*), 10-oz. pkg. 532

ham (*Morton*), 10-oz. pkg. 440

Italian style

   (*Banquet International Favorite's*), 12-oz. pkg. 597

lasagna:

   (*Armour Dinner Classics*), 10-oz. pkg. 380

   (*Swanson*), 13-oz. pkg. 420

   w/meat (*Swanson Hungry-Man*), 18¾-oz. pkg. 680

macaroni:

   and beef (*Morton*), 10-oz. pkg. 260

   and beef (*Swanson*), 12-oz. pkg. 370

   and cheese (*Morton*), 11-oz. pkg. 320

   and cheese (*Swanson*), 12¼-oz. pkg. 380

meatballs, Swedish

   (*Armour Dinner Classics*), 11½-oz. pkg. 470

meat loaf:

   (*Banquet American Favorite's*), 11-oz. pkg. 437

   (*Banquet Extra Helpings*), 19-oz. dinner 984

   (*Morton*), 11-oz. pkg. 340

   (*Swanson*), 11-oz. pkg. 510

Mexican style:

   (*Banquet International Favorite's*), 12-oz. pkg. 483

   (*Morton*), 11-oz. pkg. 300

   (*Patio*), 12¼-oz. pkg. 510

   (*Swanson Hungry-Man*), 22-oz. pkg. 910

(*Van de Kamp's*), 11½-oz. pkg. 421
combination
  (*Banquet International Favorite's*), 12-oz. pkg. 518
  combination (*Patio*), 11¼-oz. pkg. 590
  combination (*Swanson*), 16-oz. pkg. 590
  fiesta (*Patio*), 12¾-oz. pkg. 510
noodles and chicken (*Swanson*), 10½-oz. pkg. 270
pepper steak:
  (*Le Menu*), 11½-oz. pkg. 360
  beef (*Armour Classic Lites*), 10-oz. pkg. 270
  veal (*Armour Classic Lites*), 11-oz. pkg. 280
peppers, stuffed green
  (*Armour Dinner Classics*), 12-oz. pkg. 360
perch, fried (*Taste O' Sea*), 9-oz. pkg. 400
Polynesian style (*Swanson*), 12-oz. pkg. 510
pork, loin of (*Swanson*), 11¼-oz. pkg. 310
pot roast, Yankee (*Le Menu*), 11-oz. pkg. 360
Salisbury steak:
  (*Armour Dinner Classics*), 11-oz. pkg. 470
  (*Banquet American Favorite's*), 11-oz. pkg. 395
  (*Banquet Extra Helpings*), 19-oz. dinner 1024
  (*Morton*), 11-oz. pkg. 290
  (*Morton Country Table*), 15-oz. pkg. 500
  (*Morton* King Size), 19-oz. pkg. 780
  (*Swanson*), 11-oz. pkg. 460
  (*Swanson Hungry-Man*), 16½-oz. pkg. 710
scallops, fried (*Taste O' Sea*), 8-oz. pkg. 380
scrod, batter-fried
  (*Taste O' Sea Batter Dipt*), 8¾-oz. pkg. 500
seafood, natural herbs
  (*Armour Classic Lites*), 11½-oz. pkg. 240
seafood Newburg
  (*Armour Dinner Classics*), 10½-oz. pkg. 270
seafood platter (*Taste O' Sea*), 9-oz. pkg. 520
shrimp, fried (*Taste O' Sea*), 7-oz. pkg. 350
shrimp chow mein (*Chun King*), 1 dinner** 300
shrimp chow mein (*La Choy*), 12-oz. pkg. 220
shrimp chow mein/beef pepper Oriental (*Chun King*),
  1 dinner** 350
sole, fried (*Taste O' Sea*), 9-oz. pkg. 330
spaghetti and meatballs (*Morton*), 11-oz. pkg. 360

Frozen Dinners, continued

spaghetti and meatballs (*Swanson*), 12¹/2-oz. pkg. 410
steak, Teriyaki
  (*Armour Dinner Classics*), 10-oz. pkg. 360
sweet and sour chicken
  (*Armour Dinner Classics*), 11-oz. pkg. 410
sweet and sour pork
  (*Armour Dinner Classics*), 12-oz. pkg. 490
Swiss steak (*Swanson*), 10-oz. pkg. 360
tacos, beef, w/chili and beans (*Patio*), 11-oz. pkg. 640
turf and surf (*Armour Classic Lites*), 10-oz. pkg. 260
turkey:
  (*Banquet American Favorite's*), 11-oz. pkg. 320
  (*Banquet Extra Helpings*), 19-oz. dinner 723
  (*Morton*), 11-oz. pkg. 340
  (*Morton Country Table*), 15-oz. pkg. 520
  (*Morton* King Size), 19-oz. pkg. 580
  (*Swanson*), 11¹/2-oz. pkg. 340
  (*Swanson Hungry-Man*) 18¹/2-oz. pkg. 630
  breast, sliced w/mushrooms
    (*Le Menu*), 11¹/4-oz. pkg. 470
  Parmesan (*Armour Classic Lites*), 11-oz. pkg. 260
veal Parmigiana:
  (*Armour Dinner Classics*), 10³/4-oz. pkg. 380
  (*Banquet Extra Helpings*), 20-oz. dinner 1092
  (*Banquet International Favorite's*), 11-oz. pkg. 413
  (*Morton*), 11-oz. pkg. 250
  (*Morton* King Size), 20-oz. pkg. 600
  (*Swanson*), 12-oz. pkg. 480
  (*Swanson Hungry-Man*), 20-oz. pkg. 560
Western style:
  (*Banquet American Favorite's*), 11-oz. pkg. 513
  (*Morton*), 11.8-oz. pkg. 400
  (*Swanson*), 12¹/4-oz. pkg. 430
  (*Swanson Hungry-Man*), 17¹/2-oz. pkg. 650

*Pay attention to package sizes
**As packaged
***Edible portion

FROZEN POT PIES, one whole pie*
See also "Frozen Dinners,"
"Meat & Poultry Entrees, Frozen"

---

calories

beef:

(*Banquet*), 8-oz. pie 557
(*Banquet Supreme*), 8-oz. pie 380
(*Morton*), 8-oz. pie 320
(*Stouffer's*), 10-oz. pie 550
(*Swanson*), 8-oz. pie 420
(*Swanson* Chunky), 10-oz. pie 580
(*Swanson Hungry-Man*), 16-oz. pie 700
steak burger (*Swanson Hungry-Man*), 16-oz. pie 830

chicken:

(*Banquet*), 8-oz. pie 557
(*Banquet Supreme*), 8-oz. pie 430
(*Morton*), 8-oz. pie 320
(*Stouffer's*), 10-oz. pie 550
(*Swanson*), 8-oz. pie 420
(*Swanson* Chunky), 10-oz. pie 570
(*Swanson Hungry-Man*), 16-oz. pie 730
(*Van de Kamp's*), 7½-oz. pie 520

macaroni and cheese (*Swanson*), 7-oz. pie 210

tuna (*Banquet*), 8-oz. pie 510

tuna (*Morton*), 8-oz. pie 370

turkey:

(*Banquet*), 8-oz. pie 526
(*Banquet Supreme*), 8-oz. pie 430
(*Morton*), 8-oz. pie 340
(*Stouffer's*), 10-oz. pie 460
(*Swanson*), 8-oz. pie 430
(*Swanson* Chunky), 10-oz. pie 540
(*Swanson Hungry-Man*), 16-oz. pie 750

Pay attention to package sizes

Chapter 12

MEAT, FISH AND POULTRY

MEAT & POULTRY ENTREES, CANNED OR REFRIGERATED

See also "Meat & Poultry Entrees, Frozen," "Frankfurters, Luncheon Meats & Sausages" and "Meat, Fish & Poultry, Freeze-Dried"

---

calories

beef:
    chopped (*Armour Star*), 12-oz. can 1190
    goulash (*Heinz*), 7½-oz. can 240
    goulash (*Hormel Short Order*), 7½-oz. can 230
    roast (*Wilson Certified Tender Made*), 3 oz. 100
    roast, w/gravy (*Armour Star*), 8 oz. 290
    stew, *see "stew," below*
chicken:
    à la king (*Swanson*), 5¼ oz. 180
    boned, chunk (*Hormel*), 6¾ oz. 340
    boned, chunk (*Swanson*), 2½ oz. 110
    and dumplings
        (*Featherweight*—low-sodium), 7½ oz. 160
    and dumplings (*Luck's*), 7¼ oz. 240
    and dumplings (*Swanson*), 7½ oz. 220
    stew, *see "stew," below*
chili con carne, *see "Mexican & Mexican-Style Foods," page 173*
corned beef hash, *see "hash," below*
ham:
    (*Armour Star*), 8 oz. 416

Meat & Poultry Entrees, Canned or Refrigerated, ham, continued

(*Armour Star Golden*), 8 oz. 304
(*Armour Star Parti Style*), 8 oz. 336
(*Black Label* — 1 1/2 lb.), 4 oz. 150
(*Black Label* — 3 lb.), 4 oz. 140
(*EXL*), 3 oz. 90
(*EXL* Deli Ham), 3 oz. 98
(*Featherweight* — low-sodium), 3 oz. 110
(*Hormel* Bone In), 8 oz. 420
(*Hormel Cure 81*), 8 oz. 320
(*Hormel Curemaster*), 8 oz. 280
(*Hormel Holiday Glaze*), 8 oz. 260
(*Oscar Mayer Jubilee*), 8 oz. 240
(*Wilson* 93% Lean), 3 oz. 110
(*Wilson Certified* — 3- or 5-lb. can)), 3 oz. 120
(*Wilson Certified* Boneless), 3 oz. 120
(*Wilson Corn King* — 3- or 5-lb. can), 3 oz. 120
(*Wilson Corn King* Boneless), 3 oz. 120
(*Wilson* Honey 93% Lean), 3 oz. 110
(*Wilson Masterpiece* — 3-lb. can), 3 oz. 100
(*Wilson Masterpiece* Boneless), 8 oz. 110
(*Wilson Tender Made*), 3 oz. 120
patties (*Hormel*), 1 patty 180
patties (*Wilson Certified*), 2 oz. 146
slice (*Oscar Mayer Jubilee*), 2-oz. slice 60
smoked (*Oscar Mayer Jubilee*), 3 oz. 150
smoked, sliced (*Oscar Mayer Jubilee*), 3 oz. 150
steak (*Oscar Mayer Jubilee*), 2-oz. slice 70
ham luncheon meat, *see "Frankfurters,*
  Luncheon Meats & Sausages," page 155
ham roll, smoked (*Hormel*), 3 oz. 128
ham, spiced (*Hormel*), 3 oz. 240
ham and cheese patties (*Hormel*), 1 patty 190
hash:
  (*Libby's*), 7 1/2 oz. 400
  corned beef (*Armour Star*), 8 oz. 435
  corned beef (*Mary Kitchen*), 7 1/2 oz. 360
  corned beef
    (*Mary Kitchen* Short Order), 7 1/2-oz. can 360
  roast beef (*Mary Kitchen*), 7 1/2 oz. 350
  roast beef
    (*Mary Kitchen* Short Order), 7 1/2-oz. can 350

Meat & Poultry Entrees, Canned or Refrigerated, continued

meatballs in brown gravy
    (*Chef Boy•ar•dee*), 7.38 oz. 290
pork:
  chopped (*Hormel*), 3 oz. 200
  roast (*Wilson Tender Made*), 3 oz. 130
  shoulder (*Wilson Certified*), 3 oz. 210
  shoulder (*Wilson Corn King*), 3 oz. 210
sausages, *see "Frankfurters, Luncheon Meats & Sausages,"*
    page 152
sloppy Joe:
  (*Hormel* Short Order), 7½-oz. can 340
  beef (*Libby's*), ⅓ cup 110
  pork (*Libby's*), ⅓ cup 120
stew:
  beef (*Armour Star*), 8 oz. 200
  beef (*Dia Mel*), 8-oz. can 200
  beef (*Dinty Moore*), 8-oz. can 220
  beef (*Dinty Moore*—40-oz. can), 8 oz. 210
  beef (*Dinty Moore* Short Order), 7½-oz. can 180
  beef (*Featherweight*), 7½-oz. can 210
  beef (*Heinz*), 7½-oz. can 210
  beef (*Libby's*), 7½ oz. 160
  chicken (*Dia Mel*), 8-oz. can 150
  chicken (*Featherweight*), 7½-oz. can 170
  chicken (*Swanson*), 7⅝ oz. 170
  chicken, w/dumplings (*Heinz*), 7½-oz. can 210
  meatball (*Chef Boy•ar•dee*), 8 oz. 330
  meatball (*Dinty Moore*), 8 oz. 240
turkey, chunk (*Hormel*), 6¾ oz. 230

MEAT & POULTRY ENTREES, FROZEN,
one whole package*, except as noted
*See also "Meat & Poultry Entrees, Canned
or Refrigerated," "FrozenDinners"
and "Meat, Fish & Poultry, Freeze-Dried"*

---

calories

beef:
  w/barbecue sauce, in pastry
    (*Pepperidge Farm*), 8¾ oz. 270
  burgundy, w/rice and carrots
    (*Green Giant* Twin Pouch Entrees),
    9-oz. pkg. 280
  chipped, creamed
    (*Banquet Cookin' Bags*), 4-oz. pkg. 125
  chipped, creamed
    (*Morton* Boil-in-Bag), 5-oz. serving 160
  chipped, creamed (*Stouffer's*), 11-oz. pkg. 470
  chop suey, *see "Oriental & Oriental-Style Foods,"
    page 176*
  chopped sirloin, mushroom sauce
    w/beans and cauliflower
    (*Weight Watchers*), 13-oz. pkg. 410
  chopped steak, green pepper and mushroom sauce
    w/carrots
    (*Weight Watchers*), 9¾-oz. pkg. 320
  enchiladas, tamales, *see "Mexican & Mexican-Style
    Foods," page 174*
  patties (*Morton* Boil-in-Bag), 5-oz. serving 200
  patties w/mushroom gravy
    (*Morton* Family Meal), 8-oz. serving 300
  patties w/onion gravy
    (*Morton* Family Meal), 8-oz. serving 300
  ribs, boneless, in barbecue sauce w/corn on cob
    (*Green Giant* Twin Pouch Entrees), 9-oz. pkg. 390
  Salisbury steak, *see "Salisbury steak," below*
  short ribs, boneless, w/vegetable gravy
    (*Stouffer's*), 11½-oz. pkg. 700
  sliced (*Morton* Boil-in-Bag), 5-oz. serving 120

Meat & Poultry Entrees, Frozen, beef, continued

sliced, bacon sauce, in pastry
   (*Pepperidge Farm*), 8¾ oz. 260
sliced, barbecue sauce w/
   (*Banquet Cookin' Bags*), 4-oz. pkg. 133
sliced, gravy and
   (*Banquet Cookin' Bags*), 4-oz. pkg. 136
sliced, gravy and
   (*Banquet Buffet Suppers*), 32-oz. pkg. 1376
sliced, gravy and
   (*Morton* Family Meal), 8-oz. serving 210
sliced, gravy and (*Swanson*), 8-oz. pkg. 200
sliced
   (*Swanson Hungry-Man* Entree), 12¼-oz. pkg. 330
steaks, breaded (*Hormel*), 4 oz. 370
stew, *see "stew," below*
Stroganoff, w/noodles
   (*Green Giant* Twin Pouch Entrees), 9-oz. pkg. 380
Stroganoff, w/parsley noodles
   (*Stouffer's*), 9¾-oz. pkg. 390
teriyaki, *see "Oriental & Oriental-Style Foods," page 178*
chili con carne, *see "Mexican & Mexican-Style Foods,"*
   page 173
chicken:
à la king (*Banquet Cookin' Bags*), 5-oz. pkg. 159
à la king (*Weight Watchers*), 5-oz. serving 230
à la king, w/biscuits
   (*Green Giant* Twin Pouch Entrees), 9-oz. pkg. 370
à la king, w/rice (*Stouffer's*), 9½-oz. pkg. 330
in barbecue sauce w/corn on cob
   (*Green Giant* Baked Entrees), 1 pkg.* 350
w/broccoli and rice in cheese sauce
   (*Green Giant* Twin Pouch Entrees),
   9½-oz. pkg. 330
cacciatore, w/spaghetti
   (*Stouffer's*), 11¼-oz. pkg. 310
cacciatore, w/spaghetti
   (*Weight Watchers*), 10-oz. pkg. 290
cacciatore, w/vermicelli
   (*Stouffer's Lean Cuisine*), 1 pkg.* 260
chow mein, *see "Oriental & Oriental-Style Foods,"*
   page 176

Meat & Poultry Entrees, Frozen, chicken, continued

creamed (*Stouffer's*), 6½-oz. pkg. 300
croquettes, w/fricassee sauce
  (*Howard Johnson's*), 12-oz. pkg. 505
divan (*Stouffer's*), 8½-oz. pkg. 335
escalloped, and noodles
  (*Stouffer's*), 11½-oz. pkg. 500
fillets, Marsala (*Buitoni*), 11-oz. pkg. 260
fried (*Banquet*), 32-oz. pkg. 1625
fried (*Morton*), 32-oz. pkg. 1500
fried (*Morton* King Size Entree), 12-oz. pkg. 640
fried (*Swanson*), 7¼ oz.** 390
fried, assortment
  (*Swanson* Plump and Juicy), 3¼ oz. 260
fried, assortment
  (*Swanson* Plump and Juicy Take Out),
  3¼ oz.** 270
fried, breast (*Banquet*), 22-oz. pkg. 1190
fried, breast (*Morton*), 22-oz. pkg. 1480
fried, breast
  (*Swanson Hungry-Man*), 11¾ oz.** 670
fried, breast
  (*Swanson* Plump and Juicy), 4½ oz.** 350
fried, dark meat
  (*Swanson Hungry-Man*), 11 oz.** 640
fried, nibbles (*Swanson*), 5 oz.** 400
fried, thighs and drumsticks
  (*Banquet*), 25-oz. pkg. 1385
fried, wings (*Banquet*), 27-oz. pkg. 1384
glazed, w/vegetable rice
  (*Stouffer's Lean Cuisine*), 8½-oz. serving 270
in herb butter, w/stuffed potato
  (*Green Giant* Baked Entree), 1 pkg.* 430
l'orange (*Stouffer's Lean Cuisine*), 1 pkg.* 280
nibbles, wings
  (*Swanson* Plump and Juicy), 3¼ oz.** 300
and noodles, w/vegetables
  (*Green Giant* Twin Pouch Entrees), 9-oz. pkg. 390
nuggets, breaded (*Banquet*), 12-oz. pkg. 932
paprikash, w/egg noodles
  (*Stouffer's*), 10½-oz. pkg. 385

Meat & Poultry Entrees, Frozen, chicken, continued

Parmigiana, w/green beans
   (*Weight Watchers*), 7¾-oz. pkg. 220
patties, breaded (*Banquet*), 12-oz. pkg. 900
patty, Parmigiana, w/vegetable medley
   (*Weight Watchers*), 8-oz. pkg. 290
patty, Southern-fried, w/vegetable medley
   (*Weight Watchers*), 6¾-oz. pkg. 260
and pea pods w/rice and vegetables, in sauce
   (*Green Giant* Twin Pouch Entrees),
     10-oz. pkg. 300
sliced, in celery sauce w/peas and onions
   (*Weight Watchers*), 8½-oz. pkg. 230
sticks, breaded (*Banquet*), 12-oz. pkg. 912
thighs and drumsticks
   (*Swanson* Plump and Juicy), 3¼ oz.** 280
w/vegetables and vermicelli
   (*Stouffer's Lean Cuisine*), 12¾-oz. serving 260
crepes:
chicken, w/mushroom sauce
   (*Stouffer's*), 8¼-oz. pkg. 390
ham and asparagus (*Stouffer's*), 6¼-oz. pkg. 325
ham and swiss, w/cream sauce
   (*Stouffer's*), 7½-oz. pkg. 410
frankfurters, *see "Frankfurters, Luncheon Meats &*
   Sausages," page 154
frankfurters, batter-wrapped
   (*Hormel Corn Dogs*), 1 weiner* 231
frankfurters, batter-wrapped
   (*Hormel Tater Dogs*), 1 weiner* 187
hash, roast beef (*Stouffer's*), 11½-oz. pkg. ...., 530
lasagna, *see "Pasta Entrees, Frozen," page 187*
meatballs:
w/brown gravy (*Swanson*), 8½-oz. pkg. 280
Swedish, w/parsley noodles
   (*Stouffer's*), 11-oz. pkg. 475
sweet and sour, w/rice and vegetables
   (*Green Giant* Twin Pouch Entrees),
   9.4-oz. serving 370
meat loaf:
(*Banquet Buffet Suppers*), 30-oz. pkg. 1510
(*Banquet Cookin' Bags*), 5-oz. pkg. 251

Meat & Poultry Entrees, Frozen, meatballs, continued

w/tomato sauce (*Morton* Family Meal),
    8-oz. serving 200
w/tomato sauce (*Swanson*), 5½-oz. pkg. 310
pork steaks, breaded (*Hormel*), 3 oz. 220
Salisbury steak:
    (*Howard Johnson's*), 4½ oz. 273
    (*Morton* Boil-in-Bag), 5-oz. serving 150
    (*Morton* King Size Entree), 10.3-oz. pkg. 500
    (*Swanson*), 5½-oz. pkg. 370
    (*Swanson Hungry-Man* Entree), 11¾-oz. pkg. 570
    (*Swanson* Main Course Entree), 10-oz. pkg. 430
    w/creole sauce
      (*Green Giant* Baked Entrees), 9-oz. pkg. 410
    gravy and
      (*Banquet Buffet Suppers*), 32-oz. pkg. 1410
    w/gravy (*Green Giant* Baked Entree), 1 pkg.* 280
    w/gravy (*Morton* Family Meal), 8-oz. serving 240
    w/Italian-style sauce and vegetables
      (*Stouffer's Lean Cuisine*), 9½-oz. pkg. 270
    w/mashed potatoes
      (*Green Giant* Twin Pouch Entree), 11-oz. pkg. 450
    w/onion gravy (*Stouffer's*), 12-oz. pkg. 500
sloppy Joe (*Morton* Boil-in-Bag), 5-oz. serving 210
steak:
    w/green peppers, rice and vegetables, in sauce
      (*Green Giant* Twin Pouch Entrees), 9-oz. pkg. 250
    green pepper, w/rice (*Stouffer's*), 10½-oz. pkg. 350
    w/green peppers
      (*Swanson* Main Course Entree), 8½-oz. pkg. 200
    Swiss, *see "Swiss steak," below*
stew:
    beef (*Banquet Buffet Suppers*), 32-oz. pkg. 1016
    beef (*Green Giant* Baked Entrees), 9-oz. pkg. 180
    beef (*Morton* Family Meal), 8-oz. serving 190
    beef (*Stouffer's*), 10-oz. pkg. 310
Swiss steak, in gravy w/stuffed potato
    (*Green Giant* Baked Entrees), 1 pkg.* 350
turkey:
    (*Swanson*), 8¾-oz. pkg. 230
    (*Swanson Hungry-Man* Entree), 13¼-oz. pkg. 370

Meat & Poultry Entrees, Frozen, turkey, continued

breast, sliced, w/white and wild rice stuffing
  (*Green Giant* Twin Pouch Entrees),
  9-oz. pkg. 460
casserole, w/gravy and dressing
  (*Stouffer's*), 9¾-oz. pkg. 370
croquettes, w/gravy
  (*Morton* Family Meal), 8-oz. serving 440
sliced (*Morton* Boil-in-Bag), 5-oz. serving 120
sliced
  (*Morton* King Size Entree), 12.3-oz. pkg. 380
sliced, gravy and
  (*Banquet Buffet Suppers*), 32-oz. pkg. 804
sliced, gravy and
  (*Banquet Cookin' Bags*), 5-oz. pkg. 137
sliced, w/gravy
  (*Morton* Family Meal), 8-oz. serving 200
sliced, w/gravy, stuffing, carrots and broccoli
  (*Weight Watchers*), 15¼-oz. pkg. 380
tetrazzini (*Stouffer's*), 12-oz. pkg. 480
tetrazzini, w/cheese, mushrooms and peppers
  (*Weight Watchers*), 10-oz. pkg. 310
turkey, ham and cheese, in pastry
  (*Pepperidge Farm*), 7¾-oz. pkg. 270
veal:
  breaded, and spaghetti in tomato sauce
    (*Swanson*), 8¼-oz. pkg. 270
  Parmigiana (*Banquet Cookin' Bags*), 5-oz. pkg. 293
  (*Morton* Boil-in-Bag), 5-oz. serving 130
  (*Morton* Family Meal), 8-oz. serving 300
  Parmigiana casserole (*Banquet*), 32-oz. pkg. 1385
  Parmigiana, w/tomato sauce
    (*Banquet Buffet Suppers*), 32-oz. pkg. 1385
  Parmigiana, w/zucchini, in tomato sauce
    (*Weight Watchers*), 9-oz. pkg. 250
  patties, Pomodoro
    (*Buitoni*), 10½-oz. serving 350
  patty, Parmigiana, w/vegetable medley
    (*Weight Watcher's*), 8⅛-oz. pkg. 230
  steaks (*Hormel*), 4 oz.* 130

  steaks, breaded (*Hormel*), 4 oz.* 240

  *As packaged
  **Edible portion

FRANKFURTERS, LUNCHEON MEATS & SAUSAGES
See also "Meat & Poultry Entrees, Canned
or Refrigerated" and "Meat, Fish & Poultry Spreads"

---

                                              calories

bacon, *see "Bacon," page 161*
banquet loaf, beef
  (*Eckrich Smorgas Pac*), 1 slice* 50
barbecue loaf:
  (*Eckrich* Calorie Watcher), 1-oz. slice 35
  (*Hormel BBQ*), 1 slice* 45
  (*Oscar Mayer Bar-B-Q*), 1 slice* 50
beef:
  (*Danola* Thin Sliced), 1 oz. 40
  (*Eckrich* Calorie Watcher Slender Sliced), 1 oz. 40
  barbecue loaf
    (*Eckrich* Calorie Watcher), 1-oz. slice 35
  bologna, *see "bologna," below*
  corned (*Danola* Thin Sliced), 1 oz. 40
  corned (*Dinty Moore*), 3 oz. 75
  corned (*Eckrich* Calorie Watcher Slender Sliced),
    1 oz. 40
  corned (*Libby's*), 2.3-oz. serving 160
  corned (*Wilson Continental Deli*), 3 oz. 75
  corned, brisket (*Vienna*), 3½ oz. 305
  corned, brisket
    (*Wilson Certified Tender Made*), 3 oz. 135
  corned, flats (*Vienna*), 3½ oz. 171
  corned, loaf
    (*Featherweight*—low-sodium), 2½ oz. 90
  corned, jellied loaf (*Oscar Mayer*), 1-oz. slice 40
  dried (*Armour Star*), 5-oz. jar 234
  dried, smoked (*Hormel*), 1 oz. 45
  frankfurters, *see "frankfurters and weiners," below*

Frankfurters, Luncheon Meats & Sausages, beef, continued

jellied loaf (*Hormel*), 1-oz. slice 45
pastrami, *see "pastrami," below*
peppered (*Vienna*), 3½ oz. 176
sausages, *see "sausage, beef," below*
sausages, smoked, *see "smoked links and sausages,"
    below*
smoked, sliced (*Hormel*), 1 oz. 50
bologna:
(*Armour Star*), 1 oz. 90
(*Eckrich*), 1 slice* 90
(*Eckrich German Brand*), 1-oz. slice 80
(*Eckrich German Brand*—chub), 1 oz. 80
(*Eckrich* Lunch Bologna—chub), 1 oz. 100
(*Eckrich Smorgas Pac*—12-oz. pkg.), ¾-oz. slice 70
(*Eckrich Smorgas Pac*—1-lb. pkg.), 1 slice* 90
(*Eckrich* Thick Sliced), 1 slice* 160
(*Eckrich* Thin Sliced), 1 slice* 55
(*Hormel*—coarse ground), 1 oz. 80
(*Hormel*—fine ground), 1 oz. 85
(*Oscar Mayer*), .8-oz. slice 75
(*Oscar Mayer German*), .8-oz. slice 55
(*Wilson Certified*), 1 slice* 90
(*Wilson Corn King*), 1 slice* 90
beef (*Eckrich*), 1-oz. slice 90
beef (*Eckrich Smorgas Pac*), 1 slice* 70
beef (*Eckrich* Thick Sliced), 1 slice* 140
beef (*Eckrich* Thin Sliced), 1 slice* 55
beef (*Hormel*—coarse ground), 1 oz. 80
beef (*Oscar Mayer*), .8-oz. slice 75
beef (*Oscar Mayer Lebanon*), .8-oz. slice 50
beef (*Vienna*), 3½ oz. 296
beef (*Wilson Certified*), 1 slice* 90
beef (*Wilson Corn King*), 1 slice* 90
beef-garlic (*Oscar Mayer*), .8-oz. slice 75
garlic (*Eckrich*), 1-oz. slice 90
meat (*Hormel*), 1 slice* 90
meat (*Wilson Certified*), 1 oz. 87
meat (*Wilson Corn King*), 1 oz. 87
ring (*Eckrich*), 1 oz. 90
ring (*Oscar Mayer Wisconsin*—coarse ground),
    1 oz. 80

Frankfurters, Luncheon Meats & Sausages, bologna, continued

ring
 (*Oscar Mayer Wisconsin*—fine ground), 1 oz. 85
ring, pickled (*Eckrich*), 1 oz. 90
sandwich (*Eckrich*), 1-oz. slice 90
bologna and cheese (*Eckrich*), 1 slice* 90
bologna and cheese (*Oscar Mayer*), .8-oz. slice 75
braunschweiger:
 (*Eckrich*—chub), 1 oz. 70
 (*Hormel*), 1 oz. 80
 (*Oscar Mayer*—sliced), 1-oz. slice 95
 (*Oscar Mayer*—tube), 1 oz. 95
 (*Oscar Mayer German Brand*—tube), 1 oz. 95
 (*Wilson Certified*), 1 oz. 90
breakfast sausage, *see "pork sausage," below*
capocollo (*Hormel*), 1 oz. 80
cervelat, *see "summer sausage," below*
chicken:
 (*Danola* Thin Sliced), 1 oz. 45
 (*Eckrich* Calorie Watcher Slender Sliced), 1 oz. 45
 (*Hormel* Sandwich Makin's), 1 oz. 50
 breast (*Eckrich* Calorie Watcher), 2 slices* 40
 breast, chunk (*Hormel*), 6¾-oz. can 350
chicken luncheon loaf (*Hormel*), 1 oz. 65
corned beef, *see "beef, corned," above*
frankfurters and wieners:
 (*Armour Star* Hot Dogs), 1 link* 142
 (*Eckrich*—12-oz. pkg.), 1.2-oz. link 120
 (*Eckrich*—1-11. pkg.), 1.6-oz. link 150
 (*Eckrich* Jumbo), 1 link* 190
 (*Kahn's* Jumbo), 1 link* 190
 (*Kahn's* Wieners), 1 link* 140
 (*Oscar Mayer* Jumbo Wieners), 2-oz. link 185
 (*Oscar Mayer* Little Wieners), .3-oz. link 30
 (*Oscar Mayer The Big One*), 4-oz. link 365
 (*Oscar Mayer* Wieners), 1 link* 145
 (*Wilson Certified* Skinless—1-lb. pkg.), 1 link* 150
 (*Wilson* Western Style—1-lb. pkg.), 1 link* 150
 beef (*Eckrich*—12-oz. pkg.), 1.2-oz. link 110
 beef (*Eckrich*—1-lb. pkg.), 1.6-oz. link 150
 beef (*Eckrich* Jumbo), 1 link* 190

frankfurters and wieners, continued

beef (*Hormel*—12-oz. pkg.), 1 link* 100
beef (*Hormel*—1-lb. pkg.), 1 link* 140
beef (*Kahn's*), 1 link* 140
beef (*Kahn's* Jumbo), 1 link* 190
beef (*Oscar Mayer*), 1.6-oz. link 145
beef (*Oscar Mayer* Jumbo), 2-oz. link 185
beef (*Oscar Mayer The Big One*), 4-oz. link 360
beef (*Wilson Certified*—1-lb. pkg.), 1 link* 150
beef
   (*Wilson Certified* Skinless—1-lb. pkg.), 1 link* 150
beef (*Wilson Corn King*—1-lb. pkg.), 1 link* 150
cheese (*Eckrich*), 1 link* 190
cheese
   (*Oscar Mayer* Cheese Hot Dogs), 1 link* 145
cheese (*Oscar Mayer* Wieners), 1 link* 145
cocktail, *see "Appetizers & Hors d'Oeuvres," page 133*
meat (*Hormel*—12-oz. pkg.), 1 link* 110
meat (*Hormel*—1-lb. pkg.), 1 link* 140
meat (*Wilson Certified*—1-lb. pkg.), 1 link* 150
meat (*Wilson Corn King*—1-lb. pkg.), 1 link* 150
smoked, *see "smoked links and sausages," below*
gourmet loaf
   (*Eckrich* Calorie Watcher), 1-oz. slice 35
gourmet loaf (*Eckrich Smorgas Pac*), 1 slice* 25
ham:
   black pepper (*Hormel* Perma-Fresh), 1 slice* 25
   chopped (*Eckrich* Calorie Watcher), 1 slice* 45
   chopped (*Eckrich Smorgas Pac*), 1 slice* 35
   chopped (*Hormel*—8-lb. can), 1 oz. 80
   chopped (*Oscar Mayer*), 1-oz. slice 65
   chopped (*Hormel* Perma-Fresh), 1 slice* 55
   chopped, canned (*Armour Star*), 12-oz. can 1004
   chopped, canned (*Hormel*), 12-oz. can 720
   chunk (*Hormel*), 6¾ oz. 310
   cooked (*Danola*), 1 oz. 30
   cooked (*Eckrich*), 1 slice* 30
   cooked
      (*Eckrich* Calorie Watcher), 1.2-oz. slice 30
   cooked (*Hormel*), 1 slice* 25
   cooked (*Oscar Mayer*), .8-oz. slice 25
   cooked (*Plumrose*), 1 oz. 30

Frankfurters, Luncheon Meats & Sausages, ham, continued

cooked, smoked
  (*Hormel* Perma-Fresh), 1 slice* 25
cured, whole or steaks, *see "Meat & Poultry Entrees,*
  Canned or Refrigerated," page 416
Danish (*Eckrich*), 1 oz. 25
glazed (*Hormel* Perma-Fresh), 1 slice* 25
red pepper (*Hormel* Perma-Fresh), 1 slice* 25
sausage roll (*Oscar Mayer*), .8-oz. slice 35
smoked
  (*Eckrich* Calorie Watcher Slender Sliced),
  1 oz. 45
smoked, sweet
  (*Eckrich* Calorie Watcher), 1 slice* 25
ham loaf (*Eckrich*), 1-oz. slice 70
ham and cheese loaf:
  (*Eckrich*), 1-oz. slice 60
  (*Hormel* Perma-Fresh), 1 slice* 65
  (*Oscar Mayer*), 1-oz. slice 75
  canned (*Hormel*), 1 oz. 87
head cheese (*Oscar Mayer*), 1-oz. slice 55
home-style loaf
  (*Eckrich* Calorie Watcher), 1 slice* 40
honey loaf:
  (*Eckrich Smorgas Pac*—12-oz. pkg.), 1 slice* 30
  (*Eckrich Smorgas Pac*—1-lb. pkg.), 1 slice* 35
  (*Hormel* Perma-Fresh), 1 slice* 45
  (*Oscar Mayer*), 1-oz. slice 35
honey roll sausage, beef
  (*Oscar Mayer*), .8-oz. slice 40
kielbasa:
  (*Eckrich* Polska), 1 oz. 95
  (*Eckrich* Polska Skinless), 2-oz. link 180
  (*Hormel* Kielbasa—skinless), 1/2 link* 180
  (*Hormel* Kolbase), 1 oz. 73
  (*Hormel* Polish Sausage), 1 sausage* 85
  (*Kahn's* Polska), 3 1/2 oz. 324
  (*Vienna*), 3 1/2 oz. 290
liver cheese (*Oscar Mayer*), 1.3-oz. slice 115
liver loaf (*Hormel*), 1 slice* 80
luncheon meat:
  (*Oscar Mayer*), 1-oz. slice 100

luncheon meat, continued

(*Spam*), 1 oz. 85
(*Treet*), 12-oz. can 1014
(*Wilson Certified*), 1-oz. slice 90
(*Wilson Corn King*), 1-oz. slice 90
w/cheese chunks (*Spam*), 1 oz. 85
smoked (*Spam*), 1 oz. 85
spiced (*Hormel*), 1 oz. 94
(*Hormel* Perma-Fresh), 1 slice* 75
luncheon sausage, pressed
(*Oscar Mayer*), .8-oz. slice 35
luncheon sausage, roll
(*Oscar Mayer*), .8-oz. slice 35
luxury loaf (*Oscar Mayer*), 1-oz. slice 40
minced roll sausage (*Eckrich*), 1-oz. slice 80
minced roll sausage (*Oscar Mayer*), 1-oz. slice 60
mortadella (*Oscar Mayer*), .5-oz. slice 50
New England loaf (*Hormel*), 1 oz. 50
New England sausage
(*Eckrich* Calorie Watcher), 1-oz. slice 35
New England sausage
(*Oscar Mayer New England*), .8-oz. slice 35
old-fashioned loaf:
(*Eckrich*), 1-oz. slice 70
(*Eckrich* Smorgas Pac — 12-oz. pkg.), 1 slice* 50
(*Eckrich* Smorgas Pac — 1-lb. pkg.), 1 slice* 70
(*Oscar Mayer*), 1-oz. slice 65
olive loaf:
(*Eckrich*), 1-oz. slice 80
(*Hormel*), 1 slice* 55
(*Oscar Mayer*), 1-oz. slice 65
pastrami:
(*Danola* Thin Sliced), 1 oz. 40
(*Eckrich* Calorie Watcher Slender Sliced), 1 oz. 40
(*Vienna*), 3½ oz. 303
peppered loaf
(*Eckrich* Calorie Watcher), 1-oz. slice 40
peppered loaf (*Oscar Mayer*), 1-oz. slice 45
pepperoni:
(*Eckrich*), 2-oz. slice 270
(*Hormel*), 1 slice* 40
(*Hormel* Chunk), 1 oz. 140

Frankfurters, Luncheon Meats & Sausages, pepperoni, continued

(*Hormel Leoni Brand*), 1 oz.	130
(*Hormel Rosa*), 1 oz.	140
(*Hormel Rosa Grande*), 1 oz.	140
pickle loaf:	
(*Eckrich*), 1-oz. slice	80
(*Eckrich Smorgas Pac*), 1 slice*	90
(*Hormel*), 1 slice*	60
beef (*Eckrich Smorgas Pac*), 1 slice*	50
pickle and pimento loaf	
(*Oscar Mayer*), 1-oz. slice	65
picnic loaf (*Oscar Mayer*), 1-oz. slice	65
Polish sausage, *see "kielbasa," above*	
pork luncheon meat (*Hormel*), 1 oz.	80
pork sausage:	
(*Eckrich*), 1 oz.	130
(*Eckrich*), 1 link*	220
(*Eckrich*), 1 patty*	240
(*Hormel Little Sizzlers*), 1 sausage*, cooked	52
(*Hormel* Midget Links), 1 sausage*	72
(*Jimmy Dean*), 1 oz.	113
(*Oscar Mayer Little Friers*),	
1 sausage*, cooked	80
(*Oscar Mayer Southern Brand*),	
1 patty*, cooked	125
(*Oscar Mayer Southern Brand*), 1 oz., cooked	85
(*Wilson Certified*), 1 oz.	85
(*Wilson Corn King*), 1 oz.	85
brown and serve (*Hormel*), 1 sausage*, cooked	70
roll, hot fresh (*Eckrich*), 1 oz.	120
smoked (*Hormel*), 1 oz.	97
pork, smoked	
(*Eckrich* Calorie Watcher Slender Sliced),	
1 oz.	45
prosciutto, boneless (*Hormel*), 1 oz.	90
salami:	
beef (*Hormel* Perma-Fresh), 1 slice*	25
beef (*Vienna*), 3½ oz.	278
beer (*Eckrich*), 1-oz. slice	70
beer (*Oscar Mayer*), .8-oz. slice	55
beer, beef (*Oscar Mayer*), .8-oz. slice	75
cooked (*Eckrich*—chub), 1 oz.	70

Frankfurters, Luncheon Meats & Sausages, salami, continued

cotto (*Eckrich*), 1-oz. slice 70
cotto (*Hormel*), 1 slice* 60
cotto (*Hormel*—chub), 1 oz. 100
cotto (*Oscar Mayer*), .8-oz. slice 50
cotto, beef (*Eckrich*), 1 slice* 50
cotto, beef (*Oscar Mayer*), .8-oz. slice 50
hard (*Eckrich*), 1 oz. 130
hard (*Hormel*), 1 slice* 40
hard (*Hormel*), 1 oz. 110
hard (*Hormel National Brand*), 1 oz. 120
hard (*Oscar Mayer*), 1 oz. or about 3 slices 105
Genoa (*Hormel*), 1 slice* 35
Genoa (*Hormel*), 1 oz. 110
Genoa (*Hormel Di Lusso*), 1 oz. 100
Genoa (*Hormel Gran Valore*), 1 oz. 110
Genoa (*Hormel San Remo Brand*), 1 oz. 118
Genoa (*Oscar Mayer*), .3-oz. slice 35
party (*Hormel*), 1 oz. 90
piccolo (*Hormel*—10-oz. stick), 1 oz. 120
sausage, beef, Polish (*Vienna*), 3½ oz. 280
sausage patties, hot (*Hormel*), 1 patty* 150
sausage patties, mild (*Hormel*), 1 patty* 150
smoked links & sausages:
  (*Eckrich* Hot Links), 1 link* 240
  (*Eckrich* Skinless Links—1-lb. pkg.), 2-oz. link 180
  (*Eckrich Smok-Y Links*—skinless), 1 link* 75
  (*Eckrich* Smoked Sausage), 1 oz. 95
  (*Hillshire Farm*), 3½ oz. 320
  (*Hormel Range Brand Wranglers*), 1 link* 170
  (*Hormel* Smokies), 1 link* 80
  (*Kahn's Jumbo Smokies*), 1 link* 175
  (*Kahn's Li'l Smokies*), 2 links* 171
  (*Kahn's Red Rookies*), 2 links* 171
  (*Oscar Mayer* Little Smokies), ⅓-oz. link 30
  (*Oscar Mayer* Smokie Links), 1½-oz. link 135
  (*Vienna*), 3½ oz. 276
  (*Wilson* 20% Less Fat), 2 oz. 160
  (*Wilson Certified*), 2 oz. 180
  (*Wilson Corn King*), 2 oz. 180
  beef (*Eckrich Smok-Y-Links*), 1 link* 70
  beef (*Eckrich* Smoked Sausage), 1 oz. 95

smoked links & sausages, continued

beef (*Hillshire Farm*), 3½ oz. 320
beef (*Hormel Wranglers*), 1 link* 170
beef (*Oscar Mayer* Smokies), 1.5-oz. link 130
w/cheese (*Eckrich*), 1 link* 240
cheese (*Eckrich*), 1 oz. 90
cheese (*Hormel Smoky Cheezers*), 1 sausage* .. 84
cheese (*Hormel Wranglers*), 1 frank* 180
cheese
   Oscar Mayer Cheese Smokies), 1½-oz. link ... 145
cheese (*Wilson 20% Less Fat*), 2 oz. 160
ham (*Eckrich Ham Smok-Y-Links*), 2 links* 150
maple-flavored (*Eckrich Smok-Y-Links*), 2 links* 150
summer sausage:
  (*Eckrich*), 1-oz. slice 90
  (*Hormel Old Smokehouse* Thuringer), 1 oz. ... 90
  (*Hormel Old Smokehouse* Thuringer—11-oz. pkg.),
    1 oz. 100
  (*Hormel* Summer Sausage), 1 slice* 70
  (*Hormel* Tangy), 1 oz. 90
  (*Hormel* Thuringer), 1 oz. 90
  (*Hormel Viking* Cervelat), 1 oz. 90
  (*Oscar Mayer* Summer Sausage), .8-oz. slice ... 75
  beef (*Hormel* Beefy Summer Sausage), 1 oz. ... 100
  beef (*Oscar Mayer* Summer Sausage),
    .8-oz. slice 70
  smoked (*Eckrich Smoky Tang*), 1 oz. 80
thuringer, *see "summer sausage," above*
turkey:
  (*Danola* Thin Sliced), 1 oz. 50
  breast (*Hormel*), 1 slice* 30
  breast (*Louis Rich*), 1 oz., cooked 45
  breast, barbecued (*Louis Rich*), 1 oz. 40
  breast, hickory-smoked (*Louis Rich*), 1 oz. ... 35
  breast, roasted (*Louis Rich*), 1 oz. 35
  breast, slices (*Louis Rich*), 1 oz., cooked ... 40
  breast, smoked (*Hormel* Perma-Fresh), 1 slice* ... 30
  breast, smoked (*Louis Rich*), 1-oz. slice ... 20
  breast, tenderloins (*Louis Rich*), 1 oz., cooked ... 40
  drumsticks (*Louis Rich*), 1 oz., cooked 60
  drumsticks, smoked (*Louis Rich*), 1 oz.** ... 40
  ground (*Louis Rich*), 1 oz., cooked 65

Frankfurters, Luncheon Meats & Sausages, turkey, continued

smoked
(*Eckrich* Calorie Watcher Slender Sliced),
  1 oz. 40
smoked (*Louis Rich*), 1-oz. slice 30
wings (*Louis Rich*), 1 oz., cooked 55
wings, smoked
(*Louis Rich Drumettes*), 1 oz.** 45
turkey bologna (*Louis Rich*), 1-oz. slice 60
turkey breakfast sausage
(*Louis Rich*), 1 oz., cooked 65
turkey franks (*Louis Rich*), 1.6-oz. link 100
turkey ham (*Louis Rich*), 1-oz. slice 35
turkey ham, chopped (*Louis Rich*), 1-oz. slice 40
turkey luncheon loaf (*Louis Rich*), 1-oz. slice 40
turkey pastrami (*Louis Rich*), 1-oz. slice 35
turkey salami, cotto (*Louis Rich*), 1-oz. slice 50
turkey sausage, smoked (*Louis Rich*), 1 oz. 55
turkey summer sausage (*Louis Rich*), 1-oz. slice 50
Vienna sausage, *see "Appetizers & Hors d'Oeuvres, Canned
or in Jars," page 132*

*As packaged
**Edible portion

BACON, one slice* cooked, except as noted

	calories
beef (*Vienna*)	36

bits, *see, "Condiments & Seasonings," page 209*
breakfast strips:
  (*Sizzlean*) 50
  beef (*Oscar Mayer Lean 'n Tasty*) 40
  pork (*Oscar Mayer Lean 'n Tasty*) 45
Canadian:
  (*Eckrich* Calorie Watcher), 1 oz. 35
  (*Festival*) 32
  (*Hormel*), 1 oz. 45
  (*Hormel* Perma-Fresh) 18
  (*Oscar Mayer*), 1 oz. 40

Bacon, continued

cured:
(*Hormel Black Label*)	30
(*Hormel Range Brand*)	55
(*Hormel Red Label*)	37
(*Lazy Maple*)	40
(*Oscar Mayer*)	35
(*Wilson Certified*)	40
(*Wilson Corn King*)	40
thick-sliced (*Oscar Mayer*)	70
thin-sliced (*Oscar Mayer*)	20

*As packaged

MEAT, FISH & POULTRY SPREADS,
one tablespoon, except as noted

---

	calories
anchovy paste (*Crosse & Blackwell*)	20
chicken salad (*Longacre*), 1/2 oz.*	32
chicken spread:	
(*Hormel*), 1/2 oz.*	30
(*Swanson*), 1/2 oz.*	30
(*Underwood*), 1/2 oz.*	32
corned beef spread:	
(*Hormel*), 1/2 oz.*	35
(*Underwood*), 1/2 oz.*	27
ham, deviled:	
(*Armour Star*)	48
(*Hormel*)	35
(*Libby's*), 1/2 oz.*	43
(*Underwood*), 1/2 oz.*	49
ham and cheese spread (*Oscar Mayer*), 1.2 oz.*	35
ham salad (*Oscar Mayer*), 1/2 oz.*	30
liverwurst spread:	
(*Hormel*), 1.2 oz.*	35
(*Underwood*), 1.2 oz.*	47
luncheon meat:	
devlied (*Deviled Spam*)	35
deviled (*Deviled Treet*)	44

Meat, Fish & Poultry Spreads, continued
meat, potted:
  (*Armour Star*) 35
  (*Hormel*) 30
  (*Libby's*), 1/2 oz.* 33
pâté, *see, "Appetizers, Hors d'Oeuvres & Snacks, Canned,
  Dried or in Jars," page 131*
roast beef spread (*Hormel*), 1/2 oz.* 31
sandwich spread (*Oscar Mayer*), 1/2 oz.* 33

*Approximately 1 tablespoon

FISH & SHELLFISH, CANNED OR IN JARS
See also "Fish & Shellfish, Frozen," Fish, Smoked"
and "Frozen Dinners"

---

calories

caviar, *see "Appetizers, Hors d'Oeuvres & Snacks, Canned,
  Dried or in Jars," page 131*
clam cocktail, *see "Appetizers, Hors d'Oeuvres & Snacks,
  Canned, Dried or in Jars," page 131*
clams:
  whole, meat only (*Doxsee*), 1 cup 194
  whole, half meat/half liquid (*Doxsee*), 1 cup 116
  chopped or minced, meat only (*Doxsee*), 1 cup 196
  chopped or minced,
    half meat/half liquid (*Doxsee*), 1 cup 118
  chopped or minced, w/liquid (*Snow's*), 6 1/2 oz. 100
  minced (*Gorton's*), 3 3/4-oz. can 80
crab cocktail, *see, "Appetizers, Hors d'Oeuvres & Snacks,
  Canned, Dried or in Jars," page 131*
fish balls, *see "Appetizers, Hors d'Oeuvres & Snacks,
  Canned, Dried or in Jars," page 131*
gefilte fish, 1 piece*:
  (*Manischewitz*—4 piece/12-oz. jar) 53
  (*Manischewitz*—8 piece/24-oz. jar) 53
  (*Manischewitz*—24 piece/4-lb. jar) 48
  (*Manischewitz* Homestyle—4 piece/12-oz. jar) 55
  (*Manischewitz* Homestyle—8 piece/24-oz. jar) 55

Fish & Shellfish, Caned or in Jars, gefilte fish, continued

(*Manischewitz* Homestyle—24 piece/4-lb. jar)	50
(*Mother's*—4 piece/12-oz. jar)	41
(*Mother's*—6 piece/15-oz. jar)	34
(*Mother's*—4 piece/1-lb. jar)	55
(*Mother's*—6 piece/1-lb. jar)	37
(*Mother's*—6 piece/24-oz. jar)	55
(*Mother's*—8 piece/24-oz. jar)	41
(*Mother's*—5 piece/27-oz. jar)	74
(*Mother's*—8 piece/2-lb. jar)	55
(*Mother's*—12 piece/2-lb. jar)	37
sweet (*Manischewitz*—4 piece/12-oz. jar)	65
sweet (*Manischewitz*—8 piece/24-oz. jar)	65
sweet (*Manischewitz*—24 piece/2-lb. jar)	59
sweet, whitefish and pike (*Manischewitz*—4 piece/12-oz. jar)	64
sweet, whitefish and pike (*Manischewitz*—8 piece/24-oz. jar)	64
sweet, whitefish and pike (*Manischewitz*—24 piece/2-lb. jar)	58
whitefish and pike (*Manischewitz*—4 piece/12-oz. jar)	49
whitefish and pike (*Manischewitz*—8 piece/24-oz. jar)	49
whitefish and pike (*Manischewitz*—24 piece/2-lb. jar)	44
miniature, *see "Appetizers, Hors d'Oeuvres & Snacks,* *Canned, Dried or in Jars," page 131*	
herring, kippered (*King Oscar*), 8-oz. can	480
herring, kippered, snacks, *see "Appetizers, Hors d'Oeuvres* *& Snacks, Canned, Dried or in Jars," page 131*	
herring, pickled:	
Bismarck (*Vita*), 5-oz. jar	210
cocktail (*Vita*), 8-oz. jar	350
lunch (*Vita*), 8-oz. jar	326
party snacks (*Vita*), 8-oz. jar	361
roll mops (*Vita*), 8-oz. jar	242
schmaltz, old-fashioned (*Vita*), 16-oz. jar	630
in sour cream (*Vita*), 8-oz. jar	415
tastee bits (*Vita*), 8-oz. jar	340
herring salad, pickled (*Vita*), 7½-oz. jar	493
oysters (*High Sea*), 4 oz.	100

Fish & Shellfish, Canned or in Jars, continued

oysters, whole (*Bumble Bee*), $\frac{1}{2}$ cup 109
salmon:
  blueback (*Icy Point*), $3\frac{3}{4}$-oz. can 181
  blueback (*Icy Point*), $7\frac{3}{4}$-oz. can 376
  coho steak (*Icy Point*), $3\frac{3}{4}$-oz. can 162
  keta (*Bumble Bee*), $\frac{1}{2}$ cup 153
  pink (*Bumble Bee*), $\frac{1}{2}$ cup 155
  pink (*Del Monte*), $\frac{1}{2}$ cup 160
  pink (*Icy Point*), $7\frac{3}{4}$-oz. can 310
  pink (*Libby's*), $7\frac{3}{4}$-oz. can 310
  pink (*Pink Beauty*), $7\frac{3}{4}$-oz. can 310
  red (*Icy Point*), $15\frac{1}{2}$-oz. can 775
  red sockeye (*Bumble Bee*), $\frac{1}{2}$ cup 188
  red sockeye (*Del Monte*), $\frac{1}{2}$ cup 180
  red sockeye (*Libby's*), $7\frac{3}{4}$-oz. can 380
  red sockeye (*Pillar Rock*), $3\frac{3}{4}$-oz. can 181
  red sockeye (*Pillar Rock*), $7\frac{3}{4}$-oz. can 376
  red sockeye (*Pillar Rock*), $15\frac{1}{2}$-oz. can 775
  low-sodium (*Featherweight*), 3 oz. 120
  low-sodium (*S & W Nutradiet*), $\frac{1}{2}$ cup 188
sardines:
  in mustard sauce (*Underwood*), $3\frac{3}{4}$-oz. can 230
  in oil (*Crown*), $3\frac{3}{4}$-oz. can, drained 192
  in oil (*King Oscar*), $3\frac{3}{4}$-oz. can, drained 205
  in oil (*Underwood*), $3\frac{3}{4}$-oz. can, drained 380
  in oil, low-sodium (*Featherweight*), $1\frac{7}{8}$ oz. 109
  in tomato sauce (*Del Monte*), $\frac{1}{2}$ cup 360
  in tomato sauce (*Underwood*), $3\frac{3}{4}$-oz. can 230
shrimp (*Blue Gulf/High Sea/Louisiana*), 4 oz. 116
shrimp cocktail, *see "Appetizers, Hors d'Oeuvres & Snacks, Canned, Dried or in Jars," page 132*
tuna:
  chunk light, in oil (*Bumble Bee*), $\frac{1}{2}$ cup 265
  chunk light, in oil
    (*Chicken of the Sea*), $6\frac{1}{2}$-oz. can 550
  chunk light, in oil (*Icy Point*), 5 oz., drained 278
  chunk light, in oil (*Pillar Rock*), 5 oz., drained 278
  chunk light, in oil (*Snow Mist*), 5 oz., drained 278
  chunk light, in water
    (*Chicken of the Sea*), $6\frac{1}{2}$-oz. can 200
  chunk light, in water (*Bumble Bee*), $\frac{1}{2}$ cup 117

Fish & Shellfish, Canned or in Jars, tuna, continued

chunk white, in oil
  (*Chicken of the Sea*), 6½-oz. can 500
chunk white, in water, low-sodium
  (*Chicken of the Sea*), 6½-oz. can 220
solid light, in oil (*Chicken of the Sea*), 7-oz. can 460
solid white, in oil (*Bumble Bee*), ½ cup 285
solid white, in oil (*Chicken of the Sea*), 7-oz. can 450
solid white, in oil (*Icy Point*), 5¼ oz., drained 290
solid white, in oil (*Pillar Rock*), 5¼ oz., drained 290
solid white, in water (*Bumble Bee*), ½ cup 126
solid white, in water
  (*Chicken of the Sea*), 7-oz. can 240

*As packaged

FISH & SHELLFISH, FROZEN
See also "Fish & Shellfish, Canned or in Jars," "Fish,
Smoked" and "Frozen Dinners"

---

                                   calories

catfish:
  breaded (*Taste O' Sea*), 2⅔-oz. serving 90
  fillets (*Mrs. Paul's*), 3⅝-oz. fillet 215
  fillets (*Taste O' Sea*), 4-oz. serving 100
  fingers (*Mrs. Paul's*), 4-oz. serving 250
clams, fried (*Howard Johnson's*), 5-oz. pkg. 395
clams, fried, light batter (*Mrs. Paul's*), 2½ oz. 230
cod:
  (*Van de Kamp's* Today's Catch), 4 oz. 80
  breaded (*Taste O' Sea*), 2⅔-oz. serving 80
  fillets (*Taste O' Sea*), 4-oz. serving 80
  portions (*Taste O' Sea*), 3-oz. portion 60
  sticks, fried (*Taste O' Sea*), 4 oz. 230
crab:
  cakes, deviled (*Mrs. Paul's*), 3-oz. cake 170
  deviled, miniatures (*Mrs. Paul's*), 7-oz. pkg. 440
  sticks, imitation (*Taste O' Sea*), 3.5 oz. 98

Fish & Shellfish, Frozen, continued

fish:

  oven-fried, w/vegetable medley

    (*Weight Watchers*), 6¾-oz. pkg. 220

  portions, batter-dipped (*Taste O' Sea*), 3 oz. 200

  portions, batter-dipped (*Van de Kamp's*), 3 oz. 190

fish and chips (*Swanson*), 5½-oz. pkg. 310

fish and chips, batter-dipped (*Taste O' Sea*), 4 oz. 250

fish cakes:

  (*Mrs. Paul's*), 4 oz. or 2 cakes 220

  (*Taste O' Sea*), 4 oz. 190

  thins (*Mrs. Paul's*), 5 oz. or 2 cakes 300

fish Dijon (*Mrs. Paul's*), 8½-oz. pkg. 210

fish fillets:

  (*Gorton's Potato Crisp*), 1 fillet* 270

  (*Mrs. Paul's Crispy Crunchy*), 2 fillets* 290

  (*Mrs. Paul's Light and Natural*), 1 fillet* 290

  (*Van de Kamp's Today's Catch*), 4 oz. 90

  au gratin, w/broccoli

    (*Weight Watchers*), 9-oz. pkg. 200

  batter-dipped (*Mrs. Paul's*), 2 fillets* 360

  batter-fried (*Gorton's*), 1 fillet* 250

  batter-fried (*Van de Kamp's*), 3-oz. fillet 190

  breaded (*Booth* Extra Crunchy), 3-oz. fillet 233

  buttered (*Mrs. Paul's*), 5 oz. or 2 fillets 210

  butter flavor (*Taste O' Sea*), 4.8 oz. 370

  buttermilk-breaded

    (*Booth* Extra Crunchy), 3-oz. fillet 248

  country-seasoned

    (*Van de Kamp's*), 2 oz. or 1 fillet 195

  crunchy (*Gorton's*), 1 fillet* 270

  crunchy, light batter (*Mrs. Paul's*), 2 fillets* 310

  French-fried, beer batter (*Booth*), 3-oz. fillet 249

  fried

    (*Van de Kamp's Light & Crispy*), 2-oz. fillet 180

  Italian style, in tomato sauce

    w/cheese and vegetable medley

    (*Weight Watchers*), 9-oz. pkg. 180

  lemon-parsley seasoned, breaded

    (*Booth* Light 'N Tender), 2.5-oz. fillet 130

  lightly breaded (*Gorton's*), 1 fillet* 200

Fish & Shellfish, Frozen, fish fillets, continued

seasoned, breaded
  (*Booth* Light 'N Tender), 2.5-oz. fillet 130
supreme light batter (*Mrs. Paul's*), 1 fillet* 220
tempura, lightly battered (*Gorton's*), 1 fillet* 200
fish Florentine (*Mrs. Paul's*), 9-oz. pkg. 200
fish kabobs, batter-dipped (*Van de Kamp's*), 4 oz. 240
fish Mornay (*Mrs. Paul's*), 10-oz. pkg. 230
fish Parmesan (*Mrs. Paul's*), 10-oz. pkg. 440
fish sticks:
  (*Booth*), 3 oz. or 3 sticks* 162
  (*Gorton's Potato Crisp*), 3 sticks* 230
  (*Mrs. Paul's* Crispy Crunchy), 4 sticks* 200
  batter-dipped (*Taste O' Sea*), 4 oz. 310
  batter-dipped (*Van de Kamp's*), 4 oz. 220
  batter-fried (*Gorton's*), 3 sticks* 230
  breaded (*Booth* Extra Crunchy), 3 sticks* 224
  butter flavor (*Taste O' Sea*), 4 oz. 310
  buttermilk-breaded
    (*Booth* Extra Crunchy), 3-oz. fillet* 223
  crunchy (*Gorton's*), 3 sticks* 180
  crunchy, light batter (*Mrs. Paul's*), 4 sticks* ... 240
  Divan
    (*Stouffer's Lean Cuisine*), 12 3/8-oz. serving .. 270
  Florentine
    (*Stouffer's Lean Cuisine*), 9-oz. serving 240
  French-fried (*Taste O' Sea*), 4 oz. 180
  French-fried, beer batter (*Booth*), 3 sticks* 263
  fried (*Van de Kamp's* Light & Crispy), 3 3/4 oz. .. 270
  jardiniere, w/souffléd potatoes
    (*Stouffer's Lean Cuisine*), 1 pkg.* 270
  lightly breaded (*Gorton's*), 3 sticks* 200
  in Newburg sauce, w/peas and onions
    (*Weight Watchers*), 9 1/4-oz. pkg. 190
  tempura, lightly battered (*Gorton's*), 3 sticks* .. 200
fishburgers (*Booth*), 3 oz. 137
fish kabobs, batter-dipped (*Taste O' Sea*), 4 oz. 225
fish nuggets (*Taste O' Sea*), 3 oz. 220
flounder:
  (*Van de Kamp's* Today's Catch), 4 oz. 80
  breaded (*Taste O' Sea*), 2 2/3-oz. portion 90
  fillets (*Mrs. Paul's* Crispy Crunchy), 2 fillets* . 280

Fish & Shellfish, Frozen, flounder, continued

fillets (*Mrs. Paul's* Light and Natural), 1 fillet* 320
fillets (*Taste O' Sea*), 4-oz. serving 90
fillets, crunchy light batter
   (*Mrs. Paul's*), 2 fillets* 310
w/lemon bread crumbs and vegetable medley
   (*Weight Watchers*), 6½-oz. pkg. 140
portions (*Taste O' Sea*), 3-oz. portion 60
stuffed (*Gorton's*), 6½-oz. pkg. 250
haddock:
au gratin (*Howard Johnson's*), 10-oz. pkg. 318
batter-dipped
   (*Van de Kamp's*), 4 oz. or 2 pieces 330
breaded (*Taste O' Sea*), 2⅔-oz. portion 80
fillets (*Mrs. Paul's* Crispy Crunchy), 2 fillets* 280
fillets (*Mrs. Paul's* Light and Natural), 1 fillet* 320
fillets (*Taste O' Sea*), 4-oz. serving 100
fillets, crunchy, light batter
   (*Mrs. Paul's*), 2 fillets* 320
portions (*Taste O' Sea*), 3-oz. portion 70
portions, batter-dipped (*Taste O' Sea*), 3 oz. 200
sticks, fried (*Taste O' Sea*), 4 oz. 220
stuffed, w/green beans
   (*Weight Watchers*), 7-oz. pkg. 210
in lemon butter (*Gorton's*), ½ pkg.* 120
halibut, batter-dipped
   (*Van de Kamp's*), 4 oz. or 3 pieces 260
lobster Newburg (*Stouffer's*), 6½-oz. pkg. 350
ocean perch, *see "perch," below*
perch:
   (*Van de Kamp's* Today's Catch), 4 oz. 110
batter-dipped
   (*Van de Kamp's*), 4 oz. or 2 pieces 290
breaded
   (*Taste O' Sea*), 2⅔-oz. portion 100
fillets (*Mrs. Paul's* Crispy Crunchy), 2 fillets* 290
fillets (*Taste O' Sea*), 4-oz. serving 100
ocean, w/lemon bread crumbs and broccoli
   (*Weight Watchers*), 6½-oz. pkg. 160
portions (*Taste O' Sea*), 3-oz. portion 100
pollock fillets (*Taste O' Sea*), 4-oz. serving 90
pollock sticks (*Taste O' Sea*), 4 oz. 250

Fish & Shellfish, Frozen, continued

scallops:
    batter-dipped (*Taste O' Sea*), 3.5 oz. 190
    French-fried (*Mrs. Paul's*), 3.5 oz. 210
    fried (*Taste O' Sea*), 4 oz. 230
    Mediterranean (*Mrs. Paul's*), 11-oz. pkg. 250
scallops and shrimp Mariner, w/rice
    (*Stouffer's*), 10¼-oz. pkg. 400
scrod, baked, stuffed (*Gorton's*), 6-oz. pkg. 240
seafood Newburg (*Mrs. Paul's*), 8½-oz. pkg. 310
seafood platter, combination
    (*Mrs. Paul's*), 9-oz. pkg. 510
shrimp:
    batter-dipped (*Taste O' Sea*), 3 oz. 310
    breaded (*Booth*—Ready to Fry), 4 oz. 160
    breaded, jumbo
      (*Booth* Gourmet Fantail Ready-to-Fry), 4 oz. 160
    croquettes, w/Newburg sauce
      (*Howard Johnson's*), 12-oz. pkg. 478
    fried (*Mrs. Paul's*), 6-oz. pkg. 380
    fried (*Taste O' Sea*), 4 oz. 270
    sticks (*Gorton*), 5 sticks* 200
shrimp Oriental, breaded
    (*Booth* Fantail Ready-to-Fry), 4 oz. 160
shrimp Oriental (*Mrs. Paul's*), 11-oz. pkg. 230
shrimp Primavera (*Mrs. Paul's*), 11-oz. pkg. 310
shrimp scampi (*Gorton's*), ½ pkg.* 130
shrimp scampi (*Taste O' Sea*), 7½ oz. 490
sole:
    baby (*Van de Kamp's* Today's Catch), 4 oz. 80
    batter-dipped
      (*Van de Kamp's*), 4 oz. or 2 pieces 280
    fillets (*Mrs. Paul's* Light and Natural), 1 fillet* 280
    fillets (*Taste O' Sea*), 4-oz. serving 90
    fillets, in cheese sauce (*Gorton's*), 7-oz. pkg. 250
    w/lemon butter (*Gorton's*), ½ pkg. 130
    in lemon butter (*Taste O' Sea*), 4½ oz. 350
    in lemon sauce, w/peas and onions
      (*Weight Watchers*), 9⅛-oz. pkg. 200
    portions (*Taste O' Sea*), 3-oz. portion 70
tuna pot pie, *see "Frozen Pot Pies," page 142*
tuna noodle casserole (*Stouffer's*), 11½-oz. pkg. 400

Fish & Shellfish, Frozen, continued

turbot fillets (*Taste O' Sea*), 4-oz. serving 160
whiting fillets (*Taste O' Sea*), 4-oz. serving 80
whiting, breaded (*Taste O' Sea*), 2²/3-oz. portion 90

*As packaged

FISH, SMOKED, two ounces
See also "Fish & Shellfish, Canned or in Jars"

---

	calories
chubs, flesh only (*Vita*)	108
eel, flesh only (*Vita*)	186
lake herring (*Vita*)	88
lake trout, flesh only (*Vita*)	178
lox, Nova (*Vita*)	122
lox, regular (*Vita*)	112
sable, flesh only (*Vita*)	74
salmon, flesh only (*Vita*)	100
whiting, flesh only (*Vita*)	96

Chapter 13

MEXICAN AND ORIENTAL FOODS

MEXICAN & MEXICAN-STYLE FOODS
See also "Frozen Dinners"

---

calories

beans, refried, *see "Vegetables, Canned or in Jars,"*
page 93
beef, Mexican style, w/chili sauce cheese filling, in pastry,
frozen
(*Pepperidge Farm*), 8¾-oz. serving 250
burrito, frozen:
beef (*Hormel*), 1 burrito* 205
beef, sirloin Grande
(*Van de Kamp's* Mexican Classic), 6 oz. 470
beef and bean (*Old El Paso*), 1 burrito* 277
beef and bean (*Patio*), 5-oz. burrito 190
beef and bean (*Patio*), 6-oz. burrito 225
beef and bean, w/chili salsa
(*Van de Kamp's* Mexican Classic), 6 oz. 280
beef and bean, w/green chili
(*Patio*), 5-oz. serving 190
beef and bean, w/green chili
(*Patio*), 6-oz. serving 225
beef and bean, w/red chili (*Patio*), 5-oz. serving 190
beef and bean, w/red chili (*Patio*), 6-oz. serving 220
cheese (*Hormel*), 1 burrito* 210
chicken and rice (*Hormel*), 1 burrito* 200
fried, w/guacamole
(*Van de Kamp's* Mexican Classic), 6 oz. 350

Mexican & Mexican-Style Foods, burrito, frozen, continued

Grande, w/rice and corn
  (*Van de Kamp's* Mexican Classic Combinations),
    14¾ oz. 531
  hot chili (*Hormel*), 1 burrito* 240
chicken Suiza, w/rice and beans, frozen
  (*Van de Kamp's* Mexican Classic Combinations),
    14¾ oz. 552
chili con carne, without beans:
  beef, canned (*Chef Boy•ar•dee*), 7½ oz. 370
  canned (*Armour Star*), 7¾ oz. 424
  canned (*Dennison's*), 7½ oz. 300
  canned (*Hormel*), 7½ oz. 370
  canned (*Hormel* Short Order), 7½-oz. can 360
  canned (*Libby's*), 7½ oz. 390
  canned (*Old El Paso*), 1 cup 349
  canned (*Van Camp*), 8 oz. 340
  hot, canned (*Hormel*), 7½ oz. 370
chili con carne, with beans:
  beef, canned (*Chef Boy•ar•dee*), 7½ oz. 330
  canned (*Armour Star*), 7¾ oz. 347
  canned (*Dennison's*), 7½ oz. 320
  canned (*Heinz*), 7¾ oz. 350
  canned (*Hormel*), 7½ oz. 310
  canned (*Hormel* Short Order), 7½-oz. can 280
  canned (*Libby's*), 7½ oz. 270
  canned (*Luck's*), 7½ oz. 350
  canned (*Old El Paso*), 1 cup 423
  canned (*Van Camp*), 8 oz. 340
  canned (*Van Camp Chilee Weenee*), 8 oz. 290
  dietetic, canned (*Dia-Mel*), 8-oz. can 360
  dietetic, canned (*Featherweight*), 7 1.2-oz. can 270
  hot, canned (*Dennison's*), 7½ oz. 310
  hot, canned (*Heinz*), 7¾ oz. 330
  hot, canned (*Hormel*), 7½ oz. 310
  hot, canned
    (*Hormel* Short Order), 7 1.2-oz. can 300
  freeze-dried (*Mountain House*), 2.75 oz. 390
  frozen (*Stouffer's*), 8¾-oz. pkg. 270
  frozen (*Weight Watchers*), 10-oz. pkg. 290
chili mac:
  canned (*Chef Boy•ar•dee*), 7½ oz. 230

Mexican & Mexican-Style Foods, chili mac, continued

canned (*Dennison's*), 7½ oz. 210
canned (*Heinz*), 7½ oz. 250
canned (*Hormel* Short Order), 7½-oz. can 200
w/beef, freeze-dried (*Mountain House*), 1.9 oz. 250

chili peppers, *see "Vegetables, Canned or in Jars," page 96*

chili sauce, *see "Condiments & Seasonings," page 210
and "Sauces," page 204*

chimichangas, beef, frozen
(*Old El Paso*), 1 piece* 400

chimichangas, chicken, frozen
(*Old El Paso*), 1 piece* 360

enchilada sauce, *see "Sauces," page 204*

enchiladas, beef, canned
(*Old El Paso*), 2.1-oz. enchilada 86

enchiladas, frozen:
beef (*Banquet Buffet Suppers*), 32-oz. pkg. 1056
beef (*Hormel*), 1 enchilada* 140
beef (*Patio*), 2.7-oz. enchilada 87
beef (*Swanson*), 11¼-oz. pkg. 470
beef (*Swanson Hungry-Man*), 16-oz. pkg. 660
beef (*Van de Kamp's* Mexican Holiday),
7½-oz. serving 250
beef
(*Van de Kamp's* Mexican Holiday—4 pack),
8½-oz. serving 340
beef, w/beef chili gravy (*Patio*), 10.65-oz. pkg. 250
beef, Mexican (*Old El Paso*), 1 enchilada* 280
beef, w/sauce, frozen
(*Banquet Cookin' Bags*), 6-oz. pkg. 215
beef, shredded
(*Van de Kamp's* Mexican Classic), 5½ oz. 180
beef, shredded, w/rice and corn
(*Van de Kamp's* Mexican Classic Combinations),
14¾ oz. 485
beef and cheese, w/rice and beans
(*Van de Kamp's* Mexican Classic Combinations),
14¾ oz. 539
cheese (*Hormel*), 1 enchilada* 151
cheese (*Old El Paso*), 2.5-oz. enchilada 57
cheese (*Van de Kamp's* Mexican Classic Ranchero),
5½ oz. 252

Mexican & Mexican-Style Foods, enchiladas, frozen, continued

cheese
  (*Van de Kamp's* Mexican Holiday),
  7½-oz. serving 270
cheese
  (*Van de Kamp's* Mexican Holiday—4 pack),
  8½-oz. serving 370
cheese, w/chili gravy (*Patio*), 12-oz. pkg. 200
cheese, Mexican (*Old El Paso*), 1 enchilada* 440
cheese, w/rice and beans
  (*Van de Kamp's* Mexican Classic Combinations),
  14¾ oz. 623
chicken
  (*Van de Kamp's* Mexican Holiday),
  7½-oz. serving 250
chicken, Mexican (*Old El Paso*), 1 enchilada* 230
chicken, w/sour cream
  (*Old El Paso*), 1 enchilada* 524
chicken Suiza
  (*Van de Kamp's* Mexican Classic), 5½ oz. 230
Sonora style
  (*Green Giant* Baked Entrees), 12-oz. pkg. 700
taco, beef, frozen (*Patio*), 2-oz. taco 80
taco, beef, snack, frozen (*Patio*), 3 tacos* 130
taco sauce, *see "Condiments & Seasonings," page 212*
taco shell (*Old El Paso*), 1 shell* 59
taco shell (*Ortega*), 1 shell* 50
tamale and beef, w/chili gravy, frozen
  (*Patio*), 10.65-oz. pkg. 280
tamales:
  canned (*Hormel* Short Order), 7½-oz. can 270
  canned (*Old El Paso*), 1 tamale* 96
  in jars (*Armour Star*), 1 tamale* 92
  beef, canned (*Hormel*), 1 tamale* 70
  beef, hot, canned
    (*Hormel* Hot 'N Spicy), 1 tamale* 70
tamalitos in chili gravy, canned
    (*Dennison's*), 7½ oz. 310
taquito, shredded beef, w/guacamole, frozen
  (*Van de Kamp's* Mexican Classic), 8 oz. 490
tortilla, frozen (*Patio*), ¾-oz. tortilla 17

Mexican & Mexican-Style Foods, continued

tostada, beef supreme, frozen
 (*Van de Kamp's* Mexican Classic), 8½ oz. 530
tostada shell (*Old El Paso*), 1 shell* 57

*As packaged

> **ORIENTAL & ORIENTAL-STYLE FOODS**
> See also "Frozen Dinners"

calories

bamboo shoots, *see "Vegetables, Canned or in Jars,"*
 page 91
bean sprouts, *see "Vegetables, Canned or in Jars," page 91*
beef, Oriental, w/vegetables and rice, in sauce, frozen
 (*Stouffer's Lean Cuisine*), 8⅝-oz. serving 280
beef, Oriental, w/vegetables and rice, frozen
 (*Weight Watchers*), 10-oz. pkg. 260
beef, Szechwan, stir-fry, frozen
 (*Green Giant* Baked Entrees), 10-oz. pkg. 290
beef and vegetables, Szechwan, w/rice, frozen
 (*Van de Kamp's* Chinese Classics), 11 oz. 370
chicken, almond, Cantonese, w/rice, frozen
 (*Van de Kamp's* Chinese Classics), 11 oz. 430
chicken, cashew, stir-fry, frozen
 (*Green Giant* Baked Entrees), 10-oz. pkg. 340
chicken, w/garden vegetables, stir-fry, frozen
 (*Green Giant* Baked Entrees), 10-oz. pkg. 250
chicken Oriental in ginger sauce,
 w/vegetables and rice, frozen
 (*Weight Watchers*), 9½-oz. pkg. 240
chop suey, beef, w/rice, frozen
 (*Stouffer's*), 12-oz. pkg. 355
chow mein, canned:
 (*Chun King* Stir Fry), ⅕ of pkg.* 230
 beef (*Chun King*—Divider Pak), ¼ of pkg.* 80
 beef (*Chun King*—Divider Pak, 24 oz.),
  ½ of pkg.* 90
 beef (*La Choy*—14-oz. can), ¾ cup 70

Oriental & Oriental-Style Foods, chow mein, canned, continued

  beef (*La Choy*—Bi-Pack), ³⁄₄ cup* 60
  chicken (*Chun King*—Divider Pak), ¹⁄₄ of pkg.* 80
  chicken
    (*Chun King*—Divider Pak, 24 oz.),
    ¹⁄₂ of pkg.* 90
  chicken (*La Choy*—14-oz. can), ³⁄₄ cup 80
  chicken (*La Choy*—Bi-Pack), ³⁄₄ cup* 70
  meatless (*La Choy*—14-oz. can), ³⁄₄ cup 35
  pork (*Chun King*—Divider Pak), ¹⁄₄ of pkg.* 110
  pork (*Hormel* Short Order), 7¹⁄₂-oz. can 140
  pork (*La Choy*—Bi-Pack), ³⁄₄ cup* 90
  shrimp (*Chun King*—Divider Pak), ¹⁄₄ of pkg.* 70
  shrimp (*La Choy*—14-oz. can), ³⁄₄ cup 60
  shrimp (*La Choy*—Bi-Pack), ³⁄₄ cup* 70
  vegetable (*La Choy*—Bi-Pack), ³⁄₄ cup* 60
chow mein, frozen:
  beef, Mandarin
    (*Van de Kamp's* Chinese Classics), 11 oz. 380
  beef, w/rice and vegetables
    (*Green Giant* Twin Pouch Entrees), 9-oz. pkg. 240
  chicken (*Chun King* Pouched Entree), ¹⁄₂ pkg. 90
  chicken (*La Choy*), 12-oz. pkg. 180
  chicken (*Stouffer's*), 8-oz. pkg. 145
  chicken, Mandarin
    (*Van de Kamp's* Chinese Classics), 11 oz. 380
  chicken, w/rice
    (*Stouffer's Lean Cuisine*), 11¹⁄₄-oz. serving 250
  chicken, w/rice and vegetables
    (*Green Giant* Twin Pouch Entrees), 9-oz. pkg. 220
  shrimp (*Chun King* Pouched Entree), ¹⁄₂ pkg. 80
  shrimp (*La Choy*), 12-oz. pkg. 120
dim sum, *see "Appetizers, Hors d'Oeuvres & Snacks,*
  Frozen," page 133
egg foo yung (*Chun King* Stir Fry), ¹⁄₆ of pkg.* 100
egg rolls, *see "Appetizers, Hors d'Oeuvres & Snacks,*
  Frozen," page 133
noodles:
  (*Chun King* Chinatown Style), 1 oz. 133
  chow mein, canned (*Chun King*), 5 oz. 100
  chow mein, canned (*La Choy*), ¹⁄₂ cup 150
  rice, canned (*La Choy*), ¹⁄₂ cup 130

Oriental & Oriental-Style Foods, continued

pepper Oriental:
  canned
    (*Chun King*—Divider Pak), ¼ of pkg.* 70
    canned (*La Choy*—14-oz. can), ¾ cup 70
    canned (*La Choy*—Bi-Pack), ¾ cup* 70
    frozen (*La Choy*), ⅔ cup 80
  frozen, beef
    (*Chun King* Pouched Entree), ½ of pkg. 80
pepper steak
    (*Chun King* Stir Fry), ⅕ of pkg.* 185
rice, fried, *see, "Rice, Flavored," page 193*
scallops Oriental, w/vegetables and rice, frozen
    (*Stouffer's Lean Cuisine*), 11-oz. pkg. 220
snow peas, *see "Vegetables, Frozen," page 108*
soy sauce, *see "Condiments & Seasonings," page 212*
sukiyaki (*Chun King* Stir Fry), ⅕ of pkg.* 220
sukiyaki, canned (*La Choy*—Bi-Pack), ¾ cup* 70
sweet and sour:
    (*Chun King* Stir Fry), ⅕ of pkg.* 270
  chicken, frozen
    (*Green Giant* Baked Entrees), 10-oz. pkg. 300
  chicken, frozen (*La Choy*), ⅔ cup 190
  chicken, w/Oriental vegetables, frozen
    (*Weight Watchers*), 9-oz. pkg. 210
  Oriental, w/chicken, canned
    (*La Choy*), ¾ cup 240
  Oriental, w/pork, canned (*La Choy*), ¾ cup 260
  pork, frozen
    (*Chun King* Pouched Entree), ½ of pkg. 200
  pork, frozen (*La Choy*), ⅔ cup 180
  pork, w/rice, frozen
    (*Van de Kamp's* Chinese Classics), 11 oz. 460
sweet and sour sauce, *see "Sauces," page 206*
teriyaki, beef, w/rice and vegetables, frozen
    (*Stouffer's*), 10-oz. pkg. 365
teriyaki, beef, stir-fry
    (*Green Giant* Baked Entrees), 10-oz. pkg. 320
teriyaki sauce, *see "Condiments & Seasonings," page 213*
vegetables, *see "Vegetables, Canned or in Jars,"
    page 91, and "Vegetables, Frozen," page 100*

Oriental & Oriental-Style Foods, continued

water chestnuts, *see "Vegetables, Canned or in Jars," page 98*

wontons, *see "Appetizers, Hors d'Oeuvres & Snacks, Frozen," page 133*

*Prepared according to package directions

Chapter 14

PIZZA, PASTA, NOODLES AND RICE

PIZZA, FROZEN, one whole pie or package*

---

	calories
Canadian bacon:	
(*Celeste* Canadian Style), 8-oz. pie	483
(*Celeste* Canadian Style), 19-oz. pie	1152
(*Totino's My Classic Pizza*), 1 pie**	1320
(*Totino's* Party Pizza), 1 pie**	680
cheese:	
(*Buitoni*—6 slice), 12-oz. pie	880
(*Buitoni* Instant Pizza), 12-oz. pkg.	960
(*Celeste*), 7-oz. pie	472
(*Celeste*), 19-oz. pie	1236
(*Celeste* Suprema), 10-oz. pie	590
(*Celeste* Suprema), 24-oz. pie	1416
(*Totino's My Classic* Deluxe Pizza), 1 pie**	1470
(*Totino's* Party Pizza), 1 pie**	700
(*Weight Watchers*), 6-oz. pie	350
on English muffin	
(*Chef Boy•ar•dee*), 13¼-oz. pkg.	680
on French bread (*Stouffer's*), 10⅜-oz. pkg.	660
nacho (*Totino's* Party Pizza), 1 pie**	680
open face (*Buitoni*), 13-oz. pie	620
combination:	
(*Celeste* Chicago Style), 1 pie**	1440
(*Celeste* Deluxe), 9-oz. pie	563
(*Celeste* Deluxe), 23½-oz. pie	1472
(*Celeste* Deluxe Sicilian Style), 26-oz. pie	1632
(*Totino's My Classic* Deluxe Pizza), 1 pie**	1830

Pizza, Frozen, combination, continued

(*Weight Watchers* Deluxe), 7¼-oz. pkg. 340
on French bread
   (*Stouffer's* Deluxe), 12⅜-oz. pkg. 800
hamburger (*Totino's* Party Pizza), 1 pie** 680
hamburger, on French bread
   (*Stouffer's*), 12¼-oz. pkg. 800
meatless (*Celeste* Suprema), 10-oz. pie 590
meatless (*Celeste* Suprema), 20-oz. pie 1088
Mexican (*Totino's* Party Pizza), 1 pie** 720
mushroom, on French bread
   (*Stouffer's*), 12-oz. pkg. 340
pepperoni:
   (*Celeste*), 7¼-oz. pie 568
   (*Celeste*), 20-oz. pie 1388
   (*Celeste* Chicago Style Deluxe), 1 pie** 1496
   (*Fox* Deluxe Pizza), 1 pie** 560
   (*Totino's My Classic* Deluxe Pizza), 1 pie** 1680
   (*Totino's* Party Pizza), 1 pie** 740
   (*Weight Watchers*), 6¼-oz. pkg. 370
   on English muffin
      (*Chef Boy•ar•dee*), 14½ oz. pkg. 800
   on French bread
      (*Stouffer's*), 11¼-oz. pkg. 820
sausage:
   (*Celeste*), 8-oz. pie 525
   (*Celeste*), 22-oz. pie 1436
   (*Celeste* Chicago Style Deluxe), 1 pie** 1528
   (*Totino's My Classic* Deluxe Pizza), 1 pie** 1680
   (*Totino's* Party Pizza), 1 pie** 800
   on English muffin
      (*Chef Boy•ar•dee*), 15½-oz. pkg. 840
   on French bread (*Stouffer's*), 12-oz. pkg. 840
sausage and mushroom:
   (*Celeste*), 9-oz. pie 555
   (*Celeste*), 24-oz. pie 1460
   on French bread (*Stouffer's*), 12½-oz. pkg. 790
sausage and pepperoni
   (*Totino's* Party Pizza), 1 pie** 800
sausage and peppers (*Buitoni*), 1 pie** 460
sausage, veal
   (*Weight Watchers*), 6¾-oz. pkg. 350

Pizza, Frozen, continued
vegetable
  (*Weight Watchers* Supreme), 7¼-oz. pkg. 400

*Note variation in sizes
**As packaged

MACARONI, NOODLES & PASTA, PLAIN, two ounces*
See also "Rice, Plain"

---

                                                  calories
macaroni:
  (*American Beauty*) 200
  (*La Rosa*) 210
  (*Mueller's*) 210
  (*Ronzoni*) 210
  spinach ribbon (*Creamette*) 200
noodles, egg:
  (*American Beauty*) 220
  (*Buitoni*) 220
  (*Creamette*) 220
  (*Mueller's*) 210
  (*Pennsylvania Dutch*) 220
  (*Ronzoni*) 220
pasta**:
  (*American Beauty*) 200
  (*Buitoni*—High Protein Brand) 210
  (*Buitoni*—Pasta Romana Brand) 210
  (*Creamette*) 210
  (*La Rosa*) 210
  (*Mueller's*) 210
  (*Ronzoni*) 210
  spinach (*Buitoni*) 210

*Uncooked weight
**Includes spaghetti, vermicelli, linguine, etc.

MACARONI ENTREES, CANNED
See also "Macaroni Entrees, Frozen"
and "Dinner & Side Dish Mixes"

calories

(*Franco-American UFO's*), 7½ oz. 180
macaroni and beef:
  (*Chef Boy•ar•dee* Beefaroni—15-oz. can),
    7 1.2 oz. 220
  (*Chef Boy•ar•dee* Beefaroni—40-oz. can),
    8 oz. 240
  in sauce (*Buitoni*), 7½ oz. 190
  in tomato sauce
    (*Franco-American BeefyOs*), 7½ oz. 220
  w/tomato sauce (*Heinz*), 7¼ oz. 200
macaroni and cheese:
  (*Franco-American*), 7⅜ oz. 170
  (*Hormel* Short Order), 7½-oz. can 170
  w/cheese sauce (*Heinz*), 7½-oz. can 190
macaroni and meatballs:
  (*Chef Boy•ar•dee* Meatball-a-roni), 7½ oz. 220
  (*Franco-American UFO's* with Meteors),
    7½ oz. 230
  in sauce
    (*Chef Boy•ar•dee* Zooroni), 7½ oz. 240
macaroni, in pizza sauce
  (*Franco-American PizzOs*), 7½ oz. 170
macaroni, shells, in tomato sauce
  (*Chef Boy•ar•dee*), 7½ oz. 150
macaroni, in tomato sauce
  (*Chef Boy•ar•dee* Zooroni), 7½ oz. 140

MACARONI ENTREES, FROZEN, one whole package*
See also "Macaroni Entrees, Canned"
and "Dinner & Side Dish Mixes"

calories

macaroni and beef, w/tomato sauce
  (*Stouffer's*), 11½-oz. pkg. 380
macaroni and cheese:
  (*Banquet Buffet Supper*), 32-oz. pkg. 1344
  (*Banquet Cookin' Bags*), 5-oz. pkg. 227
  (*Green Giant* Baked Entree), 9-oz. pkg. 290
  (*Howard Johnson's*), 10-oz. pkg. 542
  (*Howard Johnson's*), 19-oz. pkg. 1029
  (*Morton* Family Meal), 8-oz. serving 260
  (*Stouffer's*), 12-oz. pkg. 520
  (*Swanson* Main Course Entree), 12-oz. pkg. 440
  casserole (*Banquet*), 8-oz. pkg. 344
  casserole (*Morton*), 8-oz. pkg. 270
  pot pie, *see "Frozen Pot Pies," page 142*

*Note variations in package sizes

NOODLE ENTREES, CANNED & FROZEN
See also "Dinner & Side Dish Mixes"

calories

(*Chef Boy•ar•dee* ABC'S & 123's), 7½ oz. 150
(*Van Camp Noodle Weenee*), 8 oz. 230
noodles and beef, canned
  (*Hormel* Short Order), 7½-oz. can 230
noodles and beef, w/sauce, canned
  (*Heinz*), 7½-oz. can 230
noodles and chicken, canned
  (*Dinty Moore* Short Order), 7½-oz. can 210
noodles and chicken,
  canned (*Heinz*), 7½-oz. can 160
noodles w/franks
  (*Chef Boy•ar•dee* ABC'S & 123's), 7½ oz. 220

Noodle Entrees, Canned & Frozen, continued

noodles w/meatballs
(*Chef Boy•ar•dee* ABC'S & 123's), 8 oz. 260
noodles w/mini meatballs
(*Chef Boy•ar•dee* ABC'S & 123's), 7½ oz. 240
noodles Romanoff, frozen (*Stouffer's*), 12-oz. pkg. 510
noodles in sauce
(*Chef Boy•ar•dee* ABC'S & 123's), 8 oz. 150
noodles and tuna, canned (*Heinz*), 7½-oz. can 170

PASTA ENTREES, CANNED
See also "Pasta Entrees, Frozen,"
"Dinner & Side Dish Mixes,"
"Macaroni Entrees, Canned"
and "Noodle Entrees, Canned & Frozen"

---

calories

cannelloni (*Chef Boy•ar•dee*), 7½ oz. 230
(*Chef Boy•ar•dee* Beef-O-Getti), 7½ oz. 220
(*Chef Boy•ar•dee* Mini Bites), 7½ oz. 260
(*Chef Boy•ar•dee* Roller Coasters), 7½ oz. 230
lasagna:
(*Chef Boy•ar•dee* –15-oz. can), 7½ oz. 220
(*Chef Boy•ar•dee*—40-oz. can), 8 oz. 240
(*Hormel* Short Order), 7½-oz. can 260
ravioli:
(*Dia Mel*), 8-oz. can 260
beef (*Chef Boy•ar•dee* Lido Club), 7½ oz. 190
beef (*Featherweight*), 8-oz. can 260
beef, in meat sauce
(*Franco-American*), 7½ oz. 230
beef, mini
(*Chef Boy•ar•dee*—15-oz. can), 7½ oz. 210
beef, mini (*Chef Boy•ar•dee*—40-oz. can), 8 oz. 220
beef, in sauce (*Chef Boy•ar•dee*), 8 oz. 220
beef, in tomato sauce
(*Chef Boy•ar•dee*), 7½ oz. 200
cheese (*Buitoni*), 15-oz. can 360

Pasta Entrees, Canned, ravioli, continued

cheese, in beef and tomato sauce
(*Chef Boy•ar•dee*), 7½ oz. 200
cheese, in tomato sauce
(*Chef Boy•ar•dee*), 7½ oz. 200
chicken (*Chef Boy•ar•dee*), 7½ oz. 180
chicken, mini
(*Chef Boy•ar•dee*), 7½ oz. 220
meat (*Buitoni*), 15-oz. can 340
sausage, in tomato and meat sauce
(*Chef Boy•ar•dee*), 7½ oz. 210
raviolios, beef, in meat sauce
(*Franco-American*), 7½ oz. 210
spaghetti:
and beef (*Hormel* Short Order), 7½-oz. can 260
and beef, in tomato sauce
(*Chef Boy•ar•dee*), 7½ oz. 220
in meat sauce (*Franco-American*), 7½ oz. 210
in meat sauce (*Heinz*), 7½ oz. 170
w/meatballs (*Buitoni*), 15-oz. can 480
w/meatballs (*Chef Boy•ar•dee*), 8½ oz. 260
w/meatballs (*Dia Mel*), 8-oz. can 220
w/meatballs (*Featherweight*), 7½-oz. can 200
w/meatballs (*Hormel* Short Order), 7½-oz. can 210
w/meatballs, in tomato sauce
(*Chef Boy•ar•dee*—15-oz. can), 7½ oz. 240
w/meatballs, in tomato sauce
(*Chef Boy•ar•dee*—40-oz. can), 8 oz. 220
w/meatballs, in tomato sauce
(*Franco-American*), 7⅜ oz. 220
w/tomato sauce and cheese
(*Chef Boy•ar•dee*—15-oz. can), 7½ oz. 150
w/tomato sauce and cheese
(*Chef Boy•ar•dee*—40-oz. can), 8 oz. 150
w/tomato sauce and cheese
(*Franco-American*), 7⅜ oz. 180
w/tomato sauce and cheese
(*Heinz*), 7¾ oz. 160
rings, w/sliced franks in tomato sauce
(*Franco-American* SpaghettiOs), 7⅜ oz. 220
rings, w/little meatballs
(*Chef Boy•ar•dee* Lido Club), 7½ oz. 220

Pasta Entrees, Canned, spaghetti, continued

rings, w/meatballs in sauce
  (*Buitoni*), 7½-oz. can 210
rings, w/little meatballs in tomato sauce
  (*Franco-American* SpaghettiOs), 7⅜ oz. 210
rings, in tomato and cheese sauce
  (*Franco-American* SpaghettiOs), 7⅜ oz. 170
twists, w/meatballs (*Buitoni*), 15-oz. can 440
twists, w/sauce (*Buitoni*), 15-oz. can 320

PASTA ENTREES, FROZEN,
one whole package*, except as noted
See also "Pasta Entrees, Canned,"
"Dinner & Side Dish Mixes,"
"Macaroni Entrees, Frozen"
and "Noodle Entrees, Canned & Frozen"

---

                                                calories

cannelloni, beef and pork, w/Mornay sauce
  (*Stouffer's Lean Cuisine*), 9⅝-oz. pkg. 260
cannelloni, cheese, w/tomato sauce
  (*Stouffer's Lean Cuisine*), 9⅛-oz. pkg. 270
fettuccine Alfredo (*Buitoni*), 10-oz. pkg. 440
fettuccine Alfredo (*Stouffer's*), 10-oz. pkg. 540
fettuccine Carbonara (*Buitoni*), 10-oz. pkg. 440
fettuccine Primavera (*Buitoni*), 10-oz. pkg. 440
lasagna:
  (*Green Giant* Baked Entrees), 9½-oz. pkg. 290
  (*Stouffer's*), 10½-oz. pkg. 385
  (*Stouffer's*), 21-oz. pkg. 770
  (*Swanson Hungry-Man* Entree), 12¾-oz. pkg. 480
  beef and mushroom
    (*Van de Kamp's* Italian Classics), 11 oz. 430
  w/cheese, meat and sauce
    (*Weight Watchers*), 12-oz. pkg. 360
  chicken
    (*Green Giant* Baked Entrees), 12-oz. pkg. 640
  deep dish (*Buitoni*), 11 oz. 390
  Florentine (*Buitoni*), 9½ oz. 480

Pasta Entrees, Frozen, lasagna, continued

Italian cheese (*Weight Watchers*), 12-oz. pkg. 360
Italian sausage
  (*Van de Kamp's* Italian Classics), 11 oz. 440
w/meat (*Banquet Buffet Suppers*), 32-oz. pkg. 1488
w/meat
  (*Swanson* Main Course Entree), 13¼-oz. pkg. 480
w/meat sauce (*Buitoni*), 14-oz. pkg. 540
w/meat and sauce
  (*Green Giant* Baked Entrees), 10½-oz. pkg. 430
w/meat sauce
  (*Green Giant* Baked Entrees—single serve),
  12-oz. pkg. 490
w/meat sauce, deep dish (*Buitoni*), 10½ oz. 400
spinach
  (*Green Giant* Baked Entrees), 12-oz. pkg. 540
spinach (*Van de Kamp's* Italian Classics), 11 oz. 400
w/veal, tomato sauce and cheese
  (*Weight Watchers*), 12¾-oz. pkg. 380
zucchini (*Stouffer's Lean Cuisine*), 11-oz. pkg. 260
linguine w/clam sauce (*Stouffer's*), 10½-oz. pkg. 285
linguine w/clam sauce
  (*Stouffer's Lean Cuisine*), 1 pkg.* 270
manicotti:
cheese, w/meat
  (*Banquet Buffet Suppers*), 32-oz. pkg. 1392
jumbo (*Buitoni*), 18-oz. pkg. 810
in sauce (*Buitoni*), 13-oz. pkg. 420
mostaccioli and meat sauce
  (*Banquet Buffet Suppers*), 32-oz. pkg. 1004
ravioli:
cheese (*Buitoni*), 15-oz. pkg. 1040
cheese, Parmigiana (*Buitoni*), 12-oz. pkg. 440
cheese, round (*Buitoni*), 11-oz. pkg. 620
meat (*Buitoni*), 15-oz. pkg. 1060
meat, Parmigiana (*Buitoni*), 12-oz. pkg. 520
meat, round (*Buitoni*), 5½ oz. 340
shells:
baked, in sauce (*Buitoni*), 8 oz. 320
stuffed, beef and spinach, w/tomato sauce
  (*Stouffer's*), 9-oz. pkg. 290
stuffed, broccoli (*Buitoni*), 5 oz. 150

Pasta Entrees, Frozen, shells, continued
  stuffed, cheese, w/meat sauce
    (*Stouffer's*), 9-oz. pkg. 320
  stuffed, chicken, w/cheese sauce
    (*Stouffer's*), 9-oz. pkg. 400
  stuffed, w/sauce (*Buitoni*), 20-oz. pkg. 700
  stuffed, spinach and cheese (*Buitoni*), 5½ oz. 160
spaghetti:
  w/beef and mushroom sauce
    (*Stouffer's Lean Cuisine*), 11-oz. pkg. 260
  and meat casserole (*Morton*), 8-oz. pkg. 220
  w/meat sauce (*Stouffer's*), 14-oz. pkg. 445
  w/meat sauce, casserole (*Banquet*), 8-oz. pkg. 270
tortellini Guido (*Buitoni*), 10 oz. 380
ziti, baked, in sauce (*Buitoni*), 10½-oz. pkg. 360
ziti, w/veal, cheese and sauce
    (*Weight Watchers*), 11¼-oz. pkg. 290

Pay attention to package sizes

DINNER & SIDE DISH MIXES
See also "Rice, Flavored"

---

                                               calories
beef:
  noodle, dry (*Hamburger Helper*), ⅕ pkg. 140
  noodle, w/meat*
    (*Hamburger Helper*), ⅕ pkg. 320
  Romanoff, dry (*Hamburger Helper*), ⅕ pkg. 160
  Romanoff, w/meat*
    (*Hamburger Helper*), ⅕ pkg. 340
  cheeseburger macaroni, dry
    (*Hamburger Helper*), ⅕ pkg. 180
  cheeseburger macaroni, w/meat*
    (*Hamburger Helper*), ⅕ pkg. 360
chicken:
  and dumplings, dry
    (*Betty Crocker Chicken Helper*), ⅕ pkg. 210
  and dumplings, w/meat*
    (*Betty Crocker Chicken Helper*), ⅕ pkg. 530

  mushroom, dry
    (*Betty Crocker Chicken Helper*), ⅕ pkg. 150
  mushroom, w/meat*
    (*Betty Crocker Chicken Helper*), ⅕ pkg. 460
  and stuffing, dry
    (*Betty Crocker Chicken Helper*), ⅕ pkg. 180
  and stuffing, w/meat*
    (*Betty Crocker Chicken Helper*), ⅕ pkg. 580
  teriyaki, dry
    (*Betty Crocker Chicken Helper*), ⅕ pkg. 170
  teriyaki, w/meat*
    (*Betty Crocker Chicken Helper*), ⅕ pkg. 480
chili tomato, dry (*Hamburger Helper*), ⅕ pkg. 150
chili tomato, w/meat*
  (*Hamburger Helper*), ⅕ pkg. 330
dumpling noodles, *see "noodles," below*
hamburger:
  w/cheese, dry
    (*Creamette* Hamburger Mate), ⅕ pkg. 170
  w/cheese, w/meat*
    (*Creamette* Hamburger Mate), ⅕ pkg. 310
  hash, dry (*Hamburger Helper*), ⅕ pkg. 130
  hash, w/meat* (*Hamburger Helper*), ⅕ pkg. 300
  pizza dish, dry (*Hamburger Helper*), ⅕ pkg. 160
  pizza dish, w/meat*
    (*Hamburger Helper*), ⅕ pkg. 340
  stew, dry (*Hamburger Helper*), ⅕ pkg. 110
  stew, w/meat* (*Hamburger Helper*), ⅕ pkg. 290
lasagna, dry (*Hamburger Helper*), ⅕ pkg. 140
lasagna, w/meat* (*Hamburger Helper*), ⅕ pkg. 320
macaroni:
  and cheese, dry (*Creamette*), 2 oz. 220
  and cheese*
    (*Golden Grain* Stir & Serve), ½ cup 183
  and cheese* (*Kraft* Deluxe Dinner), ¾ cup 260
  and cheese* (*Kraft* Dinner), ¾ cup 300
  and cheese*
    (*Kraft* Dinner—Family Size), ¾ cup 300
  and cheese* (*Lipton*), ½ cup 210
  and cheese, freeze-dried
    (*Mountain House*), 1.05 oz. 200

Dinner & Side Dish Mixes, macaroni, continued

spiral, and cheese* (*Kraft*), ¾ cup 300
w/cheese and meat, *see "cheeseburger macaroni," above*
noodles:
Alfredo, w/sauce* (*Lipton* Deluxe), ½ cup 220
beef flavor, w/sauce* (*Lipton*), ½ cup 190
butter, w/sauce* (*Lipton*), ½ cup 190
butter and herb, w/sauce* (*Lipton*), ½ cup 180
cheese, w/sauce* (*Lipton*), ½ cup 200
w/cheese sauce and tuna, dry
  (*Tuna Helper*), ⅕ pkg. 170
w/cheese sauce and tuna, w/tuna*
  (*Tuna Helper*), ⅕ pkg. 230
and chicken, freeze-dried
  (*Mountain House*), 2 oz. 270
chicken Bombay, w/sauce*
  (*Lipton* Deluxe), ½ cup 190
chicken flavor, w/sauce* (*Lipton*), ½ cup 190
creamy, and tuna, dry (*Tuna Helper*), ⅕ pkg. 220
creamy, and tuna, w/tuna*
  (*Tuna Helper*), ⅕ pkg. 280
dumpling, and tuna, dry (*Tuna Helper*), ⅕ pkg. 170
dumpling, and tuna, w/tuna*
  (*Tuna Helper*), ⅕ pkg. 230
egg, and cheese* (*Kraft*), ⅔ cup 250
egg, w/chicken* (*Kraft*), ¾ cup 240
fettuccine Alfredo*
  (*Betty Crocker* International), ¼ pkg. 220
Oriental beef flavor (*Ramen Pride*), 3-oz. pkg. 396
Oriental chicken flavor
  (*Ramen Pride*), 3-oz. pkg. 401
Parisienne*
  (*Betty Crocker* International), ¼ pkg. 170
Parmesano, w/sauce* (*Lipton* Deluxe), ½ cup 210
Parmesano* (*Noodle-Roni*), ¾ cup 195
Romanoff*
  (*Betty Crocker* International), ¼ pkg. 230
Romanoff* (*Noodle-Roni*), ½ cup 181
sour cream and chive, w/sauce*
  (*Lipton*), ½ cup 190
Stroganoff*
  (*Betty Crocker* International), ¼ pkg. 240

Dinner & Side Dish Mixes, noodles, continued

Stroganoff, w/sauce* (*Lipton* Deluxe), 1/2 cup 200
Stroganoff, w/meat* (*Noodle-Roni*), 1/2 cup 120
potatoes:
au gratin, dry (*Hamburger Helper*), 1/5 pkg. 140
au gratin, w/meat* (*Hamburger Helper*), 1/5 pkg. 320
Stroganoff, dry (*Hamburger Helper*), 1/5 pkg. 140
Stroganoff, w/meat*
    (*Hamburger Helper*), 1/5 pkg. 320
rice mixes, *see "Rice, Flavored," page 193*
spaghetti:
(*Kraft* American Style Dinner), 1 cup* 270
dry (*Hamburger Helper*), 1/5 pkg. 150
w/meat* (*Hamburger Helper*), 1/5 pkg. 330
w/meat sauce*
    (*Kraft* Spaghetti With Meat Sauce Dinner),
    3/4 cup 250
w/meat sauce, freeze-dried
    (*Mountain House*), 1.7 oz. 260
Italian style
    (*Kraft* Tangy Italian Style Dinner), 1 cup 270
tamale pie, dry (*Hamburger Helper*), 1/5 pkg. 190
tamale pie, w/meat* (*Hamburger Helper*), 1/5 pkg. ... 370
tuna Tetrazzini, dry (*Tuna Helper*), 1/5 pkg. 150
tuna Tetrazzini, w/tuna* (*Tuna Helper*), 1/5 pkg. ... 260

Prepared according to package directions

RICE, PLAIN, 1/2 cup cooked*
See also "Rice, Flavored"

---

                                              calories
brown:
(*Mahatma*) 110
(*River Brand*) 110
parboiled, long grain (*Uncle Ben's*) 100
white:
(*Carolina*) 100
(*Comet*) 102
(*Mahatma*) 100
(*River*) 100

Rice, Plain, white, continued

(*Success*)	100
(*Uncle Ben's* Converted)	97
(*Water Maid*)	100
parboiled (*Comet*)	90
precooked (*Carolina*)	110
precooked (*Minute Rice*)	90
precooked (*Uncle Ben's* Quick)	89

*Cooked according to package directions, without butter

RICE, FLAVORED, ½ cup, except as noted
See also "Rice, Plain"

---

calories

beef flavor:

freeze-dried (*Mountain House*), 2.25 oz.	390
mix* (*Comet*)	100
w/sauce, mix* (*Lipton*)	160
w/vermicelli, mix (*Make-It-Easy*), 1.3 oz.	130
w/vermicelli, mix* (*Minute Rice* Rib Roast)	150
w/vermicelli, mix* (*Rice-A-Roni*)	160
w/broccoli in cheese sauce, frozen (*Green Giant* Rice Originals)	140
brown and wild rice, mix* (*Uncle Ben's*)	150
w/cheese flavor sauce and vermicelli, mix* (*Rice-A-Roni*)	145

chicken flavor:

w/sauce, mix* (*Lipton*)	150
w/vermicelli, mix (*Make-It-Easy*), 1.3 oz.	130
w/vermicelli, mix* (*Minute Rice* Drumstick)	150
w/vermicelli, mix* (*Rice-A-Roni*)	160
curry (*R. M. Quiggs*), 4.5 oz.	150
French onion, mix* (*R. M. Quiggs*), 4.5 oz.	160
French style, frozen (*Birds Eye* International), 3.6 oz.	100

fried, Chinese:

canned (*La Choy*), ¾ cup	190
mix** (*Durkee* Seasoning Mix)	108
mix* (*Minute Rice*)	160
frozen (*Birds Eye*), 3.6 oz.	100

Rice, Flavored, fried, Chinese, continued

frozen (*Chun King* Stir Fry), ⅕ pkg. 130
w/pork, frozen (*Chun King*), 5 oz. 180
w/vermicelli, mix* (*Rice-A-Roni*) 187
herb butter sauce, frozen
(*Green Giant Rice Originals*) 150
herb and butter, w/sauce, mix* (*Lipton*) 160
Italian blend, w/spinach in cheese sauce, frozen
(*Green Giant Rice Originals*) 160
Italian style, frozen
(*Birds Eye* International), 3.6 oz. 130
long grain and wild rice:
mix* (*Minute Rice*) 150
mix* (*R. M. Quiggs*), 4.5 oz. 150
mix* (*Uncle Ben's*) 113
mix* (*Uncle Ben's* Fast) 127
w/white, frozen (*Green Giant Rice Originals*) 110
Oriental style:
fried, *see "fried, Chinese," above*
frozen (*Birds Eye* International), 3.6 oz. 130
mix*** (*Hamburger Helper*), ⅕ pkg. 340
paella, mix* (*R. M. Quiggs*), 4½ oz. 160
pilaf:
frozen (*Green Giant Rice Originals*) 120
mix* (*Uncle Ben's* Greek Style) 144
rice medley, frozen (*Green Giant Rice Originals*) 120
saffron-seasoned (*Mahatma*) 100
Spanish:
canned (*Comstock*) 60
canned (*Featherweight*), 7½-oz. can 140
canned (*Heinz*), 7¼-oz. can 150
canned (*Van Camp*) 80
frozen (*Birds Eye* International), 3.6 oz. 120
mix** (*Durkee* Seasoning Mix) 137
mix* (*Minute Rice*) 150
w/sauce, mix* (*Lipton*) 140
turkey flavor, w/vermicelli, mix* (*Rice-A-Roni*) 182
wild rice, w/vermicelli, mix* (*Rice-A-Roni*) 134

Prepared according to package directions
**Prepared according to package directions, with rice*
***Prepared according to package directions, with hamburger*

Chapter 15

FATS, OILS
AND SALAD DRESSINGS

FATS & OILS, one tablespoon, except as noted

---

calories

butter:
  (*Land O Lakes*) 100
  (*Meadow Gold*) 100
  (*Sealtest*) 102
  whipped (*Breakstone's*) 67
margarine:
  (*Blue Bonnet*—stick or soft) 100
  (*Fleischmann's*—stick or soft) 100
  (*I Can't Believe It's Not Butter*) 90
  (*Kraft Miracle Brand*) 60
  (*Mazola*) 100
  (*Mazola*—unsalted) 100
  (*Mrs. Filbert's*—stick or soft) 100
  (*Nucoa*) 100
  (*Nucoa*—soft) 90
  (*Parkay*—stick or soft) 100
  (*Promise*—stick or soft) 90
  diet (*Blue Bonnet*) 50
  diet (*Fleischmann's*) 50
  diet (*Imperial*) 50
  diet (*Mazola*) 50
  diet (*Mrs. Filbert's*) 50
  diet (*Parkay*) 50
  diet (*Weight Watchers*—stick) 60
  diet (*Weight Watchers*—tub) 50
safflower oil (*Hain*) 100

Fats & Oils, margarine, continued

safflower oil (*Hain*—unsalted) 100
spread (*Blue Bonnet* Light Tasty) 80
spread (*Fleischmann's*) 80
spread (*Mrs. Filbert's* Family Spread) 70
spread (*Mrs. Filbert's* 25) 80
spread (*Parkay* Light) 70
squeeze (*Fleischmann's*) 100
squeeze (*Squeeze Parkay*) 100
whipped (*Blue Bonnet*—stick or soft) 70
whipped (*Parkay*—cup or stick) 60

oil:

all-blend (*Hain*) 120
almond (*Hain*) 120
apricot kernel (*Hain*) 120
butter flavor
  (*Orville Redenbacher* Gourmet Popping Oil) 120
cod liver (*Hain*) 120
cod liver, flavored (*Hain*) 120
corn (*Fleischmann's*) 120
corn (*Hain*) 120
corn (*Mazola*) 125
cottonseed (*Hain*) 120
olive (*Filippo Berio*) 125
olive (*Hain*) 120
peanut (*Hain*) 120
peanut (*Planters*) 130
popcorn (*Planters*) 130
safflower (*Hain*) 120
sesame (*Hain*) 120
soy (*Hain*) 120
sunflower (*Hain*) 120
sunflower (*Sunlite*) 120
vegetable (*Crisco*) 120
vegetable (*Puritan*) 120
vegetable (*Wesson*) 120
walnut (*Hain*) 120
wheat germ (*Hain*) 120

oil, cooking spray
  (*Mazola No Stick*), 2-second spray 7
oil and garlic (*Hain*) 120

Fats & Oils, continued
shortening:
   (*Crisco*) 110
   (*Fluffo*) 110
   (*Snowdrift*) 110

SALAD DRESSINGS, one tablespoon, except as noted

---

                                                    calories

avocado goddess, bottled
   (*Marie's Specialty Brands*) 96
bacon, creamy, bottled (*Seven Seas*) 60
bacon, low-calorie, bottled (*Kraft*) 30
bacon and buttermilk, bottled (*Kraft*) 80
bacon and buttermilk, bottled (*Seven Seas*) 60
bacon and Parmesan, bottled (*Seven Seas*) 60
bacon and tomato:
   bottled (*Kraft*) 70
   bottled (*Seven Seas*) 60
   low-calorie, bottled (*Kraft*) 30
(*Bama* Salad Dressing) 50
blue cheese:
   bottled (*Marie's Specialty Brands*) 100
   bottled (*Roka Brand*) 60
   buttermilk, bottled (*Hain Naturals*) 70
   chunky, bottled (*Kraft*) 70
   chunky, bottled (*Seven Seas*) 70
   chunky, bottled (*Wish-Bone*) 70
   low-calorie, bottled (*Dia-Mel*) 2
   low-calorie, bottled (*Featherweight Neu Bleu*) .. 4
   low-calorie, bottled (*Marie's Specialty Brands*) . 35
   low-calorie, bottled (*Roka Brand*) 14
   low-calorie, bottled (*S & W Nutradiet*) 25
   low-calorie, chunky, bottled (*Kraft*) 30
   low-calorie, chunky, bottled (*Walden Farms*) ... 27
   low-calorie, chunky, bottled (*Wish-Bone* Lite) .. 40
   low-calorie, mix* (*Weight Watchers*) 10
   mix* (*Hain Natural No Oil*) 6
bottled (*Seven Seas Capri*) 70

Salad Dressings, continued

buttermilk:
- bottled (*Seven Seas* Buttermilk Recipe) 80
- creamy, bottled (*Kraft*) 80
- old-fashioned, bottled (*Hain Naturals*) 70
- mix* (*Hain Natural No Oil*) 11
- low-calorie, bottled (*Wish-Bone* Lite) 50
- low-calorie, creamy, bottled (*Kraft*) 30

buttermilk and chives, creamy, bottled (*Kraft*) 80

buttermilk spice, bottled
(*Marie's Specialty Brands*) 93

Caesar:
- bottled (*Kraft* Golden) 70
- bottled (*Seven Seas*) 60
- bottled (*Wish-Bone*) 70
- creamy, bottled (*Hain Naturals*) 60
- creamy, bottled (*Hain Naturals* — no salt added) 60
- low-calorie, creamy (*Featherweight*) 14
- mix* (*Hain Natural No Oil*) 4

Cheddar and bacon, bottled (*Wish-Bone*) 70

cheese avocado, bottled (*Hain Naturals*) 70

coleslaw (*Kraft*) 70

cucumber:
- bottled (*Kraft Philadelphia Brand*) 70
- creamy, bottled (*Kraft*) 70
- creamy, bottled (*Wish-Bone*) 80
- low-calorie, creamy, bottled (*Dia-Mel*) 2
- low-calorie, creamy, bottled (*Featherweight*) 12
- low-calorie, creamy, bottled (*Kraft*) 30
- low-calorie, creamy, bottled (*S & W Nutradiet*) 20
- low-calorie, creamy, bottled (*Wish-Bone* Lite) 40

cucumber-dill, bottled (*Hain Naturals*) 80

French:
- bottled (*Hain Naturals* Olé French) 60
- bottled (*Kraft*) 60
- bottled (*Kraft Catalina Brand*) 60
- bottled (*Wish-Bone* De Luxe) 50
- bottled (*Wish-Bone* Sweet 'n Spicy) 70
- creamy, bottled (*Hain Naturals*) 60
- w/herbs (*Wish-Bone*) 60
- mix* (*Hain Natural No Oil*) 12
- low-calorie, bottled (*Dia-Mel*) 2

Salad Dressings, French, continued

  low-calorie, bottled (*Featherweight*) 6
  low-calorie, bottled (*Kraft*) 20
  low-calorie, bottled (*S & W Nutradiet*) 18
  low-calorie, bottled (*Walden Farms*) 33
  low-calorie, bottled (*Wish-Bone* Lite) 30
  low-calorie, bottled (*Wish-Bone* Sweet 'n Spicy) 30
  low-calorie, mix* (*Weight Watchers*) 4
garlic:
  creamy, bottled (*Wish-Bone*) 80
  and cheese, mix* (*Hain Natural No Oil*) 6
  and chive, bottled (*Kraft Philadelphia Brand*) 70
  and oil, bottled (*Hain Naturals*) 120
  and sour cream, bottled (*Hain Naturals*) 70
  mix* (*Good Seasons*) 80
  low-calorie, creamy, bottled (*Dia-Mel*) 2
garlic-Caesar, low-calorie, bottled (*Estee*) 6
garlic-French, bottled (*Seven Seas*) 60
green goddess, bottled (*Lawry's*) 59
green goddess, bottled (*Seven Seas*) 60
Hawaiian, bottled (*Lawry's*) 77
herb:
  bottled (*Hain Naturals* Savory—no salt added) 30
  and spices, bottled (*Seven Seas*) 60
  low-calorie, bottled (*Estee* Herb Garden) 6
  low-calorie, mix* (*Hain Natural No Oil*) 2
honey and sesame, bottled (*Hain Naturals*) 60
Italian:
  bottled (*Bennett's*) 60
  bottled (*Hain*) 64
  bottled (*Hain Naturals* Traditional) 80
  bottled
    (*Hain Naturals* Traditional—no salt added) 60
  bottled (*Kraft* Golden Blend) 70
  bottled (*Kraft* Zesty Italian) 80
  bottled (*Seven Seas* Mild) 70
  bottled (*Seven Seas* Viva) 70
  bottled (*Wish-Bone*) 70
  bottled (*Wish-Bone* Robusto) 80
  w/cheese, bottled (*Marie's Specialty Brand*) 62
  creamy, bottled (*Hain Naturals*) 80
  creamy, bottled (*Hain Naturals*—no salt added) 80

Salad Dressings, Italian, continued

creamy, bottled (*Seven Seas*) 70
creamy, bottled (*Wish-Bone*) 60
creamy, w/sour cream, bottled (*Kraft*) 60
garlic, bottled (*Marie's Specialty Brands*) 100
herb, bottled (*Kraft Philadelphia Brand*) 70
w/herbs, bottled (*Wish-Bone*) 70
mix* (*Good Seasons*) 80
mix* (*Good Seasons* Mild) 90
mix* (*Good Seasons Thick 'n Creamy*) 85
low-calorie, bottled (*Dia-Mel*) 2
low-calorie, bottled (*Estee* Spicy Italian) 6
low-calorie, bottled (*Featherweight*) 4
low-calorie, bottled (*Kraft*) 6
low-calorie, bottled (*Kraft*—oil-free) 4
low-calorie, bottled (*S & W Nutradiet*—no oil) 2
low-calorie, bottled (*Walden Farms*) 9
low-calorie, bottled
  (*Walden Farms*—no sugar added) 6
low-calorie, bottled (*Wish-Bone* Lite) 30
low-calorie, creamy, bottled (*Dia-Mel*) 2
low-calorie, creamy, bottled (*Kraft*) 25
low-calorie, creamy, bottled (*S & W Nutradiet*) 10
low-calorie, creamy, bottled (*Wish-Bone* Lite) 30
low-calorie, creamy, bottled (*Weight Watchers*) 50
low-calorie, mix* (*Good Seasons*) 8
low-calorie, mix* (*Hain Natural No Oil*) 4
low-calorie, mix* (*Weight Watchers*) 2
low-calorie, creamy, mix* (*Weight Watchers*) 4
mayonnaise:
bottled (*Bama*) 100
bottled (*Bennett's*) 110
bottled (*Best Foods*) 100
bottled (*Cains*) 100
bottled (*Hellmann's*) 100
bottled (*Kraft*) 100
bottled (*Mrs. Filbert's*) 100
imitation, bottled (*Dia-Mel*) 106
imitation, bottled (*Kraft Miracle Whip*) 70
imitation, bottled (*Mrs. Filbert's*) 40
imitation, eggless, bottled (*Hain Naturals*) 85

Salad Dressings, mayonnaise, continued

    imitation, eggless, bottled
      (*Hain Naturals*—no salt added) 110
    low-calorie, bottled (*S & W Nutradiet*) 25
    reduced calorie, bottled (*Bennett's*) 40
    reduced calorie, bottled (*Featherweight*) 60
    reduced calorie, bottled (*Light n' Lively*) 40
    reduced calorie, bottled (*Weight Watchers*) 40
oil and vinegar, bottled (*Kraft*) 70
onion, mix* (*Good Seasons*) 80
onion, toasted, bottled
    (*Kraft Philadelphia Brand*) 70
onion and chive, creamy, bottled (*Kraft*) 70
onion and chive, low-calorie, bottled
    (*Wish-Bone* Lite) 40
onion and cucumber, low-calorie, bottled (*Estee*) 6
Parmesan, bottled (*Seven Seas Viva Parmesan*) 60
Parmesan, creamy, bottled (*Seven Seas*) 60
ranch, bottled (*Marie's Specialty Brands*) 105
red wine and vinegar, low-calorie, bottled
    (*Dia-Mel*) 2
red wine and vinegar, low-calorie, bottled
    (*Featherweight*) 6
red wine vinegar and oil, bottled (*Seven Seas*) 60
Romano, bottled (*Hain Naturals* Robust Romano) 70
Roquefort, bottled (*Marie's Specialty Brands*) 105
Russian:
    bottled (*Hain Naturals* Tangy Russian) 60
    bottled (*Kraft*) 60
    bottled (*Marie's Specialty Brands*) 88
    bottled (*Wish-Bone*) 60
    w/bacon, bottled
      (*Wish-Bone* Southern Recipe) 60
    creamy, bottled (*Seven Seas*) 80
    low-calorie, bottled (*Kraft*) 30
    low-calorie, bottled (*S & W Nutradiet*) 25
    low-calorie, bottled (*Wish-Bone* Lite) 25
    low-calorie, mix* (*Weight Watchers*) 4
sour cream and bacon, bottled (*Wish-Bone*) 70
Tahiti, low-calorie, bottled (*Dia-Mel*) 2
Thousand Island:
    bottled (*Hain Naturals*) 50

Salad Dressings, Thousand Island, continued

bottled (*Kraft*)	70
bottled (*Marie's Specialty Brands*)	88
bottled (*Seven Seas*)	50
bottled (*Wish-Bone*)	60
bottled (*Wish-Bone* Southern Recipe)	70
mix* (*Good Seasons Thick 'n Creamy*)	75
mix* (*Hain Natural No Oil*)	12
low-calorie, bottled (*Dia-Mel*)	2
low-calorie, bottled (*Diet Delight*)	18
low-calorie, bottled (*Kraft*)	30
low-calorie, bottled (*S & W Nutradiet*)	25
low-calorie, bottled (*Walden Farms*)	24
low-calorie, bottled (*Wish-Bone* Lite)	25
low-calorie, mix* (*Weight Watchers*)	12
Yogurt-buttermilk, low-calorie, bottled (*Dia-Mel*)	2

Prepared according to package directions

Chapter 16

SAUCES, GRAVIES, CONDIMENTS AND SEASONINGS

SAUCES, 1/2 cup, except as noted
*See also "Gravies," "Condiments & Seasonings"
and "Seasoning & Roasting Mixes, Dry"*

	calories
à la king, mix* (*Durkee*)	67
barbecue, in jars:	
(*Cris & Pitt's*)	120
(*Estee*), 1 tbsp.	16
(*Featherweight*), 1 tbsp.	7
(*French's* Cattlemens)	200
(*Heinz*)	160
(*Hunt's* All Natural)	160
(*Kraft*)	180
(*Open Pit*), 4 oz.**	104
garlic (*Kraft*)	140
hickory (*Hunt's* All Natural)	200
hickory smoke flavor (*Heinz*)	160
hickory smoke flavor (*Kraft*)	160
hickory smoke flavor (*Open Pit*), 4 oz.**	106
hickory smoke flavor, w/onion bits (*Kraft*)	200
hot (*Heinz*)	160
hot (*Kraft*)	160
hot hickory smoke (*Kraft*)	160
hot and zesty (*Hunt's* All Natural)	200
smoky flavor (*French's* Cattlemens)	200
w/mushrooms (*Heinz*)	160
onion (*Hunt's* All Natural)	160

Sauces, barbecue, in jars, continued

w/onion bits (*Kraft*) 200
w/onions (*Heinz*) 160
w/onions (*Open Pit*), 4 oz.** 109
browning sauce, microwave:
  beef (*Holland House*), 1/2 oz. 28
  chicken (*Holland House*), 1/2 oz. 31
  pork (*Holland House*), 1/2 oz. 33
cheese:
  mix* (*Durkee*) 158
  mix* (*French's*) 160
  mix* (*McCormick/Schilling*) 154
chili:
  canned (*Featherweight*), 1 tbsp. 8
  canned (*Heinz*), 1/2 cup 136
  hot dog w/beef, canned
    (*Chef Boy•ar•dee*), 1 oz. 30
clam, red, canned (*Buitoni*), 5 1/8 oz. 130
clam, white, canned (*Buitoni*), 5 1/8 oz. 180
enchilada:
  mix* (*Durkee*) 29
  green chili (*Old El Paso*), 1/4 cup 18
  hot or mild, canned (*Del Monte*) 45
  hot, canned (*Old El Paso*) 52
  mild, canned (*Old El Paso*) 50
fondue (*Swiss Knight*), 1 oz. 60
hollandaise:
  mix* (*Durkee*) 115
  mix* (*French's*) 3 tbsp. 45
  mix* (*McCormick/Schilling*) 170
Italian, *see "spaghetti or pasta," below*
marinara, *see "spaghetti or pasta," below*
picante (*Tostitos*), 3 1/8 oz. 45
pizza:
  canned (*Buitoni*), 4 oz.** 72
  canned (*Ragu Pizza Quick*), 3 tbsp. 45
  w/cheese, canned (*Chef Boy•ar•dee*), 2.63 oz. 70
  w/pepperoni slices, canned
    (*Chef Boy•ar•dee*), 2.6 oz. 110
  w/sausage, canned (*Chef Boy•ar•dee*), 2.6 oz. 90
  burrito (*Del Monte*), 1/4 cup 20
  green chile, mild (*Del Monte*), 1/4 cup 20

Sauces, pizza, continued

Picante, hot (*Del Monte*), ¼ cup	20
Picante, hot and chunky (*Del Monte*), ¼ cup	15
Roja, mild (*Del Monte*), ¼ cup	20
portovista sauce:	
(*Chef Boy•ar•dee*), 3.5 oz.	60
w/meat (*Chef Boy•ar•dee*), 3.5 oz.	60
w/mushrooms (*Chef Boy•ar•dee*), 3.5 oz.	60
sour cream, mix* (*French's*), 2½ tbsp.	60
sour cream, mix* (*McCormick/Schilling*), ¼ cup	73
spaghetti or pasta:	
canned (*Hunt's*—salt-free), 4 oz.**	80
canned (*Hunt's Prima Salsa*), 4 oz.**	60
canned (*Prego*), 4 oz.**	140
canned (*Prego*—no salt added), 4 oz.**	100
canned (*Ragu*), 4 oz.**	80
canned (*Ragu* Homestyle), 4 oz.**	70
canned (*S & W Nutradiet*)	50
mix* (*Durkee*)	45
mix* (*McCormick/Schilling*)	53
mix* (*Spatini*), 4 oz.**	80
dietetic salt-free, canned (*Featherweight*), ⅓ cup	50
w/ground beef, canned (*Chef Boy•ar•dee*), 4 oz.**	90
Italian style, canned (*Hain Naturals*), 4 oz.**	70
Italian style, mix* (*French's*), ⅝ cup	100
Italian style, w/mushrooms, canned (*Hain Naturals*), 4 oz.**	80
marinara, canned (*Buitoni*), 4 oz.**	75
marinara, canned (*Ragu*), 4 oz.**	90
meat flavor, canned (*Buitoni*), 4 oz.**	85
meat flavor, canned (*Hunt's Prima Salsa*), 4 oz.**	80
meat flavor, canned (*Prego*), 4 oz.**	150
w/meat, canned (*Chef Boy•ar•dee*), 4 oz.**	140
w/meat, canned (*Chef Boy•ar•dee* Original), 3¾ oz.	120
w/meat, canned (*Ragu* Extra Thick and Zesty), 4 oz.**	100
meatless, canned (*Buitoni*), 4 oz.**	69
meatless, canned (*Chef Boy•ar•dee*), 3¾ oz.	60

Sauces, spaghetti or pasta, continued

meatless, in jars (*Chef Boy•ar•dee*), 4 oz.** 60
mushroom, canned (*Buitoni*), 4 oz.** 64
w/mushrooms, canned
  (*Chef Boy•ar•dee*), 4 oz.** 70
w/mushrooms, canned
  (*Chef Boy•ar•dee* Original), 3¾ oz. 80
w/mushrooms, canned
  (*Hunt's Prima Salsa*), 4 oz.** 60
w/mushrooms, canned (*Prego*), 4 oz.** 140
w/mushrooms, canned (*Ragu*), 4 oz.** 90
w/mushrooms, canned
  (*Ragu* Homestyle), 4 oz.** 70
w/mushrooms, in jars
  (*Chef Boy•ar•dee*), 4 oz.** 70
w/mushrooms, mix* (*Durkee*) 39
w/mushrooms, mix* (*French's*), ⅝ cup 100
thick, mix*
  (*French's* Homemade Style), ⅞ cup 170
w/tomato paste, mix*
  (*Durkee* Extra Thick & Rich) 47
soy, *see "Condiments & Seasonings," page 212*
Stroganoff, mix* (*French's*), ⅓ cup 110
sweet dessert sauces, *see "Syrups & Toppings," page 257*
sweet and sour, mix* (*Durkee*) 115
sweet and sour, mix* (*French's*) 55
taco sauce, *see "Condiments & Seasonings," page 212*
teriyaki, *see "Condiments & Seasonings," page 213*
tomato:
canned (*Del Monte*) 35
canned (*Hunt's*), 4 oz.** 30
canned (*Hunt's* Special), 4 oz.** 35
canned (*S & W Nutradiet*) 45
canned (*Tri/Valley*) 40
canned (*Tri/Valley*—unsalted) 45
w/bits, canned (*Hunt's*), 4 oz.** 30
w/cheese, canned (*Hunt's*), 4 oz.** 45
herb, canned (*Hunt's*), 4 oz.** 80
Italian style, canned (*Hunt's*), 4 oz.** 60
w/mushrooms, canned (*Hunt's*), 4 oz.** 25
w/onions, canned (*Del Monte*) 50
w/onions, canned (*Hunt's*), 4 oz.** 40

Sauces, tomato, continued

   pizza sauce, *see "pizza," above*
   spaghetti sauce, *see "spaghetti or pasta," above*
tomato paste or puree, *see "Tomato Paste & Puree," page 112*
Welsh rarebit, canned (*Snow's*) 170
white sauce, mix* (*Durkee*) 159
worcestershire, *see "Condiments & Seasonings," page 213*

  Prepared according to package directions
**Approximately 1/2 cup*

GRAVIES, 1/2 cup, except as noted
See also "Condiments & Seasonings," "Sauces"
and "Seasoning & Roasting Mixes, Dry"

---

                          calories
au jus:
  canned (*Franco-American*), 4 oz.** 10
  mix* (*Durkee*) 16
  mix* (*French's*) 16
  mix* (*McCormick/Schilling*) 15
beef, canned (*Franco-American*), 4 oz.** 50
beef, brown, canned (*Howard Johnson's*) 51
brown:
  in jars (*Heinz*), 4 oz.** 60
  mix* (*Ehler's*) 44
  mix* (*Durkee*) 30
  mix* (*French's*) 40
  mix* (*McCormick/Schilling*) 59
  mix* (*McCormick/Schilling* Lite) 20
  mix* (*Pillsbury*) 30
  mix* (*Spatini* Family Style), 4 oz.** 32
  w/mushrooms, mix* (*Durkee*) 30
  w/onion, canned (*Franco-American*), 4 oz.** .. 50
  w/onion, mix* (*Durkee*) 33
chicken:
  canned (*Franco-American*), 4 oz.** 100
  in jars (*Heinz*), 4 oz.** 80
  mix* (*Durkee*) 46

Gravies, chicken, continued

mix* (*Ehler's*) 42
mix* (*French's*) 50
mix* (*McCormick/Schilling*) 48
mix* (*McCormick/Schilling* Lite) 20
mix* (*Pillsbury*) 50
creamy, mix* (*Durkee*) 78
chicken giblet, canned
    (*Franco-American*), 4 oz.** 60
herb, mix* (*McCormick/Schilling*) 41
home-style:
mix* (*Durkee*) 35
mix* (*French's*) 50
mix* (*Pillsbury*) 30
mushroom:
canned (*Franco-American*), 4 oz.** 50
in jars (*Heinz*), 4 oz.** 60
mix* (*Durkee*) 30
mix* (*French's*) 40
mix* (*McCormick/Schilling*) 40
onion:
in jars (*Heinz*), 4 oz.** 70
mix* (*Durkee*) 42
mix* (*French's*) 50
mix* (*McCormick/Schilling*) 51
pork:
canned (*Franco-American*), 4 oz.** 80
in jars (*Heinz*) 60
mix* (*Durkee*) 35
mix* (*French's*) 40
Swiss steak, mix* (*Durkee*) 23
turkey:
canned (*Franco-American*), 4 oz.** 60
in jars (*Heinz*) 80
mix* (*Durkee*) 44
mix* (*French's*) 50
mix* (*McCormick/Schilling*) 41
turkey giblet, canned (*Howard Johnson's*) .. 55

Prepared according to package directions
**Approximately 1/2 cup*

CONDIMENTS & SEASONINGS
See also "Sauces," "Gravies,"
"Seasoning & Roasting Mixes, Dry,"
"Pure Herbs & Spices, Ground" and "Salad Dressings"

calories

bacon bits:
 (*Hormel*), 1 tbsp. 30
 (*Oscar Mayer*), 1/2 oz. 40
 imitation (*Bac*Os*), 1 tbsp. 40
 imitation (*Durkee*), 1 tsp. 8
 imitation (*French's Crumbles*), 1 tsp. 6
 imitation (*McCormick/Schilling*), 1 tbsp. 30
bacon chips (*Durkee*), 1 tbsp. 44
bacon crumbles
 (*Libby's* Produce Partners), 1 tbsp. 25
barbecue sauce, *see "Sauces," page 203*
barbecue seasoning (*French's*), 1 tsp. 6
(*Bennett's* Special Sauce), 1 tbsp. 50
bitters (*Angostura*), 1/4 tsp. 4
browning sauce, microwave, *see "Sauces," page 204*
brown seasoning and broth
 (*G. Washington's*), .14 oz. 6
brown seasoning and broth
 (*G. Washington's* Kosher), .14 oz. 6
burger sauce (*Hellmann's Big H*), 1 tbsp. 70
butter flavor, imitation (*Durkee*), 1 tsp. 3
butter flavor, imitation (*Ehler's*), 1 tsp. 8
capers (*Crosse & Blackwell*), 1 tbsp. 6
catsup:
 (*Del Monte*), 1 tbsp. 15
 (*Heinz*), 1 tbsp. 18
 (*Hunt's*), 1 tbsp. 16
 hot (*Heinz*), 1 tbsp. 18
 low-calorie (*Dia-Mel*), 1 tbsp. 6
 low-calorie (*Featherweight*), 1 tbsp. 6
 low-calorie (*Heinz* Lite), 1 tbsp. 8
 low-calorie (*Heinz* Lite—salt-free), 1 tbsp. 8
celery salt, *see "salt, flavored," below*
chili powder (*Mexene*), 1 tbsp. 24

Condiments & Seasonings, continued

chili sauce, canned (*Del Monte*), ¼ cup 70
chili sauce (*Bennett's*), 1 tbsp. 15
chutney, Major Grey's
    (*Crosse & Blackwell*), 1 tbsp. 53
cocktail seafood sauce:
    (*Bennett's*), 1 tbsp. 18
    (*Crosse & Blackwell*), 1 tbsp. 22
    (*Del Monte*), 1 tbsp. 18
    (*Estee*), 1 tbsp. 10
    (*Sau-Sea*), 1 tbsp. 16
coconut, cream of
    (*Holland House Coco Casa*), 1 tbsp. 59
curry powder (*Crosse & Blackwell*), 1 tbsp. 26
(*Durkee Famous Sauce*), 1 tbsp. 69
fish-poultry seasoning (*Estee*), 1 tsp. 0
garlic flavoring, liquid (*Burton's*), ½ tsp. 21
garlic, salt, *see "salt, flavored," below*
garlic spread (*Lawry's*), 1 tbsp. 88
golden seasoning and broth
    (*G. Washington's*), .13 oz. 6
golden seasoning and broth
    (*G. Washington's* Kosher), .13 oz. 6
(*Gravymaster*), 1 tsp. 12
horseradish (*Kraft*), 1 tbsp. 12
horseradish, cream style (*Kraft*), 1 tbsp. 8
horseradish sauce (*Kraft*), 1 tbsp. 50
hot sauce (*Frank's*), 1 tsp. 1
hot sauce (*Tabasco*), 1 tsp. 1
hot sauce relish (*Bennett's*), 1 tbsp. 16
lemon-pepper seasoning (*French's*), 1 tsp. 6
marinade, meat, mix* (*Durkee*), ½ cup 47
marinade, meat, dry form, *see "Seasoning & Roasting
   Mixes, Dry," page 214*
mayonnaise, *see "Salad Dressings," page 200*
meat-fish-poultry sauce:
    (*A.1.*), 1 tbsp. 12
    (*Crosse & Blackwell*), 1 tbsp. 21
    (*Escoffier Sauce Diable*), 1 tbsp. 20
    (*Escoffier Sauce Robert*), 1 tbsp. 20
    (*Heinz 57*), 1 tbsp. 15

Condiments & Seasonings, meat-fish-poultry sauce, continued

(*Steak Supreme* Steak Sauce), 1 tbsp.	20
meat seasoning (*Estee*), 1 tsp.	0
mint sauce (*Crosse & Blackwell*), 1 tbsp.	16
mustard, prepared:	
(*Featherweight*), 1 tbsp.	15
(*French's* Bold 'n Spicy), 1 tbsp.	16
(*French's* Medford), 1 tbsp.	16
(*Grey Poupon*), 1 tbsp.	18
(*Heinz* Pourable), 1 tbsp.	15
brown (*Heinz*), 1 tbsp.	24
creamy mild (*Gulden's*), 1/4 oz.	6
diablo (*Gulden's*), 1/4 oz.	8
Dijon (*Gulden's*), 1/4 oz.	10
w/horseradish (*French's*), 1 tbsp.	16
w/horseradish (*Kraft*), 1 tbsp.	12
hot (*Mister Mustard*), 1 tbsp.	33
mild (*Heinz*), 1 tbsp.	15
w/onion (*French's*), 1 tbsp.	25
pure (*Kraft*), 1 tbsp.	12
spicy brown (*Gulden's*), 1/4 oz.	8
yellow (*French's*), 1 tbsp.	10
onion flavoring, liquid (*Burton's*), 1/2 tsp.	21
onion salt, *see "salt, flavored," below*	
onion seasoning and broth (*G. Washington's*), .18 oz.	12
onion seasoning and broth (*G. Washington's* Kosher), .18 oz.	12
pepper, seasoned (*French's*), 1 tsp.	8
pepper, seasoned (*Lawry's*), 1 tsp.	8
pimento spread (*Price's*), 1 oz	80
pizza seasoning (*French's*), 1 tsp.	4
potato toppers (*Libby's* Produce Partners), 1 tbsp.	30
relish, *see specific kinds, and "Pickles & Relishes," page 114*	
salad crunchies (*Libby's* Produce Partners), 1 tbsp.	35
salad dressing:	
(*Durkee*), 1 tsp.	4
(*Mrs. Filbert's*), 1 tbsp.	70
w/cheese (*Durkee*), 1 tsp.	10
salad seasoning (*French's*), 1 tsp.	6

Condiments & Seasonings, continued

salt, flavored:

butter, imitation (*French's*), 1 tsp.	8
butter, imitation (*McCormick/Schilling*), 1 tsp.	2
celery (*French's*), 1 tsp.	2
garlic (*French's*), 1 tsp.	4
garlic, parslied (*French's*), 1 tsp.	6
hickory smoke (*French's*), 1 tsp.	2
onion (*French's*), 1 tsp.	6
seasoned (*Lawry's*), 1 tsp.	1
seasoning (*French's*), 1 tsp.	2

sandwich spread:

(*Bennett's*), 1 tbsp.	45
(*Best Foods*), 1 tbsp.	55
(*Hellmann's*), 1 tbsp.	55
(*Kraft*), 1 tbsp.	50
(*Mrs. Filbert's*), 1 tbsp.	60

seafood sauce, *see "cocktail seafood sauce," above, and "tartar sauce," below*

seafood seasoning (*French's*), 1 tsp.	2

soy sauce:

(*Chun King*), 1 tbsp.	6
(*Kikkoman*), 1 tbsp.	12
(*Kikkoman* Lite), 1 tbsp.	10
(*La Choy*), 1 tbsp.	8
stock base, beef flavor (*French's*), 1 tsp.	8
stock base, chicken flavor (*French's*), 1 tsp.	8

sweet and sour sauce, *see "Sauces," page 206*

taco sauce:

(*Ortega*), 1 tbsp.	22
hot or mild (*Del Monte*), 1/4 cup	15
hot (*Old El Paso*), 1 tbsp.	6
mild (*Old El Paso*), 1 tbsp.	6
taco starter (*Del Monte*), 8 oz.	140

tartar sauce:

(*Bennett's*), 1 tbsp.	70
(*Best Foods*), 1 tbsp.	70
(*Kraft*), 1 tbsp.	70
(*Hellmann's*), 1 tbsp.	70
mix* (*Van de Kamp's*), 1/2 oz.	80
tenderizer, meat (*French's*), 1 tsp.	2
tenderizer, meat, seasoned (*French's*), 1 tsp.	2

Condiments & Seasonings, continued

teriyaki sauce:
  (*Chun King*), 1 tbsp. 12
  (*Kikkoman*), 1 tbsp. 16
  mix* (*French's*), 1 tbsp. 18
vegetable seasoning (*Estee*), 1 tsp. 0
vinegar:
  cider (*Heinz*), 1 tbsp. 3
  red wine (*Regina*), 1 fl. oz. 4
  red wine, w/garlic (*Regina*), 1 fl. oz. 4
  white (*Heinz*), 1 tbsp. 3
  white wine (*Regina*), 1 fl. oz. 4
wine, cooking:
  burgundy (*Regina*), 1/4 cup 2
  Marsala (*Holland House*), 1 tbsp. 18
  red (*Holland House*), 1 tbsp. 13
  sauterne (*Regina*), 1/4 cup 2
  sherry (*Holland House*), 1 tbsp. 20
  sherry (*Regina*), 1/4 cup .... trace
  white (*Holland House*), 1 tbsp. 13
worcestershire sauce:
  (*Crosse & Blackwell*), 1 tbsp. 15
  (*French's*), 1 tbsp. 10
  (*Heinz*), 1 tbsp. 11
  (*Lea & Perrins*), 1 tbsp. 12
  smoky (*French's*), 1 tbsp. 10

**Prepared according to package directions*

SEASONING & ROASTING MIXES, DRY, 1 packet*
See also "Sauces," "Gravies"
and "Seasoned Coating Mixes"

---

                                    calories
au jus (*Durkee Roastin' Bag*), 1-oz. packet 64
beef:
  ground (*Durkee*), 1 1/8-oz. packet 91
  ground, w/onion (*Durkee*), 1 1/8-oz. packet 102
  ground, w/onion (*French's*), 1 packet 100

Seasoning & Roasting Mixes, Dry, sloppy joe, continued

    (*McCormick/Schilling*), 1⁵/₁₆-oz. packet 102
    Italian (*Durkee*), 1¹/₂-oz. packet 99
sparerib sauce
    (*Durkee Roastin' Bag*), 1.9-oz. packet 162
Stroganoff (*Durkee*), 1¹/₄-oz. packet 90
Stroganoff
    (*McCormick/Schilling*), 1¹/₂-oz. packet 113
Swiss steak
    (*Durkee Roastin' Bag*), 1¹/₂-oz. packet 115
Swiss steak (*McCormick/Schilling*), 1-oz. packet 44
taco:
    (*Durkee*), 1¹/₈-oz. packet 67
    (*French's*), 1 packet 120
    (*McCormick/Schilling*), 1¹/₄-oz. packet 61
    (*Old El Paso*), 1 packet 101
tuna casserole
    (*McCormick/Schilling*), 1¹/₂-oz. packet 104

*Note variation in packet sizes

PURE HERBS & SPICES, GROUND, 1 teaspoon
See also "Condiments & Seasonings"

Note: Since the composition of pure herbs and spices
should not vary in caloric content by brand, it is assumed
that the following values are the same for all brands—
Durkee, Ehler's, McCormick/Schilling, etc.

---

                                                    calories
allspice (all brands) 6
basil leaves (all brands) 3
bay leaves (all brands) 5
caraway seed (all brands) 8
cardamom seed (all brands) 6
celery seed (all brands) 11
cinnamon (all brands) 6
cloves (all brands) 7
coriander seed (all brands) 6

Pure Herbs & Spices, Ground, continued

cumin seed (all brands)	7
dill seed (all brands)	9
fennel seed (all brands)	8
garlic powder (all brands)	5
ginger (all brands)	6
mace (all brands)	10
marjoram (all brands)	4
mustard powder (all brands)	9
nutmeg (all brands)	11
onion powder (all brands)	8
oregano (all brands)	6
paprika, domestic (all brands)	7
parsley flakes (all brands)	4

pepper:

black (all brands)	9
chili (all brands)	9
red (all brands)	9
white (all brands)	9
poppy seed (all brands)	13
rosemary leaves (all brands)	5
sage (all brands)	4
savory (all brands)	5
sesame seed (all brands)	9
tarragon (all brands)	5
thyme (all brands)	5
turmeric (all brands)	7

Chapter 17

PUDDINGS, CUSTARDS
AND GELATINS

CUSTARDS, PUDDINGS & PIE FILLINGS,
½ cup, except as noted
See also "Gelatin Desserts" and "Pie Fillings, Canned"

---

	calories
banana:	
(*Del Monte Pudding Cup*), 5-oz. container	180
(*Hunt's Snack Pack*), 5-oz. container	210
cream, freeze-dried (*Mountain House*), 1.25 oz.	130
cream, mix* (*Jell-O*), ⅙ of 8″ pie**	100
cream, mix* (*Jell-O Instant*)	170
cream, mix* (*Royal*)	160
cream, mix* (*Royal Instant*)	180
butterscotch:	
(*Del Monte Pudding Cup*), 5-oz. container	180
(*Hunt's Snack Pack*), 5-oz. container	210
(*Rich's*), 3-oz. container	130
(*Swiss Miss*), 4-oz. container	150
freeze-dried (*Mountain House*), 1.25 oz.	130
mix* (*Jell-O*)	170
mix* (*Jell-O Instant*)	170
mix* (*My-T-Fine*)	143
mix* (*Royal*)	160
mix* (*Royal Instant*)	180
low-calorie, mix* (*D-Zerta*)	70
low-calorie, mix* (*Dia-Mel*)	50
low-calorie, mix* (*Estee*)	70

Custards, Puddings & Pie Fillings, butterscotch, continued

low-calorie, mix* (*Featherweight*) 60
chocolate:
    (*Del Monte Pudding Cup*), 5-oz. container 190
    (*Hunt's Snack Pack*), 5-oz. container 210
    (*Rich's*), 3-oz. container 140
    freeze-dried (*Mountain House*), 1.25 oz. 180
    mix* (*Jell-O*) 160
    mix* (*Jell-O* Instant) 180
    mix* (*My-T-Fine*) 133
    mix* (*Royal*) 180
    mix* (*Royal* Instant) 190
    low-calorie, mix* (*D-Zerta*) 60
    low-calorie, mix* (*Dia-Mel*) 50
    low-calorie, mix* (*Estee*) 70
    low-calorie, mix* (*Featherweight*) 60
chocolate, dark, mix* (*Royal Dark 'N Sweet*) 180
chocolate, dark, mix*
(*Royal Dark 'N Sweet* Instant) 190
chocolate, German
(*Hunt's Snack Pack*), 5-oz. container 220
chocolate, milk, mix* (*Jell-O*) 170
chocolate, milk, mix* (*Jell-O* Instant) 180
chocolate almond, mix* (*My-T-Fine*) 169
chocolate fudge:
    (*Del Monte Pudding Cup*), 5-oz. container 190
    (*Hunt's Snack Pack*), 5-oz. container 200
    mix* (*Jell-O*) 160
    mix* (*Jell-O* Instant) 180
    mix* (*My-T-Fine*) 151
chocolate marshmallow
(*Hunt's Snack Pack*), 5-oz. container 200
chocolate mint, mix* (*Royal* Instant) 190
chocolate mousse, low-calorie, mix*
(*Featherweight*) 100
chocolate sundae (*Swiss Miss*), 4-oz. container 180
coconut:
    cream, mix* (*Jell-O*), 1/6 of 8" pie** 110
    cream, mix* (*Jell-O* Instant) 180
    toasted, mix* (*Royal* Instant) 170
custard:
    mix* (*Royal*) 150

custard, continued

egg (*Swiss Miss*), 4-oz. container 150
golden egg, mix* (*Jell-O Americana*) 160
low-calorie, mix* (*Featherweight*) 80
flan, mix* (*Royal*) 150
lemon:
  (*Hunt's Snack Pack*), 5-oz. container 180
  mix* (*Jell-O*), ⅙ of 9″ pie** 170
  mix* (*Jell-O* Instant) 180
  mix* (*My-T-Fine*) 164
  mix* (*Royal*) 160
  mix* (*Royal* Instant) 180
  low-calorie, mix* (*Dia-Mel*) 14
  low-calorie, mix* (*Estee*) 70
lime, key, mix* (*Royal*) 160
pineapple cream, mix* (*Jell-O* Instant) 170
pistachio, mix* (*Jell-O* Instant) 180
pistachio, mix* (*Royal* Instant) 170
plum (*Crosse & Blackwell*), 4 oz. 340
plum (*Richardson & Robbins*) 300
raspberry, low-calorie, mix* (*Estee*) 70
rice pudding:
  (*Comstock*) 110
  (*Hunt's Snack Pack*), 5-oz. container 220
  mix* (*Jell-O Americana*) 170
strawberry, low-calorie, mix* (*Estee*) 70
strawberry-banana, low-calorie, mix* (*Estee*) ... 70
tapioca:
  (*Del Monte Pudding Cup*), 5-oz. container 180
  (*Hunt's Snack Pack*), 5-oz. container 140
  (*Swiss Miss*), 4-oz. container 140
  banana cream, mix* (*Hain*) 170
  carob cream, mix* (*Hain*) 170
  chocolate, mix* (*Jell-O Americana*) 170
  custard, mix* (*Hain*) 200
  vanilla, mix* (*Jell-O Americana*) 160
  vanilla, mix* (*My-T-Fine*) 130
  vanilla, mix* (*Royal*) 160
  vanilla, French, mix* (*Hain*) 210
vanilla:
  (*Del Monte Pudding Cup*), 5-oz. container 180
  (*Hunt's Snack Pack*), 5-oz. container 210

Custards, Puddings & Pie Fillings, vanilla, continued

(*Rich's*), 3-oz. container	130
(*Swiss Miss* Sundae), 4-oz. container	170
mix* (*Jell-O*)	170
mix* (*Jell-O* Instant)	170
mix* (*My-T-Fine*)	133
mix* (*Royal*)	160
mix* (*Royal* Instant)	180
low-calorie, mix* (*D–Zerta*)	70
low-calorie, mix* (*Dia-Mel*)	50
low-calorie, mix* (*Estee*)	70
low-calorie, mix* (*Featherweight*)	60
French, mix* (*Jell-O*)	170
French, mix* (*Jell-O* Instant)	170

Prepared according to package directions
**Prepared according to package directions, without crust*

PUDDING BARS, FROZEN
See also "Ice Cream and Frozen Confections"

---

calories

all flavors

(*Good Humor Pudding Stix*), 1.75 fl.-oz. bar	90
banana (*Jell-O Pudding Pops*), 1 bar*	90
banana, chocolate-peanut coated	
(*Swiss Miss*), 1 bar*	160
chocolate (*Jell-O Pudding Pops*), 1 bar*	90
chocolate, w/coating and crunch	
(*Swiss Miss*), 2 fl.-oz. bar	160
chocolate-vanilla swirl	
(*Jell-O Pudding Pops*), 1 bar*	90
vanilla (*Jell-O Pudding Pops*), 1 bar*	90
vanilla (*Swiss Miss*), 1.75 fl.-oz. bar	90
vanilla, w/coating and crunch	
(*Swiss Miss*), 2 fl-oz. bar	160

As packaged

GELATIN DESSERTS, 1/2 cup, except as noted
See also "Gelatin, Unflavored"

 |calories
---|---
all flavors, low-calorie (*Dia-Mel*) .... | 8
all flavors, mix*: |
  (*Jell-O*) .... | 80
  (*Royal*) .... | 80
  low-calorie (*D–Zerta*) .... | 8
  low-calorie (*Dia-Mel*) .... | 8
  low-calorie (*Dia-Mel Gel-A-Thin*) .... | 8
  low-calorie (*Estee*) .... | 8
  low-calorie (*Featherweight*) .... | 10
orange, drinking (*Knox*), 1 envelope .... | 70

Prepared according to package directions

GELATIN, UNFLAVORED, one envelope*
See also "Gelatin Desserts"

 |calories
---|---
(*Knox*) .... | 25

As packaged

Chapter 18

CAKES, COOKIES PIES AND PASTRIES

DESSERT CAKES, FROZEN*
See also "Dessert Cakes, Mixes,"
"Dessert Pies, Frozen"
and "Pastries, Cakes & Pies, Frozen & Refrigerated"

---

calories

apple walnut, w/cream cheese icing
  (*Pepperidge Farm* Old Fashioned),
  1/8 of 12-3/4-oz. cake 150
banana
  (*Pepperidge Farm* Cake Supreme),
  1/4 of 11-1/2-oz. cake 280
black forest (*Sara Lee*), 1/8 of cake 190
Boston cream
  (*Pepperidge Farm* Cake Supreme),
  1/4 of 11-1/2-oz. cake 290
Boston cream pie, *see "Dessert Pies, Frozen," page 227*
butterscotch pecan
  (*Pepperidge Farm*), 1/8 of 17-oz. cake 200
carrot w/cream cheese icing
  (*Pepperidge Farm* Old Fashioned),
  1/8 of 12-3/4-oz. cake 130
carrot w/icing (*Weight Watchers*), 3-oz. serving 180
cheesecake:
  (*Sara Lee Elegant Endings*), 1/6 of cake 350
  (*Weight Watchers*), 4-oz. serving 200
  cherry, black (*Weight Watchers*), 4-oz. serving 190

Dessert Cakes, Frozen, cheesecake, continued

chocolate chip
   (*Sara Lee Elegant Endings*), 1/6 of cake 420
cream cheese (*Sara Lee* French), 1/8 of cake 260
pecan praline
   (*Sara Lee Elegant Endings*), 1/6 of cake 430
strawberry (*Weight Watchers*), 4-oz. serving 180
strawberry, cream cheese
   (*Sara Lee* French), 1/8 of cake 250
chocolate:
   (*Pepperidge Farm* Cake Supreme),
   1/4 of 12-oz. cake 310
   Dutch (*Pepperidge Farm* Cake Supreme),
   1/8 of 21-oz. cake 285
   fudge (*Pepperidge Farm*), 1/8 of 17-oz. cake 225
   German (*Pepperidge Farm*), 1/8 of 17-oz. cake 225
chocolate-mint
   (*Pepperidge Farm*), 1/8 of 17-oz. cake 213
chocolate mousse
   (*Sara Lee* Bavarian), 1/8 of cake 250
coconut (*Pepperidge Farm*), 1/8 of 17-oz. cake 225
coffee cake, pecan (*Sara Lee*), 1/8 of cake 160
coffee cake, walnut (*Sara Lee*), 1/8 of cake 170
devil's food (*Pepperidge Farm*), 1/8 of 17-oz. cake 225
golden layer (*Pepperidge Farm*), 1/8 of 17-oz. cake 225
Grand Marnier (*Pepperidge Farm* Cake Supreme),
   1/8 of 19 oz. cake 240
lemon-coconut (*Pepperidge Farm* Cake Supreme),
   1/4 of 12-oz. cake 280
peach melba
   (*Pepperidge Farm* Cake Supreme),
   1/4 of 12 1/2-oz. cake 270
pineapple cream
   (*Pepperidge Farm* Cake Supreme),
   1/8 of 24-oz. cake 285
pound cake:
   butter (*Pepperidge Farm*), 1/10 of 10 1/2-oz. cake 130
   chocolate chip (*Sara Lee*), 1/10 of cake 130
   raisin walnut (*Sara Lee*), 1/10 of cake 140
raspberry mocha
   (*Pepperidge Farm* Cake Supreme),
   1/4 of 10 1/4-oz. cake 310

Dessert Cakes, Frozen, continued

strawberry cheese, *see "cheesecake," above*
strawberry shortcake (*Sara Lee*), ⅛ of cake 190
vanilla (*Pepperidge Farm*), ⅛ of 17-oz. cake 238
walnut
    (*Pepperidge Farm* Cake Supreme),
      ¼ of 10-oz. cake 300

*Note variations in sizes

DESSERT CAKES, MIXES*,
1/12 of whole cake, except as noted
See also "Dessert Cakes, Frozen,"
"Snack & Coffee Cakes, Mixes,"
"Cake Frosting, Ready to Spread"
and "Cake Frostings, Mixes"

---

                                              calories

angel food:
    (*Duncan Hines*) 140
    lemon chiffon (*Betty Crocker*) 190
    raspberry (*Pillsbury*) 140
    white (*Pillsbury*) 140
apple cinnamon (*Betty Crocker Supermoist*) 260
apple, Dutch (*Pillsbury Streusel Swirl*) 347
applesauce spice (*Pillsbury Plus*) 250
banana:
    (*Betty Crocker Supermoist*) 260
    (*Pillsbury Plus*) 250
    (*Pillsbury Streusel Swirl*) 347
    supreme (*Duncan Hines* Layer) 260
Black Forest, German (*Betty Crocker* Classics) 180
Boston cream (*Pillsbury Bundt*) 360
brown sugar-pecan (*Pillsbury Streusel Swirl*) 347
butter:
    (*Betty Crocker Supermoist Butter Brickle*) 260
    (*Pillsbury Plus* Butter Recipe) 240
    fudge (*Duncan Hines* Layer) 270
    golden (*Duncan Hines* Layer) 270

Dessert Cakes, Mixes, butter, continued

rich (*Pillsbury Streusel Swirl*) 347
butter pecan (*Betty Crocker Supermoist*) 250
carrot:
  (*Betty Crocker Supermoist*) 260
  (*Duncan Hines* Layer) 250
  and spice (*Pillsbury Plus*) 260
cheesecake, *see "Pies, Mixes," page 229*
cherry chip (*Betty Crocker Supermoist*) 180
cherry supreme (*Duncan Hines* Layer) 260
cinnamon (*Betty Crocker Stir 'N Streusel*) 120
cinnamon (*Pillsbury Streusel Swirl*) 347
chocolate:
  dark (*Pillsbury Plus*) 260
  deep (*Duncan Hines* Layer) 280
  fudge (*Betty Crocker Supermoist*) 250
  German (*Betty Crocker Stir 'N Streusel*) 120
  German (*Betty Crocker Supermoist*) 260
  German (*Pillsbury Plus*) 250
  German (*Pillsbury Streusel Swirl*) 347
  macaroon (*Pillsbury Bundt*) 333
  milk (*Betty Crocker Supermoist*) 250
  mint (*Pillsbury Plus*) 260
  sour cream, *see "sour cream," below*
  Swiss (*Duncan Hines* Layer) 280
  dietetic (*Dia-Mel*), 1/10 of cake 100
  reduced-calorie (*Estee*), 1/10 of cake 100
chocolate chip:
  (*Betty Crocker Supermoist*) 190
  (*Duncan Hines* Layer) 260
  chocolate (*Betty Crocker Supermoist*) 250
devil's food:
  (*Betty Crocker Supermoist*) 270
  (*Duncan Hines* Layer) 280
  (*Pillsbury Plus*) 250
fudge:
  (*Pillsbury Bundt Tunnel of Fudge*) 360
  marble (*Duncan Hines* Layer) 260
  marble (*Pillsbury Plus*) 270
  marble (*Pillsbury Streusel Swirl*) 347
  nut crown (*Pillsbury Bundt*) 293

Dessert Cakes, Mixes, continued

lemon:
(*Betty Crocker Supermoist*) 260
(*Pillsbury Bundt Tunnel of Lemon*) 360
(*Pillsbury Plus*) 260
(*Pillsbury Streusel Swirl*) 360
supreme (*Duncan Hines* Layer) 260
dietetic (*Dia-Mel*), 1/10 of cake 100
reduced-calorie (*Estee*), 1/10 of cake 100
lemon-blueberry (*Pillsbury Bundt*) 267
marble (*Betty Crocker Supermoist*) 260
marble, fudge, *see "fudge," above*
marble supreme (*Pillsbury Bundt*) 333
oats 'n brown sugar (*Pillsbury Plus*) 260
orange (*Betty Crocker Supermoist*) 260
orange supreme (*Duncan Hines* Layer) 260
pineapple supreme (*Duncan Hines* Layer) 260
pineapple upside-down
(*Betty Crocker* Classics), 1/9 of cake 270
pound:
(*Dromedary*), 3/4" slice 210
(*Pillsbury Bundt*) 307
golden (*Betty Crocker*) 200
diatetic (*Dia-Mel*), 1/10 of cake 100
sour cream:
chocolate (*Betty Crocker Supermoist*) 260
chocolate (*Duncan Hines* Layer) 280
white (*Betty Crocker Supermoist*) 180
spice:
(*Betty Crocker Supermoist*) 260
(*Duncan Hines* Layer) 260
dietetic (*Dia-Mel*), 1/10 of cake 100
strawberry:
(*Betty Crocker Supermoist*) 260
(*Pillsbury Plus*) 260
supreme (*Duncan Hines* Layer) 260
vanilla, golden (*Duncan Hines* Layer) 260
white:
(*Betty Crocker Supermoist*) 250
(*Duncan Hines* Layer) 250
(*Pillsbury Plus*) 240
reduced-calorie (*Estee*), 1/10 of cake 100

Dessert Cakes, Mixes, continued
yellow:
   (*Betty Crocker Supermoist*) 260
   (*Duncan Hines* Layer) 250
   (*Pillsbury Plus*) 260
   butter recipe (*Betty Crocker Supermoist*) 260

*Prepared according to package directions, without added frosting

---

DESSERT PIES, FROZEN, ¹/6 of whole pie*
See also "Pies, Mixes"
and "Pastries, Cakes & Pies, Frozen & Refrigerated"

---

                          calories
apple:
   (*Banquet* Family Size), ¹/6 of 20 oz. pie 253
   (*Morton*), ¹/6 of 24-oz. pie 290
   (*Mrs. Smith's*), ¹/6 of 46-oz. pie 520
   lattice
     (*Mrs. Smith's* Thaw 'n Serve), ¹/6 of 36-oz. pie 467
   natural juice (*Mrs. Smith's*), ¹/6 of 42-oz. pie 490
   old-fashioned (*Mrs. Smith's*), ¹/6 of 50-oz. pie 487
   streusel, natural juice
     (*Mrs. Smith's*), ¹/6 of 47-oz. pie 490
banana cream:
   (*Banquet*), ¹/6 of 14-oz. pie 177
   (*Morton*), ¹/6 of 16-oz. pie 170
   (*Mrs. Smith's* Thaw 'n Serve), ¹/6 of 24-oz. pie 320
blackberry
   (*Banquet* Family Size), ¹/6 of 20-oz. pie 268
blueberry:
   (*Banquet* Family Size), ¹/6 of 20-oz. pie 266
   (*Morton*), ¹/6 of 24-oz. pie 280
   (*Mrs. Smith's*), ¹/6 of 46-oz. pie 507
Boston cream
     (*Mrs. Smith's* Thaw 'n Serve),
     ¹/6 of 24-oz. pie 347
Boston cream cake, *see "Dessert Cakes, Frozen," page 222*

Dessert Pies, Frozen, continued

cherry:
  (*Banquet* Family Size), 1/6 of 20-oz. pie 252
  (*Morton*), 1/6 of 24-oz. pie 300
  (*Mrs. Smith's*), 1/6 of 46-oz. pie 533
  lattice
    (*Mrs. Smith's* Thaw 'n Serve), 1/6 of 36-oz. pie 467
  natural juice (*Mrs. Smith's*), 1/6 of 42-oz. pie 547
cheesecake, *see "Dessert Cakes, Frozen," page 222*
chocolate cream:
  (*Banquet*), 1/6 of 14-oz. pie 185
  (*Morton*), 1/6 of 16-oz. pie 200
  (*Mrs. Smith's* Thaw 'n Serve), 1/6 of 24-oz. pie 360
coconut:
  cream (*Banquet*), 1/6 of 14-oz. pie 187
  cream (*Morton*), 1/6 of 16-oz. pie 190
  cream
    (*Mrs. Smith's* Thaw 'n Serve), 1/6 of 24-oz. pie 360
  custard (*Mrs. Smith's*), 1/6 of 44-oz. pie 440
custard, egg (*Mrs. Smith's*), 1/6 of 44-oz. pie 400
lemon:
  cream (*Banquet*), 1/6 of 14-oz. pie 173
  cream
    (*Mrs. Smith's* Thaw 'n Serve), 1/6 of 24-oz. pie 327
  meringue
    (*Mrs. Smith's* Thaw 'n Serve), 1/6 of 34-oz. pie 413
mince (*Morton*), 1/6 of 24-oz. pie 310
mincemeat
  (*Banquet* Family Size), 1/6 of 20-oz. pie 258
peach:
  (*Banquet* Family Size), 1/6 of 20-oz. pie 244
  (*Morton*), 1/6 of 24-oz. pie 280
  (*Mrs. Smith's*), 1/6 of 46-oz. pie 487
pecan
  (*Mrs. Smith's* Thaw 'n Serve), 1/6 of 36-oz. pie 680
pumpkin:
  (*Banquet* Family Size), 1/6 of 20-oz. pie 197
  (*Morton*), 1/6 of 24-oz. pie 230
  custard (*Mrs. Smith's*), 1/6 of 46-oz. pie 413
strawberry cream (*Banquet*), 1/6 of 14-oz. pie 168

*Note variations in sizes

PIES, MIXES*

See also "Dessert Pies, Frozen,"
and "Snack Cakes & Pies, Packaged"
and "Pastries, Cakes & Pies, Frozen & Refrigerated"

---

calories

banana cream (*Jell-O*), 1/6 of 8" pie** 110
Boston cream (*Betty Crocker*), 1/8 pie or pkg. 260
cheesecake (*Jell-O*), 1/8 of 8" pie 300
cheesecake (*Royal*), 1/8 of pie or pkg. 230
chocolate mint (*Royal*), 1/8 of pie 260
coconut cream (*Jell-O*), 1/6 of 8" pie 110
lemon (*Jell-O*), 1/6 of 9" pie** 180

*Prepared according to package directions
**Prepared according to package directions with whole milk—
  does not include crust

SNACK CAKES & PIES, PACKAGED,
one piece*, except as noted
See also "Pastries, Cakes & Pies, Frozen & Refrigerated,"
"Snack and Coffee Cakes, Mixes" and "Cookies"

---

calories

apple-nut
  (*Pepperidge Farm* Snack Bars), 1 piece* 170
apricot cake (*El Molino*), 2-oz. piece 250
apricot-raspberry
  (*Pepperidge Farm* Snack Bars), 1 piece* 170
banana
  (*Hostess Suzy Q's*), 2 1/4-oz. piece 240
blueberry
  (*Pepperidge Farm* Snack Bars), 1 piece* 170
brownie:
  carob (*El Molino*), 2-oz. piece 220
  nut (*Pepperidge Farm* Snack Bars), 1 piece* 190
  nut fudge (*Frito-Lay*), 1/8-oz. brownie 220

Snack Cakes & Pies, Packaged, continued

butterscotch (*Tastykake Krimpets*), 1¾-oz. pkg. 192
chocolate or devil's food:
  (*Drake's Devil Dogs*), 1 piece* 170
  (*Drake's Funny Bones*), 1 piece* 160
  (*Drake's Ring Ding Jr.*), 1 piece* 160
  (*Drake's Swiss Roll*), 3-oz. piece 350
  (*Drake's Yodels*), .9-oz. piece 120
  (*Hostess Big Wheels*), 1⅓-oz. piece 170
  (*Hostess Chip Flips*), 1¾-oz. piece 330
  (*Hostess Choco-Dile*), 2-oz. piece 240
  (*Hostess Ding Dongs*), 1⅓-oz. piece 170
  (*Hostess Ho Ho's*), 1-oz. piece 120
  (*Hostess Suzy Q's*), 2¼-oz. piece 240
  (*Nabisco*), 1 piece* 100
  (*Tastykake* Chocolate Cream Tempty),
    2-oz. pkg. 197
  (*Tastykake* Chocolate Creamies), 2⅓-oz. pkg. 257
  (*Tastykake* Chocolate Juniors), 2¾-oz. pkg. 307
  (*Tastykake* Chocolate Tasty Klairs), 4-oz. pkg. 435
  (*Tastykake* Kandy Kake), 1⅓-oz. pkg. 181
chocolate chip macaroon
  (*Pepperidge Farm* Snack Bars), 1 piece* 210
cinnamon crumb cake (*El Molino*), 2-oz. piece 250
coffee cake:
  (*Drake's*), 1 piece* 220
  (*Hostess* Crumb Cakes), 1¼-oz. piece 130
  (*Tastykake* Koffee Kake), 2-oz. pkg. 247
  (*Tastykake* Koffee Kake Juniors),
    2½-oz. pkg. 313
coconut
  (*Tastykake* Coconut Juniors), 2¾-oz. pkg. 330
coconut macaroon
  (*Nabisco* Soft Cakes), 1 piece* 140
coconut macaroon
  (*Pepperidge Farm* Snack Bars), 1 piece* 210
cup cakes:
  (*Hostess Dessert Cups*), 1 piece* 60
  chocolate (*Drake's Yankee Doodles*), 1 piece* 110
  chocolate (*Hostess*), 1¾-oz. piece 170
  chocolate (*Tastykake*), 2-oz. pkg. 200
  orange (*Hostess*), 1½-oz. piece 150

Snack Cakes & Pies, Packaged, continued

danish:
  (*Hostess* Butterhorn), 1 piece* 330
  apple (*Hostess*), 1 piece* 360
  raspberry (*Hostess*), 1 piece* 300
date cake (*El Molino*), 2-oz. piece 240
date nut (*Pepperidge Farm* Snack Bars), 1 piece 190
doughnuts:
  chocolate-coated (*Hostess*), 1 piece* ..../.... 130
  chocolate-coated, miniature
     (*Hostess Donettes*), 1 piece* 60
  cinnamon (*Hostess*), 1-oz. piece 110
  krunch (*Hostess*), 1-oz. piece 110
  old-fashioned (*Hostess*), 1½-oz. piece 180
  old-fashioned, glazed (*Hostess*), 1 piece* 230
  plain (*Hostess*), 1-oz. piece 110
  powdered-sugar (*Hostess*), 1-oz. piece 110
  powdered-sugar, miniature
     (*Hostess Donettes*), 1 piece* 40
fruit (*Hostess* Fruit Loaf), 1 piece* 400
fruit and spice cake (*El Molino*), 2-oz. piece 230
granola cake (*El Molino*), 2-oz. piece 220
honey and bran cake (*El Molino*), 1½-oz. piece 160
honeybun, glazed (*Hostess*), 3¾-oz. piece 450
(*Hostess O's*), 1 piece* 240
(*Hostess Lil' Angels*), 1 piece 90
(*Hostess Twinkies*), 1½-oz. piece 160
(*Hostess Sno Ball*), 1½-oz. piece 150
(*Hostess Tiger Tail*), 2¼-oz. piece 210
jelly (*Tastykake* Jelly Krimpets), 1¾-oz. pkg. 168
lemon (*Tastykake* Lemon Juniors), 2¾-oz. pkg. 297
oatmeal raisin bar (*Tastykake*), 1¾-oz. pkg. 267
peanut (*Hostess Peanut Putters*), 1 piece* 410
peanut, filled (*Hostess Peanut Putters*), 1 piece* 360
pie:
  apple (*Banquet*), 8-oz. piece 578
  apple (*Drake's*), 1 piece* 220
  apple (*Hostess*), 4½-oz. piece 390
  apple (*Tastykake*), 4-oz. pkg. 348
  apple, French (*Tastykake*), 4¼-oz. pkg. 405
  berry (*Hostess*), 4½-oz. piece 370
  blueberry (*Hostess*), 4½-oz. piece 390

pies, continued

blueberry (*Tastykake*), 4-oz. pkg. 366
cherry (*Banquet*), 8-oz. piece 575
cherry (*Hostess*), 4½-oz. piece 390
cherry (*Tastykake*), 4-oz. pkg. 381
lemon (*Hostess*), 4½-oz. piece 400
lemon (*Tastykake*), 4-oz. pkg. 370
peach (*Banquet*), 8-oz. piece 553
peach (*Hostess*), 4½-oz. piece 400
peach (*Tastykake*), 4-oz. pkg. 349
pecan (*Frito-Lay*), 3-oz. pkg. 350
strawberry (*Hostess*), 1 piece* 340
pound cake, butter (*Drake's*), 1-oz. piece 100
raisin spice
  (*Pepperidge Farm* Snack Bars), 1 piece* 180
raspberry crumb cake (*El Molino*), 2-oz. piece 260
spice cake
  (*Tastykake* Spice Creamie), 2¾-oz. pkg. 272
strawberry-filled cake (*El Molino*), 2-oz. piece 240

Note variations in sizes

PASTRIES, CAKES & PIES, FROZEN & REFRIGERATED,
one piece*
See also "Dessert Cakes, Frozen"
and "Dessert Pies, Frozen"

---

calories

apple criss-cross pastry, frozen
  (*Pepperidge Farm*), 2-oz. piece 180
apple square, frozen
  (*Pepperidge Farm* Fruit Squares), 1 square** 230
blueberry square, frozen
  (*Pepperidge Farm* Fruit Squares), 1 square** 220
buns, honey, frozen (*Morton*), 2.3-oz. piece 230
buns, honey, mini, frozen (*Morton*), 1.3-oz. piece 130
cheesecake:
  cherry, frozen
    (*Morton* Great Little Desserts), 6-oz. piece 460

Pastries, Cakes & Pies, Frozen & Refrigerated, cheesecake, continued

cream, frozen
  (*Morton* Great Little Desserts), 6-oz. piece 480
pineapple, frozen
  (*Morton* Great Little Desserts), 6-oz. piece 460
strawberry, frozen
  (*Morton* Great Little Desserts), 6-oz. piece 470
cherry square, frozen
  (*Pepperidge Farm* Fruit Squares), 1 square** 230
croissants, *see "Rolls, Biscuits & Muffins," page 40*
danish:
  almond, deep-dish, frozen
    (*Pepperidge Farm*), 1 piece** 240
  apple, frozen (*Sara Lee* Individual), 1 piece** 120
  apple, refrigerator
    (*Pillsbury Pipin' Hot*), 1 piece** 250
  apple, deep-dish, frozen
    (*Pepperidge Farm*), 1 piece** 180
  blueberry, deep-dish, frozen
    (*Pepperidge Farm*), 1 piece** 200
  caramel, w/nuts, refrigerator
    (*Pillsbury*), 1 piece** 155
  cheese, frozen (*Sara Lee* Individual), 1 piece** 130
  cheese, deep-dish, frozen
    (*Pepperidge Farm*), 1 piece** 280
  cherry, deep-dish, frozen
    (*Pepperidge Farm*), 1 piece** 200
  cinnamon raisin, refrigerator
    (*Pillsbury*), 1 piece** 145
  orange, refrigerator (*Pillsbury*), 1 piece** 145
devil's food cake, frozen
  (*Morton Donut Holes*), 1½-oz. piece 160
doughnuts:
  Bavarian creme, frozen (*Morton*), 2-oz. piece 180
  Boston creme, frozen (*Morton*), 2⅓-oz. piece 210
  chocolate-iced, frozen (*Morton*), 1½-oz. piece 150
  chocolate-iced, frozen
    (*Morton* Morning Light), 2-oz. piece 200
  glazed, frozen (*Morton*), 1½-oz. piece 150
  glazed, frozen
    (*Morton* Morning Light), 2-oz. piece 200
  jelly, frozen (*Morton*), 1.8-oz. piece 180

Pastries, Cakes & Pies, Frozen & Refrigerated, doughnuts, continued

jelly, frozen
   (*Morton* Morning Light), 2.6-oz. piece 250
mini, frozen (*Morton*), 1.1-oz. piece 120
dumpling, apple, frozen
   (*Pepperidge Farm*), 1 piece** 260
éclair, chocolate, frozen (*Rich's*), 2-oz. piece 210
honey wheat cake, frozen
   (*Morton Donut Holes*), 1½-oz. piece 160
muffins, sweet:
   blueberry, frozen
      (*Howard Johnson's Toastee*), 1 piece** 121
   blueberry, frozen (*Morton*), 1½-oz. piece 120
   blueberry, frozen
      (*Pepperidge Farm* Old Fashioned), 1 piece** 180
   blueberry, rounds, frozen
      (*Morton*), 1.58-oz. piece 110
   bran, w/raisin, frozen
      (*Pepperidge Farm* Old Fashioned), 1 piece** 180
   carrot walnut, frozen
      (*Pepperidge Farm* Old Fashioned), 1 piece** 170
   cinnamon swirl, frozen
      (*Pepperidge Farm* Old Fashioned), 1 piece** 190
   corn, frozen
      (*Howard Johnson's Toastee*), 1 piece** 112
   corn, frozen (*Morton*), 1.6-oz. piece 130
   corn, frozen
      (*Pepperidge Farm* Old Fashioned), 1 piece** 180
   orange-cranberry, frozen
      (*Pepperidge Farm* Old Fashioned), 1 piece** 190
pies, frozen:
   apple (*Morton* Great Little Desserts), 8-oz. pie 590
   apple (*Pet•Ritz* Fancy Crust), 5-oz. piece 360
   apple (*Pet•Ritz* Fruit Pies), 4.33-oz. piece 330
   apple, Dutch
      (*Morton* Great Little Desserts), 7¾-oz. pie 600
   banana cream
      (*Morton* Great Little Desserts), 3½-oz. pie 250
   banana cream (*Pet•Ritz*), 2.33-oz. piece 170
   blueberry
      (*Morton* Great Little Desserts), 8-oz. pie 580
   blueberry (*Pet•Ritz* Fancy Crust), 5-oz. piece 340

pies, frozen, continued

blueberry (*Pet•Ritz* Fruit Pies), 4.33-oz. piece 370
cherry (*Morton* Great Little Desserts), 8-oz. pie 590
cherry (*Pet•Ritz* Fancy Crust), 5-oz. piece 360
cherry (*Pet•Ritz* Fruit Pies), 4.33-oz. piece 300
chocolate cream
  (*Morton* Great Little Desserts), 3½-oz. pie 270
chocolate cream (*Pet•Ritz*), 2.33-oz. piece 190
coconut cream
  (*Morton* Great Little Desserts), 3½-oz. pie 270
coconut cream (*Pet•Ritz*), 2.33-oz. piece 190
coconut custard
  (*Morton* Great Little Desserts), 6½-oz. pie 370
lemon cream
  (*Morton* Great Little Desserts), 3½-oz. pie 250
lemon cream (*Pet•Ritz*), 2.33-oz. piece 190
Neapolitan cream (*Pet•Ritz*), 2.33-oz. piece 180
peach (*Morton* Great Little Desserts), 8-oz. pie 590
peach (*Pet•Ritz* Fancy Crust), 5-oz. piece 340
peach (*Pet•Ritz* Fruit Pies), 4.33-oz. piece 320
pecan (*Pet•Ritz*), 3-oz. piece 310
strawberry cream (*Pet•Ritz*), 2.33-oz. piece 170
sweet potato (*Pet•Ritz*), 3.3-oz. piece 150
puffs, vanilla (*Rich's*), 2.17-oz. piece 167
rolls, sweet:
cinnamon, refrigerator
  (*Pillsbury Pipin' Hot*), 1 piece** 220
cinnamon, iced, refrigerator
  (*Hungry Jack Butter Tastin'*), 1 piece** 145
cinnamon, iced, refrigerator
  (*Pillsbury*), 1 piece** 115
strudel, apple, frozen
  (*Pepperidge Farm*), 3-oz. piece 240
turnovers:
apple, frozen (*Pepperidge Farm*), 1 piece** 310
apple, refrigerator (*Pillsbury*), 1 piece** 170
blueberry, frozen (*Pepperidge Farm*), 1 piece** 320
blueberry, refrigerator (*Pillsbury*), 1 piece** 170
cherry, frozen (*Pepperidge Farm*), 1 piece** 310
cherry, refrigerator (*Pillsbury*), 1 piece** 170
peach, frozen (*Pepperidge Farm*), 1 piece** 320
raspberry, frozen (*Pepperidge Farm*), 1 piece** 320

Pastries, Cakes & Pies, Frozen & Refrigerated, continued

vanilla cake, frozen
    (*Morton Donut Holes*), 1½-oz. piece 160

*Note variations in size
**As packaged

> **SNACK & COFFEE CAKES, MIXES***
> See also "Snack Cakes & Pies, Packaged," "Pies, Mixes"
> and "Dessert Cakes, Mixes"

---

calories

applesauce raisin
    (*Betty Crocker Snackin' Cake*), ⅑ pkg. 180
banana walnut
    (*Betty Crocker Snackin' Cake*), ⅑ pkg. 190
brownies, *see "Cookies, Frozen, Mixes," page 245*
butter pecan
    (*Betty Crocker Snackin' Cake*), ⅑ pkg. 190
carrot, w/cream cheese frosting
    (*Betty Crocker Stir n' Frost*), ⅙ pkg. 230
carrot nut (*Betty Crocker Snackin' Cake*), ⅑ pkg. 180
cheesecake, *see "Pies, Mixes," page 229*
chocolate:
    (*Betty Crocker* Pudding Cake), ⅙ pkg. 230
    chip, w/chocolate frosting
      (*Betty Crocker Stir n' Frost*), ⅙ pkg. 230
    chip, fudge
      (*Betty Crocker Snackin' Cake*), ⅑ pkg. 190
    chip, golden
      (*Betty Crocker Snackin' Cake*), ⅑ pkg. 190
    chocolate chip, w/chocolate chocolate chip frosting
      (*Betty Crocker Stir n' Frost*), ⅙ pkg. 230
    devil's food, w/chocolate frosting
      (*Betty Crocker Stir n' Frost*), ⅙ pkg. 230
    fudge, w/vanilla frosting
      (*Betty Crocker Stir n' Frost*), ⅙ pkg. 230
    German, coconut pecan
      (*Betty Crocker Snackin' Cake*), ⅑ pkg. 180

Snacks & Coffee Cakes, Mixes, continued

coconut pecan
    (*Betty Crocker Snackin' Cake*), 1/9 pkg. 190
coffee cake:
    apple cinnamon (*Pillsbury*), 1/8 cake 240
    butter pecan (*Pillsbury*), 1/8 cake 310
    cinnamon streusel (*Pillsbury*), 1/8 cake 250
    sour cream (*Pillsbury*), 1/8 cake 270
cup cake (*Flako*), 1 cake 150
devil's food, *see "chocolate," above*
fudge, peanut butter chip
    (*Betty Crocker Snackin' Cake*), 1/9 pkg. 200
lemon (*Betty Crocker* Pudding Cake), 1/6 pkg. 230
mint fudge chip
    (*Betty Crocker Snackin' Cake*), 1/9 pkg. 190
spice, w/vanilla frosting
    (*Betty Crocker Stir n' Frost*), 1/6 pkg. 280

**Prepared according to package directions, without frosting
unless indicated*

COOKIES, one piece*, except as noted
See also "Cookies, Frozen, Mixes & Refrigerated"

---

                                         calories
almond:
    (*Nabisco* Windmill) 43
    (*Pepperidge Farm* Almond Supreme) 70
    (*Stella D'Oro* Almond Toast—Mandel) 56
    (*Stella D'Oro* Breakfast Treats) 102
    (*Stella D'Oro* Chinese Desert) 178
almond fudge-chocolate chip (*Duncan Hines*) 55
animal crackers:
    (*Barnum's*) 12
    (*Dixie Belle*) 9
    (*Keebler*) 12
    (*Ralston*) 9
    (*Sunshine*) 11
anise flavor:
    (*Stella D'Oro* Anisette Sponge) 52

Cookies, continued

kettle (*Nabisco* Famous Cookie Assortment) 33
lemon:
  (*Archway* Frosty Lemon) 122
  (*Girl Scout* Lemon Pastry Creme) 51
  (*Sunshine* Lemon Coolers) 29
  low-calorie (*Estee* Thins) 17
  low-calorie (*Featherweight*) 40
lemon-coconut (*Archway* Family Style) 78
lemon-nut crunch (*Pepperidge Farm*) 57
(*Mayfair* English Style Tea Biscuits) 26
marshmallow:
  (*Frito-Lay's Marshmallow Pie*), 2-oz. serving . . . 240
  chocolate-covered (*Mallomars*) 65
  chocolate-covered (*Nabisco* Puffs) 120
  chocolate-covered (*Pinwheels*) 130
  w/chocolate sprinkles (*Sunshine* Sprinkles) 59
  w/coconut (*Sunshine Mallo Puffs*) 62
  sandwich (*Nabisco*) 30
mint:
  chocolate (*Girl Scout* Thin Mint) 38
  patty (*Girl Scout* Mint Creme Pattie) 55
  sandwich (*FFV*) 81
  sandwich (*Pepperidge Farm* Mint Milano) 77
  sandwich, chocolate-covered (*Mystic*) 75
mint-chocolate chip (*Duncan Hines*) 55
molasses:
  (*Archway* Homestyle Old Fashioned) 120
  (*Grandma's*), 3 oz. 350
  (*Nabisco Pantry*) 65
  (*Pepperidge Farm* Crisps) 33
oatmeal:
  (*Archway* Homestyle) 116
  (*Drake's*) 63
  (*Pepperidge Farm*—large) 120
  (*Pepperidge Farm* Irish Oatmeal) 47
  (*Sunshine*) 61
  apple spice (*Grandma's*), 3 oz. 350
  coconut and raisin (*Nabisco*) 47
  date-filled (*Archway* Homestyle) 106
  and nut (*Archway* Family Style) 71
  raisin (*Pepperidge Farm*) 57

Cookies, oatmeal, continued

raisin, low-calorie (*Estee*) 17
orange (*Pepperidge Farm*) 57
orange sandwich
    (*Pepperidge Farm* Orange Milano) 53
peach-apricot (*Stella D'Oro* Pastry) 97
peach-apricot
    (*Stella D'Oro* Pastry—dietetic salt-free) 90
peanut bar, chocolate (*Ideal*) 75
peanut brittle (*Nabisco*) 47
peanut butter:
    (*Grandma's*—large), 3 oz. 410
    (*Frito-Lay's*), 1.75-oz. bar 270
    (*Pepperidge Farm* Star Wars) 35
    (*Sunshine* Wafers) 39
    chip (*Archway* Family Style) 80
    chip (*Pepperidge Farm* Old Fashioned) 57
    chip (*Pepperidge Farm*—large) 130
    fudge (*Nabisco*) 47
    fudge-chocolate chip (*Duncan Hines*) 55
    patty (*Girl Scouts*) 76
    sandwich (*Girl Scouts*) 56
    sandwich (*Nutter Butter*) 70
    sandwich, chocolate-filled
        (*Pepperidge Farm* Nassau) 85
pecan-chocolate chip (*Girl Scouts*) 42
pecan-chocolate chunk (*Pepperidge Farm*) 65
pecan shortbread, *see "shortbread," below*
prune (*Stella D'Oro* Pastry—dietetic salt-free) 90
raisin:
    (*Grandma's* Soft), 3 oz. 350
    (*Stella D'Oro* Golden Bars) 109
    (*Sunshine* Golden Fruit) 60
raisin-bran (*Pepperidge Farm*) 53
rum and brandy flavor
    (*Stella D'Oro* Roman Egg Biscuits) 125
sesame (*Stella D'Oro* Regina) 48
sesame (*Stella D'Oro* Regina—dietetic salt-free) 43
shortbread:
    (*Buttercup*) 24
    (*Girl Scouts*) 32
    (*Lorna Doone*) 35

Cookies, shortbread, continued

Cookies, vanilla, continued

low-calorie (*Sug'r Like* Creme Wafer) 49
chocolate center (*Stella D'Oro* Swiss Fudge) 67
chocolate-laced
   (*Pepperidge Farm* Pirouette Rolls) 37
chocolate-covered (*Pepperidge Farm* Orleans) 30
sandwich, chocolate-covered
   (*Pepperidge Farm* Orleans Sandwich) 60
sandwich, chocolate-filled
   (*Pepperidge Farm* Brussels) 53
sandwich, chocolate-filled
   (*Pepperidge Farm* Lido) 95
sandwich, chocolate-filled
   (*Pepperidge Farm* Milano) 60
sandwich, chocolate-mint-filled
   (*Pepperidge Farm* Brussels Mint) 67
wafers, *see specific flavors*
wafers, assorted, low-calorie (*Estee*) 30

**As Packaged. Bear in mind that cookies are available in
dozens of sizes and shapes; therefore, it is hard—indeed,
just about impossible—to accurately compare the caloric
content of different brands and types. (See "What You Should
Know About Using This Book," pages 13–17)*

COOKIES, FROZEN, MIXES* & REFRIGERATOR,
one piece, except as noted
See also "Cookies"

---

                                                    calories
brownies:
   mix (*Betty Crocker* Fudge), 1/16 of pkg. 150
   mix (*Betty Crocker* Fudge Family Size),
      1/24 of pkg. 130
   mix
      (*Betty Crocker* Supreme Fudge), 1/24 of pkg. 120
   mix (*Duncan Hines* Double Fudge) 130
   mix (*Pillsbury*), 2″ square 150
   mix (*Pillsbury* Family Size), 2″ square 150

Cookies, Frozen, Mixes & Refrigerator, brownies, continued

   mix (*Pillsbury* Fudge), 2″ square 140
   golden, mix
     (*Betty Crocker* Supreme Family Size),
     1/24 of pkg. 110
   low-calorie, mix (*Estee*), 2″ square 45
   w/walnuts, mix (*Betty Crocker*), 1/16 of pkg. 160
   w/walnuts, mix
     (*Betty Crocker* Family Size), 1/24 of pkg. 130
   w/walnuts, mix
     (*Pillsbury* Family Size), 2″ square 160
   refrigerator (*Pillsbury* Fudge) 140
chocolate chip:
   frozen (*Mrs. Goodcookie*) 57
   mix (*Betty Crocker Big Batch*) 60
   mix (*Duncan Hines*) 75
   refrigerator (*Pillsbury*) 57
   double, mix (*Duncan Hines*) 70
chocolate fudge, frozen (*Mrs. Goodcookie*) 57
coconut macaroons, mix
     (*Betty Crocker* Dessert Mix), 1/24 of pkg. 80
date bar, mix (*Betty Crocker*), 1/32 of pkg. 60
fudge-oatmeal:
   brown sugar, mix
     (*Pillsbury Fudge Jumbles*), 1 bar 100
   chocolate chip, mix
     (*Pillsbury Fudge Jumbles*), 1 bar 100
   coconut, mix (*Pillsbury Fudge Jumbles*), 1 bar 100
   peanut butter, mix
     (*Pillsbury Fudge Jumbles*), 1 bar 100
gingerbread:
   mix (*Betty Crocker* Dessert Mix), 1/9 of pkg. 210
   mix (*Dromedary*), 2″ square 100
   mix (*Pillsbury*), 3″ square 190
oatmeal:
   mix (*Betty Crocker Big Batch*) 65
   w/raisins, frozen (*Mrs. Goodcookie*) 53
   w/raisins, mix (*Duncan Hines*) 65
peanut butter:
   frozen (*Mrs. Goodcookie*) 60
   mix (*Duncan Hines*) 70
   refrigerator (*Pillsbury*) 50

Cookies, Frozen, Mixes & Refrigerator, continued
sugar:
  frozen (*Mrs. Goodcookie*) 53
  mix (*Betty Crocker Big Batch*) 60
  mix (*Duncan Hines* Golden Sugar) 65
  refrigerator (*Pillsbury*) 57
Vienna bar, mix
    (*Betty Crocker* Vienna Dream Bar),
    1/24 of pkg. 90

Prepared according to package directions

TOASTER PASTRIES, one piece*

---

	calories
all varieties (*Nabisco Toastettes*)	190

apple, Dutch, frosted
    (*Kellogg's Frosted Pop-Tarts*) 210
blueberry:
  (*Kellogg's Pop-Tarts*) 210
  (*Pillsbury Toaster Strudel*) 190
  frosted (*Kellogg's Frosted Pop-Tarts*) 200
brown sugar-cinnamon:
  (*Kellogg's Pop-Tarts*) 210
  frosted (*Kellogg's Frosted Pop-Tarts*) 210
cherry:
  (*Kellogg's Pop-Tarts*) 210
  frosted (*Kellogg's Frosted Pop-Tarts*) 210
chocolate fudge, frosted
    (*Kellogg's Frosted Pop-Tarts*) 200
chocolate-vanilla creme, frosted
    (*Kellogg's Frosted Pop-Tarts*) 220
cinnamon (*Pillsbury Toaster Strudel*) 190
grape, Concord, frosted
    (*Kellogg's Frosted Pop-Tarts*) 210
raspberry:
  (*Pillsbury Toaster Strudel*) 190
  frosted (*Kellogg's Frosted Pop-Tarts*) 210
strawberry:
  (*Kellogg's Pop-Tarts*) 200

Toaster Pastries, strawberry, continued
   (*Pillsbury Toaster Strudel*) 190
   frosted (*Kellogg's Frosted Pop-Tarts*) 200

*As packaged

FOOD STICKS & BARS, one piece*
See also "Breakfast Bars & Beverages"

---

	calories
caramel nut (*Figurines*)	138
chocolate:	
(*Figurines*)	138
(*Pillsbury Milk Break*)	230
(*Slender*)	138
double (*Figurines*)	138
chocolate caramel (*Figurines*)	138
chocolate mint (*Figurines*)	138
chocolate mint (*Pillsbury Milk Break*)	230
chocolate peanut butter (*Figurines*)	138
chocolate peanut butter (*Slender*)	138
cinnamon (*Slender*)	138
lemon yogurt (*Figurines*)	138
natural (*Pillsbury Milk Break*)	230
peanut butter (*Pillsbury Milk Break*)	220
strawberry yogurt (*Figurines*)	138
vanilla (*Figurines*)	138
vanilla (*Slender*)	138

*As packaged

CAKE FROSTINGS, READY TO SPREAD,
1/12 of container, except as noted
See also "Cake Frostings, Mixes"

                                                                    calories
butter pecan (*Betty Crocker Creamy Deluxe*) 160
caramel pecan (*Pillsbury Frosting Supreme*) 160
cherry (*Betty Crocker Creamy Deluxe*) 160
chocolate and fudge:
   (*Betty Crocker Creamy Deluxe*) 170
   double Dutch (*Pillsbury Frosting Supreme*) 150
   dark Dutch fudge
     (*Betty Crocker Creamy Deluxe*) 160
   fudge (*Pillsbury Frosting Supreme*) 150
   milk chocolate (*Betty Crocker Creamy Deluxe*) 160
   milk chocolate (*Pillsbury Frosting Supreme*) 150
chocolate chip (*Betty Crocker Creamy Deluxe*) 170
chocolate chocolate chip
   (*Betty Crocker Creamy Deluxe*) 160
chocolate mint (*Pillsbury Frosting Supreme*) 150
chocolate nut (*Betty Crocker Creamy Deluxe*) 160
coconut almond (*Pillsbury Frosting Supreme*) 150
coconut pecan (*Betty Crocker Creamy Deluxe*) 170
coconut pecan (*Pillsbury Frosting Supreme*) 160
cream cheese (*Betty Crocker Creamy Deluxe*) 160
cream cheese (*Pillsbury Frosting Supreme*) 160
decorator, all colors (*Pillsbury*), 1 tbsp. 70
lemon (*Betty Crocker Creamy Deluxe*) 160
lemon (*Pillsbury Frosting Supreme*) 160
orange (*Betty Crocker Creamy Deluxe*) 160
sour cream:
   chocolate (*Betty Crocker Creamy Deluxe*) 170
   vanilla (*Pillsbury Frosting Supreme*) 160
   white (*Betty Crocker Creamy Deluxe*) 160
strawberry (*Pillsbury Frosting Supreme*) 160
vanilla (*Betty Crocker Creamy Deluxe*) 160
vanilla (*Pillsbury Frosting Supreme*) 160

CAKE FROSTINGS, MIXES*, 1/12 of package
See also "Cake Frostings, Ready to Serve"

---

          calories

banana (*Betty Crocker Chiquita* Fluffy) 170
butter (*Betty Crocker Butter Brickle* Fluffy) 170
butter pecan (*Betty Crocker* Fluffy) 170
caramel (*Pillsbury Rich 'n Easy*) 140
cherry, creamy (*Betty Crocker* Fluffy) 170
chocolate and fudge:
  chocolate (*Duncan Hines*) 160
  dark fudge (*Betty Crocker*) 170
  double Dutch (*Pillsbury Rich 'n Easy*) 150
  fudge (*Betty Crocker*) 170
  fudge (*Pillsbury Rich 'n Easy*) 150
  fudge, dark Dutch (*Duncan Hines*) 160
  milk chocolate (*Betty Crocker*) 170
  milk chocolate (*Duncan Hines*) 160
  milk chocolate (*Pillsbury Rich 'n Easy*) 150
chocolate almond fudge (*Betty Crocker*) 180
coconut almond (*Betty Crocker*) 140
coconut almond (*Pillsbury*) 160
coconut pecan (*Betty Crocker* Fluffy) 140
coconut pecan (*Pillsbury*) 150
cream cheese and nuts (*Betty Crocker*) 150
lemon (*Betty Crocker*) 170
lemon (*Pillsbury Rich 'n Easy*) 140
sour cream, chocolate fudge (*Betty Crocker*) 170
sour cream, white (*Betty Crocker*) 170
strawberry (*Pillsbury Rich 'n Easy*) 140
vanilla (*Duncan Hines*) 160
vanilla (*Pillsbury Rich 'n Easy*) 150
white:
  (*Betty Crocker* Fluffy) 60
  (*Pillsbury* Fluffy) 60
  creamy (*Betty Crocker* Fluffy) 180

**Prepared according to package directions*

PIE FILLINGS, CANNED, 3½ ounces*, except as noted
See also "Custards, Puddings & Pie Fillings"

calories

apple (*Comstock*) 120
apple (*Comstock* Lite) 80
apricot (*Comstock*) 110
banana cream (*Comstock*) 110
blueberry (*Comstock*) 110
blueberry (*Comstock* Lite) 75
boysenberry (*Comstock* Lite) 120
cherry (*Comstock*) 110
cherry (*Comstock* Lite) 75
chocolate (*Comstock*) 130
coconut cream (*Comstock*) 120
lemon (*Comstock*) 140
mincemeat:
  (*Borden None Such*), ¼ of pkg. 220
  (*Comstock*) 150
  w/brandy and rum
    (*Borden None Such*), ¼ of pkg. 220
peach (*Comstock*) 110
pineapple (*Comstock*) 100
pumpkin (*Comstock*), 4½ oz. 100
pumpkin (*Stokely*) 117
raisin (*Comstock*) 120
strawberry (*Comstock*) 100

*Approximately ½ cup

PASTRY SHELLS & PIE CRUSTS

calories

pastry sheet, frozen
  (*Pepperidge Farm*), ¼ sheet 260
pastry shell (*Stella D'Oro*), 1 shell* 147
patty shell, frozen (*Pepperidge Farm*), 1 shell* 210

Pastry Shells & Pie Crusts, continued

pie crusts:

frozen (*Mrs. Smith's*), 1/6 of 9⅝" crust 173

frozen (*Pet•Ritz*), 1/6 of crust 110

mix (*Betty Crocker*), 1/16 of pkg. 120

mix** (*Flako*), 1/6 of 9" crust 260

mix** (*Pillsbury*), 1/6 of 2-crust pie 270

refrigerator

  (*Pillsbury* All Ready), 1/8 of 2-crust pie 240

sticks (*Betty Crocker*), 1/8 of stick 120

sticks** (*Pillsbury*), 1/6 of 2-crust pie 270

deep-dish, frozen (*Pet•Ritz*), 1/6 of crust 130

graham cracker, frozen (*Pet•Ritz*), 1/6 of crust 110

whole grain, frozen (*Pet•Ritz*), 1/6 of crust 130

*As packaged
**Prepared according to package directions

Chapter 19

NUT BUTTERS, JAMS AND JELLIES

NUT BUTTERS, one tablespoon, except as noted

---

	calories
almond butter, raw:	
unsalted (*Hain*)	95
blanched, unsalted (*Hain*)	95
blanched, toasted, unsalted (*Hain*)	105
cashew butter, raw, unsalted (*Hain*)	95
cashew butter, toasted, unsalted (*Hain*)	95
peanut butter:	
creamy or crunchy (*Bama*)	100
creamy or crunchy (*Hain* Old Fashioned)	105
creamy or smooth (*Jif*)	95
creamy or smooth (*Peter Pan*)	95
creamy or smooth (*Planters*)	95
creamy or smooth (*Smucker's*)	90
creamy or smooth (*Skippy*)	95
creamy or smooth (*Velvet*)	95
crunchy or chunk (*Jif*)	95
crunchy or chunk (*Peter Pan*)	95
crunchy or chunk (*Planters*)	95
crunchy or chunk (*Skippy*)	95
crunchy or chunk (*Smucker's*)	90
low-sodium (*Cellu*), 1/2 oz.	90
low-sodium (*Estee*)	100
low-sodium (*Peter Pan*)	95
low-sodium (*S & W Nutradiet*)	93
low-sodium (*Teddie*)	100
natural (*Elam's*)	102

Nut Butters, peanut butter, continued

natural (*Smucker's*) 100
natural, raw, unsalted (*Hain*) 90
toasted, unsalted (*Hain*) 95
toasted, creamy, unsalted (*Hain*) 95
peanut butter w/grape jelly
    (*Smucker's Goober Grape*) 90
sesame butter, raw, unsalted (*Hain*) 90
sesame butter, toasted, unsalted (*Hain*) 100
sesame paste tahini (*Sahadi*) 95
sunflower butter, raw, unsalted (*Hain*) 90

JAMS, JELLIES & PRESERVES, one tablespoon

calories

butter, apple:
  (*Bama*) 38
  (*Ma Brown*) 32
  (*Musselman's*) 33
  (*Smucker's* Natural Cider) 38
butter, peach (*Smucker's*) 45
jams:
  all flavors (*Bama*) 45
  all flavors (*Kraft*) 54
  all flavors (*Smucker's*) 53
  grape (*Welch's*) 53
  strawberry (*Musselman's*) 54
  strawberry (*Welch's*) 53
  low-calorie, all flavors (*Dia-Mel*) 6
  low-calorie, all flavors (*S & W Nutradiet*) ... 12
  low-calorie, all flavors (*Smucker's Slenderella*) ... 21
  low-calorie, strawberry, imitation (*Smucker's*) ... 6
jellies:
  all flavors (*Crosse & Blackwell*) 51
  all flavors (*Kraft*) 48
  all flavors (*Ma Brown*) 49
  all flavors (*Musselman's*) 53
  all flavors (*Smucker's*) 53
  apple, mint-flavored (*Bama*) 45

Chapter 20

SYRUPS, TOPPINGS AND SWEET BAKING INGREDIENTS

SUGAR, one tablespoon, except as noted
See also "Honey, Molasses & Syrups"

---

	calories
brown, firm-packed (all brands)	52
cinnamon (*French's*), 1 tsp.	16
granulated (all brands)	46
powdered, stirred (all brands)	31

HONEY, MOLASSES & SYRUPS,
one tablespoon, except as noted
See also "Sugar," "Dessert Toppings & Syrups"
and *"Sweet Flavorings & Extracts"*

---

	calories
honey, strained or extracted (all brands)	64
molasses (*Brer Rabbit* Green Label), 1 oz.	67
molasses (*Grandma's* Unsulphured)	60
syrups:	
corn, dark (*Karo*)	60
corn, light (*Karo*)	60
maple, blended (*Log Cabin*)	52
maple, imitation (*Karo*)	55
maple, reduced-calorie (*Cary's* Lite)	30
maple, low-calorie (*Cary's*)	6

Honey, Molasses & Syrups, continued

pancake syrup, maple-flavored:
    (*Aunt Jemima*) 51
    (*Golden Griddle*) 50
    (*Happy Jack*) 50
    (*Karo*) 60
    (*Log Cabin Country Kitchen*) 50
    (*Smucker's*) 43
    buttered (*Log Cabin*) 54
    buttered (*Mrs. Butterworth's*) 53
    w/honey (*Log Cabin* Maple Honey) 50
    low-calorie (*Dia-Mel*) 1
    low-calorie (*Featherweight*) 12
    low-calorie (*S & W Nutradiet*) 12

DESSERT TOPPINGS & SYRUPS,
one tablespoon, except as noted
See also "Honey, Molasses & Syrups"

---

                           calories

all flavors (*Smucker's* Magic Shell) 98
blueberry, low-calorie (*Dia-Mel*) 1
blueberry, low-calorie (*Featherweight*) 14
butterscotch (*Kraft*) 60
butterscotch (*Smucker's*) 70
caramel:
    (*Kraft*) 50
    (*Smucker's*) 70
    hot (*Smucker's*) 75
chocolate:
    (*Bosco* Milk Amplifier) 50
    (*Hershey* Syrup) 40
    (*Kraft*) 50
    (*Milk Mate*) 50
    (*Smucker's*) 65
    low-calorie (*Dia-Mel*) 1
chocolate caramel (*Kraft*) 50
chocolate fudge:
    (*Hershey* Topping) 50
    (*Kraft*) 70

Dessert Toppings & Syrups, chocolate fudge, continued

(*Smucker's*)	65
(*Smucker's* Swiss Milk)	70
hot (*Smucker's*)	55
cream, *see "whipped," below*	
fruit, all flavors, except pineapple and strawberry	
(*Smucker's*)	50
hard sauce (*Crosse & Blackwell*)	64
marshmallow creme (*Kraft*), 1 oz.	90
marshmallow creme (*Marshmallow Fluff*)	177
nut (*Planters*), 1 oz.	180
peanut butter caramel (*Smucker's*)	75
pecans, in syrup (*Smucker's*)	65
pineapple (*Kraft*)	50
pineapple (*Smucker's*)	65
strawberry (*Kraft*)	45
strawberry (*Smucker's*)	60
walnuts, in syrup (*Kraft*)	90
walnuts, in syrup (*Smucker's*)	65
whipped:	
(*Birds Eye Dover Farms*)	16
cream (*Kraft* Real Cream Topping), ¼ cup	25
cream (*Reddi-Wip*)	8
non-dairy (*Birds Eye Cool Whip*)	14
non-dairy (*Birds Eye Cool Whip* Extra Creamy)	16
non-dairy (*Kraft* Whipped Topping), ¼ cup	35
non-dairy (*LaCreme*)	12
non-dairy (*Lucky Whip*)	12
non-dairy (*Pet*)	14
non-dairy (*Rich's* Aerosol), ¼ oz.	20
non-dairy (*Rich's Spoon 'N Serve*), ¼ oz.	24
non-dairy, low-calorie (*Estee*)	4
non-dairy, low-calorie (*Featherweight*)	2
non-dairy, mix* (*Dream Whip*)	10
non-dairy, mix* (*D-Zerta*)	8

*Prepared according to package directions

SWEET FLAVORINGS & EXTRACTS*, one teaspoon
See also "Honey, Molasses & Syrups"
and *"Dessert Toppings & Syrups"*

calories

almond extract:
  (*Virginia Dare*) 7
  pure (*Durkee*) 13
  pure (*Ehlers*) 12
anise extract, pure (*Durkee*) 16
anise extract, pure (*Ehlers*) 26
banana extract, imitation (*Durkee*) 15
banana extract, imitation (*Ehlers*) 20
black walnut flavor (*Durkee*) 4
brandy flavor (*Durkee*) 15
brandy flavor (*Ehlers*) 16
cherry extract, pure (*Burton's*) 9
cherry extract, imitation (*Ehlers*) 16
chocolate flavor (*Durkee*) 7
chocolate flavor (*Ehlers*) 10
coconut flavor (*Durkee*) 8
coconut flavor (*Ehlers*) 17
coffee flavor, pure (*Burton's*) 9
grenadine (*Garnier*) 17
grenadine (*Holland House*) 15
lemon extract:
  (*Virginia Dare*) 14
  imitation (*Durkee*) 17
  pure (*Ehlers*) 30
maple extract, imitation (*Durkee*) 6
maple extract, imitation (*Ehlers*) 9
orange extract:
  (*Virginia Dare*) 15
  imitation (*Durkee*) 14
  pure (*Ehlers*) 30
orgeat syrup (*Garnier*) 17
peppermint extract:
  imitation (*Durkee*) 15
  pure (*Ehlers*) 24

Sweet Flavorings & Extracts, continued

pineapple:
    extract, imitation (*Ehlers*) 14
    flavor, imitation (*Durkee*) 6
    flavor, pure (*Burton's*) 12
raspberry extract:
    imitation (*Burton's*) 10
    imitation (*Ehlers*) 14
    pure (*Burton's*) 8
rose extract, pure (*Burton's*) 9
rum:
    extract, imitation (*Burton's*) 11
    flavor, imitation (*Durkee*) 14
    flavor, pure (*Ehlers*) 19
strawberry extract:
    imitation (*Durkee*) 12
    imitation (*Ehlers*) 16
    pure (*Burton's*) 10
vanilla:
    extract (*Virginia Dare*) 7
    extract, imitation (*Durkee*) 3
    extract, imitation (*Gold Medal*) .... trace
    extract, pure (*Durkee*) 8
    extract, pure (*Ehlers*) 13
    flavor, imitation (*Durkee*) 3

*Note: If a flavoring that contains alcohol is added to a recipe before cooking, the alcohol (which frequently contributes a major portion of the calories) will be evaporated and the calories reduced.

MISCELLANEOUS SWEET BAKING INGREDIENTS,
one ounce, except as noted

---

                      calories
butterscotch (*Nestlé* Morsels) 150
chocolate:
    baking (*Hershey*) 190
    milk (*Hershey* Chips) 147

Miscellaneous Sweet Baking Ingredients, chocolate, continued

milk (*Nestlé* Morsels) 150
pre-melted (*Nestlé Choco-Bake*) 170
semisweet (*Baker's*) 130
semisweet (*Baker's* Chips) 127
semisweet (*Borden* Chips) 150
semisweet (*Ghirardelli* Chips) 150
semisweet (*Hershey* Chips/Mini Chips) 147
semisweet (*Nestlé* Morsels) 150
sweet (*Baker's* German) 140
unsweetened (*Baker's*) 140
coconut, dried:
cookie (*Baker's* Cookie Coconut) 142
flaked (*Baker's Angel Flake*) 134
flaked, canned (*Baker's Angel Flake*) 124
shredded (*Baker's* Premium Shred) 137
shredded (*Durkee*), 1 cup 277
shredded, Southern style
(*Baker's* Premium Shred) 124

Chapter 21

CANDY AND
CHEWING GUM

CANDY

	calories
almonds, w/chocolate, see "chocolate, w/fruit and/or nuts," below	
(*Baby Ruth*), 1 oz.	130
(*Black Cow* Sucker), 1 oz.	103
(*Bonkers*), 1 piece*	23
bridge mix:	
(*Nabisco*), 1 oz.	135
(*Nabisco*), 1 piece*	10
low-calorie (*Estee* TV Mix), 1 piece*	9
(*Butterfinger*), 1 oz.	140
(*Butternut*), 1.75-oz. bar	230
(*Butternut*), 1.5-oz. bar	194
butterscotch:	
(*Nestlé* Morsels), 1 oz.	150
(*Rothchild's*), 1 piece*	19
drops (*Lifesavers*), 1 piece*	10
drops (*Nabisco* Skimmers), 1 oz.	116
drops (*Nabisco* Skimmers), 1 piece*	25
candy corn (*Heide*), 1 piece*	4
(*CaraCoa Nuggets*), 1 oz.	140
caramel:	
(*CaraCoa*), 1 oz.	110
(*Kraft*), 1 piece*	35
(*Pearson* Caramel Nip), 1 oz.	120
(*Whirligigs*), .22-oz. piece	26

Candy, caramel, continued

chocolate (*Sugar Daddy* Junior), .45-oz. piece 51
chocolate center (*Tootsie Pops/Pop Drops*), 1 oz. 113
vanilla (*Sugar Babies*), 1 oz. 110
vanilla (*Sugar Babies*), 1 piece* 6
vanilla (*Sugar Daddy*), 1 oz. 110
vanilla (*Sugar Mama*), 1 oz. 125
caramel, chocolate-covered:
  (*Milk Duds*), 1 oz. 111
  (*Pom Poms*), 1 oz. 125
  (*Pom Poms*), 1 piece* 16
  (*Rolo*), 1 oz. or 5 pieces 140
  w/cookies (*Twix*), .93-oz. bar 130
carob-coated bars:
  (*CaraCoa* Milk Free), 1-oz. bar 145
  (*CaraCoa* Natural), 1-oz. bar 160
  (*Tiger's Milk*), 2-oz. bar 250
  crunchy (*CaraCoa*), 7/8-oz. bar 140
  fruit and nut (*CaraCoa*), 1-oz. bar 155
  mint (*CaraCoa*), 1-oz. bar 160
  peanut (*CaraCoa*), 1-oz. bar 160
  peanut butter (*Tiger's Milk*), 1.7-oz. bar 210
  peanut butter and honey
    (*Tiger's Milk*), 1.7-oz. bar 210
  peanut butter and jelly
    (*Tiger's Milk*), 1.7-oz. bar 210
  orange (*CaraCoa*), 1-oz. bar 160
carob-coated mix (*CaraCoa* Party Mix), 1 oz. 145
(*Charleston Chew*—all flavors), 1 oz. 120
cherries, chocolate-covered:
  dark chocolate (*Cortina*), 1 piece* 96
  dark chocolate (*Nabisco/Welch's*), 1 oz. 113
  dark chocolate (*Nabisco/Welch's*), 1 piece* 67
  milk chocolate (*Nabisco/Welch's*), 1 oz. 112
  milk chocolate (*Nabisco/Welch's*), 1 piece* 66
chocolate, solid:
  milk (*Cadbury*), 1 oz. 150
  milk (*Ghirardelli* Bars), 1 oz. 150
  milk (*Ghirardelli* Block), 1 oz. 149
  milk (*Hershey*), 1.45-oz. bar 220
  milk (*Hershey* Chips), 1.5 oz. or 1/4 cup 220
  milk (*Hershey* Kisses), 1 oz. or 6 pieces 150

Candy, chocolate, solid, continued

milk (*Nabisco* Stars), 1 oz. or 13 pieces 160
milk (*Nestlé*), 1 oz. 150
mint (*Ghirardelli*), 1 oz. 150
semisweet (*Eagle*), 1 oz. 149
semisweet (*Ghirardelli* Chips), 1 oz. 150
semisweet (*Hershey* Chips), 1.5 oz. or ¼ cup 220
semisweet
  (*Hershey* Mini Chips), 1.5 oz. or ¼ cup 220
semisweet (*Hershey Special Dark*), 1.2-oz. bar 180
semisweet (*Lindt Excellence*), 1 oz. 162
semisweet (*Nestlé* Morsels), 1 oz. 150
semisweet, w/vanilla (*Lindt*), 1 oz. 163
low-calorie, bittersweet (*Estee*), 1 square* 30
low-calorie, milk (*Estee*), 1 square* 30
low-calorie, milk (*Featherweight*), 1 piece* 45
chocolate, w/bran, low-calorie (*Estee*), 1 square* 30
chocolate, w/caramel (*Cadbury Caramello*), 1 oz. 140
chocolate, candy-coated (*M & M's*), 1.69-oz. pkg. 240
chocolate-coated candy, *see specific kinds (fudge, coconut, etc.)*
chocolate, w/coconut, low-calorie
  (*Estee*), 1 square* 30
chocolate, w/crisps:
  (*Ghirardelli*), 1 oz. 150
  (*Krackel*), 1.45-oz. bar 220
  (*Nestlé Crunch*), 1 oz. 150
  low-calorie (*Estee* Crunch), 1 square* 30
  low-calorie (*Featherweight*), 1 piece* 50
chocolate, w/fruit and/or nuts:
  w/almonds (*Cadbury*), 1 oz. 150
  w/almonds (*Ghirardelli*), 1 oz. 152
  w/almonds (*Hershey*), 1.45-oz. bar 230
  w/almonds (*Nestlé*), 1 oz. 150
  w/almonds, toasted
    (*Hershey Golden Almond*), 1 oz. 160
  w/Brazil nuts (*Cadbury*), 1 oz. 150
  w/fruit and nuts (*Cadbury*), 1 oz. 150
  w/fruit and nuts (*Chunky*), 1 oz. 135
  w/hazelnuts (*Cadbury*), 1 oz. 150
  w/peanuts (*Mr. Goodbar*), 1.65-oz. bar 250
  w/raisins (*Ghirardelli*), 1 oz. 142

Candy, chocolate, w/fruit and/or nuts, continued

   low-calorie, w/almonds (*Estee*), 1 square* 30
   low-calorie, w/fruit and nuts (*Estee*), 1 square* 30
chocolate parfait (*Pearson*), 1 piece* 30
coconut, chocolate-covered:
   (*Mounds*), 1 oz. 130
   (*Nabisco* Coconut Squares), 1 oz. 135
   (*Welch's*), 1.07-oz. bar 132
   w/almonds (*Almond Joy*), 1 oz. 140
coffee (*Pearson* Coffee Nip), 1 oz. 120
coffee (*Pearson Coffioca* Parfait), 1 piece* 30
cough drops:
   (*Beech-Nut*), 1 piece* 10
   (*Halls* — Square and Oval), 1 piece* 15
   assorted, honey and wild cherry
     (*Pine Brothers*), 1 piece* 10
   low-calorie (*Estee*), 1 piece* 13
crisps, chocolate-covered, w/caramel
     (*Caravelle*), 1 oz. 137
crisps, chocolate-covered, w/caramel
     (*$100,000*), 1 oz. 133
dates, carob-coated (*CaraCoa*), 1 oz. 125
(*Forever Yours*), 1.37-oz. bar 175
fruit chews (*Starburst*), 1 oz. 110
fruit flavor (*Skittles*), 1.72-oz. pkg. 200
fruit roll, *see "Fruit, Dried," page 81*
fudge:
   (*Kraft* Chocolate Fudgies), 1 piece* 35
   (*Nabisco* Home Style), .7-oz. bar 90
   chocolate-covered (*Nabisco*), 1 bar* 63
   chocolate-covered (*Welch's*), 1.07-oz. bar 144
   w/nuts (*Nabisco*), .54-oz. bar 70
   w/nuts (*Nabisco* Squares), 1 oz. 130
   w/nuts (*Nabisco* Squares), 1 piece* 65
(*Good & Fruity*), 1.5-oz. pkg. 136
gum candy, *see "jellied and gum candy," below*
hard candy (*see also specific flavors*):
   all flavors (*Beech-Nut*), 1 piece* 10
   all flavors (*Bonomo*), 1 oz. 110
   all flavors (*Jolly Rancher Stix* Bars), 1 oz. 102
   all flavors (*Jolly Rancher Stix* Kisses), 1 oz. 110
   all flavors (*Lifesavers* Drops), 1 piece* 10

hard candy, continued

all flavors (*Lifesavers* Sours), 1 piece*	10
all flavors (*Reed's*), 1 oz.	110
low-calorie, all flavors (*Estee*), 1 piece*	13
halvah (*Joyva*), 1 oz.	160
halvah (*Sahadi*), 1 oz.	150
(*Heide Chocolate Babies*), 1 piece*	9
(*Heide Red Hot Dollars*), 1 piece*	15
(*Heide Witchcraft*), 1 piece*	5
honey nougat (*Bit-O-Honey*), 1 oz.	116

jellied and gum candy:

(*Chuckles JuJu Softees*), 1 piece*	12
(*Chuckles* Bar), 1 piece*	40
(*Chuckles* Variety Pack), 2-oz. pkg.	205
(*Heide Jujubes*), 1 piece*	3
(*Just Born*), 1.25 oz.	117
(*Mason Dots*), 1 oz.	95
(*Mason Crows*), 1 oz.	95
beans, all flavors (*Chuckles*), 1 oz.	105
beans, all flavors (*Heide*), 1 piece*	9
cherry flavor (*Chuckles*), 1 piece	24
cinnamon (*Chuckles Cinnamon Softees*), 1 piece*	7
fruit flavor (*Chuckles Berries*), 1 piece*	12
fruit flavor (*Jujyfruits*), 1 piece*	9
licorice, see "licorice," below	
mint (*Chuckles Mint Softees*), 1 piece	20
orange flavor slices (*Chuckles*), 1 oz.	105
orange flavor slices (*Chuckles*), 1 piece*	35
rings (*Chuckles*), 1 oz.	105
rings (*Chuckles*), 1 piece*	35
spearmint flavor leaves (*Chuckles*), 1 oz.	105
spearmint flavor leaves (*Chuckles*), 1 piece*	35
spice flavor (*Chuckles*), 1 oz.	105
spice flavor sticks or drops (*Chuckles*), 1 piece*	11
low-calorie, gumdrops, all flavors (*Estee*), 1 piece*	3
(*KitKat*), 1.5-oz. bar	210

licorice:

(*Chuckles Licorice Softees*), 1 piece*	8
(*Pearson* Licorice Nip), 1 oz.	120
(*Switzer*), 1 oz.	101

Candy, licorice, continued

    candy-coated (*Good & Plenty*), 1.5-oz. pkg. 136
    drops (*Diamond*), 1 piece* 14
    jellies (*Chuckles*), 1 oz. 100
    jellies (*Chuckles*), 1 piece* 33
    red (*Switzer*), 1 oz. 101
lollipops, all flavors (*Lifesavers*), 1 piece* 45
lollipops, low-calorie, all flavors (*Estee*), 1 piece* 12
(*Marathon*), 1.37-oz. bar 179
(*Marathon* Fun Size), .44-oz. bar 58
(*Mars*), 1.87-oz. bar 260
malted milk balls (*Deran*), 1 oz. 140
malted milk crunch (*Nabisco*), 1 piece* 8
marshmallows:
    (*Campfire*), 2 large* or 24 mini* 40
    (*Just Born*), 1.1-oz. pkg. 94
    (*Kraft* Jet-Puffed), 1 piece* 25
    (*Kraft Funmallows*), 1 piece* 25
    miniature (*Kraft*), 10 pieces* 25
    miniature (*Kraft Funmallows*), 10 pieces* 25
(*Mary Jane*), 1 oz. 74
(*Mary Jane* Bite Size), 1/4-oz. piece 18
(*Milky Way*), 2.10-oz. bar 270
mints:
    (*Beech-Nut*), 1 piece* 10
    (*Certs* Clear), 1 piece* 8
    (*Certs* Pressed), 1 piece* 6
    (*Clorets*), 1 piece* 6
    (*Cortina* Thin Mints), 1 piece* 40
    (*Delson* Merri-Mints), 1 piece* 25
    (*Delson* Thin Mints), 1 piece* 52
    (*Jamaica* Mints), 1 oz. 113
    (*Jamaica* Mints), 1 piece* 24
    (*Kraft* Party Mints), 1 piece* 8
    (*Lifesavers*), 1 piece* 10
    (*Nabisco* Liberty Mints), 1 oz. 113
    (*Nabisco* Liberty Mints), 1 piece* 24
    (*Pearson* Mint Parfait), 1 oz. 120
    (*Rolaids*), 1 piece* 4
    (*Tic Tac*), 1 piece* 2
    (*Trident*), 1 piece* 8
    butter (*Kraft*), 1 piece* 8

Candy, mints, continued

butter (*Richardson*), 1 oz. 109
butter creme (*Lifesavers*), 1 piece* 10
chocolate-covered (*Junior*), 1 oz. 120
chocolate-covered (*Junior*), 1 piece* 10
chocolate-covered
  (*Nabisco* Mint Wafers), 1 piece* 10
chocolate-covered
  (*Nabisco* Peppermint Patties), 1 oz. 110
chocolate-covered
  (*Nabisco* Peppermint Patties), 1 piece* 55
chocolate-covered
  (*Nabisco* Thin Mints), 1 piece* 42
chocolate-covered (*Royals*), 1.52-oz. piece 210
chocolate-covered
  (*York* Peppermint Patties), 1 oz. 120
jelly center (*Richardson*), 1 oz. 104
midget (*Richardson*), 1 oz. 109
striped (*Richardson*), 1 oz. 109
low-calorie (*Estee* Peppermint), 1 piece* 13
low-calorie, sugar-free (*Estee* 5-Pak), 1 piece* 4
(*Nabisco* Coco-Mello), .7-oz. bar 91
(*Nabisco* Crispy Clusters), 1 oz. 114
(*Nabisco* Crispy Clusters), 1 piece* 65
(*Nabisco* Nutty Crunch), .54-oz. bar 71
(*Nestlé Choco Lite*), 1 oz. 150
(*Payday*), 1.75-oz. bar 239
(*Payday*), 1.5-oz. bar 200
peanut bar (*Munch*), 1.5-oz. bar 240
peanut brittle:
  (*Kraft*), 1 oz. 140
  (*Planters* Jumbo Block), 1 oz. 150
  (*Stuckey's*), 1 oz. 122
peanut butter:
  (*Pearson* Parfait), 1 piece* 30
  candy-coated (*Reese's Pieces*), 1 oz. 140
  chocolate-covered (*Peter Paul*), 1 oz. 157
  chocolate-covered
    (*Reese's Peanut Butter Cups* Plain or Crunchy),
    2 pieces* 240
  chocolate-covered
    (*Reese's Peanut Butter Flavor Chips*), 1.5 oz. 230

Candy, peanut butter, continued
    chocolate-covered, w/cookies
       (*Twix* Bars), .85-oz. bar 130
    low-calorie (*Estee* Cups), 1 piece* 45
peanut clusters, chocolate-covered:
    (*Deran*), 1 oz. 150
    (*Royal Cluster*), 1 oz. 137
    (*Royal Cluster*), 1 piece* 78
peanut crunch (*Sahadi*), .75-oz. bar 110
peanuts, carob-coated (*CaraCoa*), 1 oz. 160
peanuts, chocolate-covered:
    (*Goober's*), 1 oz. 153
    (*Nabisco*), 1 oz. 160
    (*Nabisco*), 1 piece* 11
    low-calorie (*Estee-ets*), 8 pieces* 55
    candy-coated (*M & M's*), 1.67-oz. pkg. 240
(*Pearson* Chocolate Parfait), 1 oz. 136
pecan roll (*Stuckey's* Log), 1 oz. 135
peppermint, *see "mints," above*
popcorn, *see "Popcorn," page 280*
popcorn, caramel-coated (*Bachman*), 1 oz. 110
popcorn, caramel-coated, w/nuts
       (*Cracker Jacks*), 1 oz. 120
(*Power House*), 1 oz. 132
praline, coconut (*Stuckey's*), 1 oz. 125
praline, maple (*Stuckey's*), 1 oz. 125
raisins, carob-coated (*CaraCoa*), 1 oz. 130
raisins, chocolate-covered:
    (*Deran*), 1 oz. 120
    (*Nabisco*), 1 oz. 130
    (*Nabisco*), 1 piece* 4
    (*Raisinets*), 1 oz. 90
    low-calorie (*Estee*), 10 pieces* 50
(*Rally*), 1 oz. 125
(*Reggie*), 2-oz. bar 290
rum wafers (*Deran*), 1 oz. 150
sesame bar (*Joyva*), 1 oz. 178
sesame crunch (*Sahadi*), .75-oz. bar 110
sesame crunch (*Flavor Tree*—in jars), 1 oz. 150
(*Snickers*), 2-oz. bar 270
soynuts, carob-coated (*CaraCoa*), 1 oz. 145
(*Snowcaps*), 1 oz. 124

Candy, continued

(*Summit*), 1.48-oz. bar	220
taffy, all flavors, except chocolate (*Bonomo*), 1 oz.	108
taffy, chocolate (*Bonomo*), 1 oz.	107
(*3 Musketeers*), 2.28-oz. bar	280
toffee:	
(*Kraft*), 1 piece*	30
chocolate (*Rothchild's*), 1 piece*	22
creamy (*Rothchild's*), 1 piece*	22
(*Tootsie Pop*), .6-oz. piece	66
(*Tootsie Pop Drops*), .18-oz. piece	20
(*Tootsie Rolls*), 1 oz.	112
(*Tootsie Flavor Rolls*), 1 oz.	117
(*Zero*), 1.8-oz. bar	230

*Average size piece, as packaged

CHEWING GUM, one piece*

	calories
(*Adams* Sour Gum)	9
(*Beechies*)	5
(*Beech-Nut*)	10
(*Big Red*)	10
(*Bubble Yum*)	25
(*Bubble Yum* Sugar Free)	20
(*Bubblicious*)	24
(*Care*Free*)	10
(*Care*Free* Bubble Gum)	10
(*Chicklets*)	6
(*Clorets*)	6
(*Dentyne*)	5
(*Doublemint*)	10
(*Featherweight*)	12
(*Freedent*)	10
(*Freshen-Up*)	10
(*Fruit Stripe*)	10
(*Juicy Fruit*)	10
(*Orbit*)	8
(*Replay*)	15

Chewing Gum, continued

*As packaged

Chapter 22

ICE CREAM AND FROZEN CONFECTIONS

ICE CREAM & FROZEN CONFECTIONS,
1/2 cup, except as noted
See also "Frozen Yogurt," "Fruit Juice Bars, Frozen"
and "Pudding Bars, Frozen"

---

          calories

frozen desserts, non-dairy:
  chocolate (*Colombo Tofu*) 130
  chocolate (*Tofutti*) 210
  honey vanilla (*Colombo Tofu*) 130
  maple walnut (*Colombo Tofu*) 130
  maple walnut (*Tofutti*) 210
  peanut butter (*Colombo Tofu*) 130
  vanilla (*Tofutti*) 210
  wild berry (*Colombo Tofu*) 130
  wild berry (*Tofutti*) 170
ice cream:
  butter almond (*Breyers*) 170
  butter almond and chocolate (*Breyers*) 160
  butter pecan (*Lady Borden*) 180
  cherry vanilla (*Breyers*) 140
  chocolate (*Breyers*) 160
  chocolate (*Foremost*) 130
  chocolate (*Häagen-Dazs*) 283
  chocolate (*Howard Johnson's*) 221
  chocolate (*Lady Borden*) 160
  chocolate (*Meadow Gold*) 129

ice cream, continued

chocolate (*Sealtest*) 140
chocolate chip (*Sealtest*) 150
chocolate-chocolate chip (*Häagen-Dazs*) 309
chocolate, Dutch (*Borden*) 130
chocolate, Dutch w/almonds
   (*Borden* All Natural) 160
chocolate éclair (*Sealtest*) 160
chocolate, freeze-dried
   (*Mountain House*), 1.25 oz. 160
chocolate peanut sundae (*Sealtest*) 170
coffee (*Breyers*) 140
coffee (*Sealtest*) 140
heavenly hash (*Sealtest*) 150
mint (*Foremost* San Francisco Mint) 140
mint chocolate chip (*Breyers*) 170
peach (*Breyers*) 140
peach (*Sealtest*) 130
peach, Alberta (*Häagen-Dazs*) 251
rum raisin (*Häagen-Dazs*) 264
strawberry (*Borden*) 120
strawberry (*Breyers*) 130
strawberry (*Foremost*) 120
strawberry (*Howard Johnson's*) 187
strawberry (*Meadow Gold*) 126
strawberry, freeze-dried
   (*Mountain House*), 1.25 oz. 170
vanilla (*Borden*) 130
vanilla (*Breyers*) 150
vanilla (*Foremost*) 130
vanilla (*Hood*) 130
vanilla (*Howard Johnson's*) 210
vanilla (*Meadow Gold*) 126
vanilla, freeze-dried (*Mountain House*), 1.25 oz. 190
vanilla, French (*Borden*) 140
vanilla, French (*Borden* All Natural) 150
vanilla, French (*Lady Borden*) 170
vanilla, w/fudge (*Breyers* Vanilla Fudge Twirl) 160
vanilla, w/fudge (*Sealtest* Fudge Royale) 150
ice cream, non-dairy, all flavors (*Meadow Gold*) 126
ice cream bars:
   (*Good Humor* Milky Pop), 1.5 fl. oz. 60

ice cream bars, continued

assorted (*Good Humor Whammy*), 1.6 fl. oz.   90
vanilla, chocolate-coated (*Eskimo Pie*), 3 fl. oz.   180
vanilla, chocolate-coated
   (*Good Humor*), 3 fl. oz.   170
vanilla, toasted almond-coated
   (*Good Humor* Toasted Almond), 3 fl. oz.   190
vanilla, toasted caramel-coated
   (*Good Humor* Toasted Caramel), 3 fl. oz.   170
vanilla w/chocolate fudge, cake-coated
   (*Good Humor* Chocolate Eclair), 3 fl. oz.   180
ice cream cookie sandwich, all flavors
   (*Good Humor*), 2.7 fl. oz.   290
ice cream cookie sandwich, all flavors
   (*Good Humor*), 4 fl. oz.   400
ice cream sandwich, mint
   (*Foremost* San Francisco Mint), 1 sandwich*   190
ice cream sandwich, vanilla
   (*Good Humor*), 2.5 fl. oz.   170
ice milk:
chocolate (*Borden* All Natural)   110
chocolate (*Foremost Big Dip*)   100
strawberry (*Borden* All Natural)   110
strawberry (*Foremost Big Dip*)   110
vanilla (*Foremost Big Dip*)   110
vanilla (*Hood Nuform*)   100
vanilla (*Meadow Gold*)   95
ice milk, non-dairy, all flavors (*Meadow Gold*)   106
ice, orange (*Sealtest*)   150
ice stripes (*Good Humor*), 1.5 fl.-oz. pop   40
sherbet:
fruit flavors (*Meadow Gold*)   120
lemon (*Borden*)   110
lemon (*Sealtest*)   140
lemon-lime (*Sealtest*)   140
lime (*Foremost*)   110
lime (*Sealtest*)   140
orange (*Borden*)   110
orange (*Foremost*)   110
orange (*Hood*)   110
orange (*Howard Johnson's*)   132
orange (*Sealtest*)   140

Ice Cream & Frozen Confections, sherbet, continued

pineapple (*Foremost*)	100
pineapple (*Sealtest*)	130
rainbow (*Sealtest*)	140
raspberry (*Foremost*)	110
raspberry, red (*Sealtest*)	140
strawberry (*Foremost*)	100
strawberry (*Sealtest*)	130
sherbet bar, fudge (*Fudgsicle*), 2½ fl. oz.	110

*As packaged

ICE CREAM CONES & CUPS, one piece, as packaged

	calories
cones, all flavors (*Comet*)	20
cones, rolled sugar (*Comet*)	40
cups, all flavors (*Comet*)	20

Chapter 23

NUTS, CHIPS, PRETZELS AND RELATED SNACKS

NUTS & SEEDS, SHELLED,
one ounce, except as noted
See also "Nut Butters"

---

                                    calories

almonds:
  (*Fisher*) 178
  (*Planters*) 170
  dry roasted (*Fisher*) 175
  dry roasted (*Planters*) 170
  raw (*Fisher*) 170
cashews:
  (*Fisher*) 159
  (*Frito-Lay*), 1-oz. pkg. 170
  (*Planters*) 170
  dry roasted (*Fisher*) 156
  dry roasted (*Planters*) 160
  dry roasted, unsalted (*Planters*) 160
  unsalted (*Planters*) 170
  w/almonds (*Fisher*) 168
granola "nuts" (*Flavor Tree*) 170
mixed nuts:
  dry roasted (*Planters*) 170
  fancy (*Fisher*) 170
  with peanuts (*Fisher*) 167
  with peanuts (*Planters*) 180
  without peanuts (*Planters*) 180
  unsalted (*Planters*) 180

Nuts & Seeds, Shelled, continued

peanuts:
   (*Planters* Lite) 90
   blanched, dry roasted (*Fisher*) 163
   blanched, roasted (*Fisher*) 166
   cocktail (*Planters*) 170
   dry roasted (*Frito-Lay*) 170
   dry roasted (*Planters*) 160
   dry roasted, unsalted (*Planters*) 170
   in shell, roasted (*Fisher*) 105
   in shell, roasted (*Planters*) 160
   in shell, salted (*Frito-Lay*) 160
   in shell, salted (*Planters*) 160
   salted (*Frito-Lay*) 170
   Spanish (*Planters*) 170
   Spanish, dry roasted (*Planters*) 160
   Spanish, raw (*Planters*) 150
   Spanish, roasted (*Fisher*) 165
   unsalted (*Planters*) 170
   w/raisins, dry roasted (*Fisher*) 130
pecans (*Planters*) 190
pecans, raw (*Fisher*) 195
pistachios, red, in shell (*Planters*) 170
pistachios, in shell (*Fisher*) 84
sesame buds w/garlic (*Flavor Tree*) 160
sesame nut mix (*Planters*) 160
sesame nut mix, dry roasted (*Planters*) 160
sesame "nuts" (*Flavor Tree*) 180
soy nuts, roasted, all varieties (*Malt-O-Meal*) 140
sunflower kernels:
   (*Frito-Lay*) 180
   dry roasted (*Planters*) 160
   roasted (*Planters*) 170
   unsalted (*Planters*) 170
   w/sesames (*Flavor Tree*) 158
sunflower seeds:
   (*Frito-Lay*) 170
   (*Planters*) 160
   dry roasted (*Fisher*) 164
   in shell, roasted (*Fisher*) 86
   shelled, dry roasted (*Fisher*) 164
tavern nuts (*Planters*) 170

Nuts & Seeds, Shelled, continued
walnuts:
  (*Diamond*) 192
  black (*Planters*) 180
  black, raw (*Fisher*) 178
  English (*Planters*) 190
  English, raw (*Fisher*) 185
wheat "nuts" (*Flavor Tree*) 190

CHIPS, PUFFS & SIMILAR SNACKS, one ounce
See also "Popcorn," "Pretzels," "Crackers"
and "Nuts & Seeds, Shelled"

---

          calories
Cheddar sticks (*Flavor Tree*) 160
corn chips:
  (*Bachmans*) 150
  (*Flavor Tree*) 150
  (*Frito's*) 160
  (*Frito's* Lite) 160
  (*Planters*) 160
  (*Wise* Corn Crunchies) 160
  barbecue flavor (*Frito's* Bar-B-Q) 160
  curls (*Buenos* Crispy) 180
corn crisps and puffs:
  (*Borden Lite-Line* Cheese Curls) 130
  (*Bugles*) 150
  (Cheddar *Flings* Crunchy) 160
  (Cheddar *Flings* Puffed) 150
  (*Cheese 'n Crunch*) 160
  (*Chee•tos* balls or puffs) 160
  (*Chee•tos* Crunchy) 160
  (*Cheez Doodles*) 160
  (*Cheez Doodles* crunchy) 160
  (*Diggers*) 150
  (*Guy's* Baked Cheese Balls) 160
  (*Jax*) 150
  (*Jax* Crunchy) 160
  (*Jax O's*) 150

Chips, Puffs & Similar Snacks, corn crisps and puffs, continued

(*Old London* Cheese Puffs) 160
(*Old London* Crunchy Cheese Puffs) 160
(*Planters* Cheez Balls) 160
(*Planters* Cheez Balls) 160
(*Planters* Cheez Curls) 160
(*Wise* Cheese Puffs) 160
nacho cheese (*Bugles*) 160
corn sticks, buttered and flavored (*Flavor Tree*) 160
(*Fiddle Faddle*) 125
party mix (*Flavor Tree*) 160
party mix (*Flavor Tree*—no salt added) 160
pork rinds, fried (*Baken•Ets*) 150
potato chips:
  (*Bachmans*) 160
  (*Chipsters*) 120
  (*Lay's*) 150
  (*Pringle's*) 170
  (*Pringle's* Light) 150
  (*Pringle's* Rippled Style) 170
  (*Ruffles*) 150
  (*Wise*) 150
  bacon and sour cream flavor (*Ruffles*) 160
  barbecue flavor (*Bachmans* Bar-B-Q) 150
  barbecue flavor (*Lay's* Bar-B-Q) 150
  barbecue flavor (*Mortons Ridgies*) 150
  barbecue flavor (*Ruffles* Bar-B-Q) 150
  barbecue flavor (*Wise*) 150
  cheese (*Pringle's Cheez-ums*) 170
  ketchup and French fry (*Buckeye*) 160
  natural (*Wise*) 160
  sour cream and onion flavor (*Bachmans*) 150
  sour cream and onion flavor (*Lay's*) 160
  sour cream and onion flavor (*Ruffles*) 160
  sour cream and onion flavor (*Wise*) 170
  unsalted (*Bachmans*) 160
  vinegar (*Bachmans*) 150
potato crisps (*Munchos*) 150
potato sticks (*O & C*) 154
onion flavor rings (*Funyuns*) 140
onion flavor rings (*Wise*) 130
(*Screaming Yellow Zonkers*) 121

Chips, Puffs & Similar Snacks, continued

sesame chips (*Flavor Tree*) 150
sesame sticks:
  (*Flavor Tree*) 150
  (*Flavor Tree* — no salt added) 160
  w/bran (*Flavor Tree*) 160
sour cream and onion sticks (*Flavor Tree*) 150
tortilla chips:
  (*Bachmans*) 140
  (*Buenos* Crispy Round) 150
  (*Buenos* — triangular) 150
  (*Doritos*) 140
  (*Doritos* Crispy Light) 150
  (*Planters*) 150
  (*Tostitos*) 140
  nacho cheese flavor (*Bachmans*) 140
  nacho cheese flavor (*Borden Lite-Line*) 130
  nacho cheese flavor (*Bravos*) 150
  nacho cheese flavor (*Buenos*) 150
  nacho cheese flavor (*Buenos* Crispy Round) 150
  nacho cheese flavor (*Buenos* — triangular) 150
  nacho cheese flavor (*Doritos*) 140
  nacho cheese flavor (*Doritos* Crispy Light) 150
  nacho cheese flavor (*Nabisco*) 140
  nacho cheese flavor (*Planters*) 150
  nacho cheese flavor (*Tostitos*) 150
  nacho cheese flavor (*Wise*) 150
  sour cream and onion flavor (*Doritos*) 140
  taco flavor (*Bachmans*) 140
  taco flavor (*Doritos*) 140
  taco flavor (*Wise*) 150

POPCORN, one ounce, except as noted

---

                                          calories

(*Bachmans*) 160
(*Jiffy Pop*), 1.5 oz. 180
butter flavor (*Jiffy Pop*), 1.5 oz. 210
butter flavor (*Wise*) 140

Popcorn, continued
cheese flavor:
  (*Bachmans*) 180
  (*Frito-Lay*) 150
  (*Wise*) 180
microwave:
  plain (*Orville Redenbacker* Gourmet Popcorn),
    1 cup 35
  plain (*Pillsbury*), 1 cup 65
  butter flavor
    (*Orville Redenbacher* Gourmet Popcorn),
    1 cup 35
  butter flavor (*Pillsbury*), 1 cup 65
  unsalted (*Pillsbury*), 1 cup 48
salted (*Frito-Lay*) 150
white (*Jiffy Pop* Popping Corn), 1.6 oz. 160
yellow (*Jiffy Pop* Popping Corn), 1.6 oz. 160

PRETZELS, one ounce, except as noted

---

                                             calories
beer (*Quinlan*) 110
bite-size:
  (*Bachmans Nutzels*) 110
  (*Old London Pretz-L Nuggets*) 110
  (*Wise*) 110
butter thins (*Bachmans*) 110
(*Estee*—unsalted), 15 pieces 75
logs (*Quinlan*) 108
(*Mr. Salty*) 110
(*Mr. Salty* Dutch) 110
nibs (*Bachmans*) 110
petites (*Bachmans*) 110
petites (*Bachmans*—low salt) 110
rings (*Bachmans*) 110
rods:
  (*Bachmans*) 110
  (*Quinlan*) 103
  (*Rold Gold*) 110
(*Rold Gold* Tiny Tim) 110

Pretzels, continued

sticks:

    (*Bachmans*) 93
    (*Mr. Salty*) 110
    (*Mr. Salty Veri-Thin*), 1 oz. or 90 sticks 110
    (*Rold Gold*) 110

thins:

    (*Quinlan* Extra Thins) 107
    (*Quinlan* Tiny Thins) 111
    unsalted (*Quinlan* Tiny Thins) 116

twists:

    (*Planters*) 110
    (*Mr. Salty*) 110
    (*Rold Gold*) 110

GRANOLA & SIMILAR SNACKS

calories

cinnamon
    (*Nature Valley Light & Crunchy*), 1 pouch* 130
honey nut
    (*Nature Valley Light & Crunchy*), 1 pouch* 140
oatmeal and apple (*Nabisco* Soft Snacks), 1 pkg.* 120
oatmeal and raspberry
    (*Nabisco* Soft Snacks), 1 pkg.* 140
oats 'n honey
    (*Nature Valley Light & Crunchy*), 1 pouch* 130
peanut butter
    (*Nature Valley Light & Crunchy*), 1 pouch* 200
w/raisins (*Nabisco* Soft Snacks), 1 pkg.* 120
raisins and nuts (*Carnation*), .9-oz. pouch 130
raspberry glaze
    (*Nature Valley Light & Crunchy*), 1 pouch* 190
trail mix (*Carnation*), .9-oz. pouch 130
vanilla glaze
    (*Nature Valley Light & Crunchy*), 1 pouch* 190

As packaged

Chapter 24

COCOA, COFFEE, TEA AND SOFT DRINKS

> **COCOA & FLAVORED MIXES, DRY,**
> one ounce, except as noted
> See also "Dessert Toppings & Syrups"
> and "Flavored Milk Beverages"

	calories
eggnog flavor (*Ovaltine*)	113
carob (*CaraCoa*), 4 heaping tsp.	45
chocolate flavor:	
(*Alba '77 Fit 'N Frosty*), 1 pouch*	70
(*Hershey* Instant), 3 tbsp.	80
(*Nestlé Quik*), 2 tsp.	90
(*Ovaltine*), ¾ oz.	80
chocolate-marshmallow	
(*Alba '77 Fit 'N Frosty*), 1 pouch*	70
cocoa:	
(*Hershey*)	120
(*Hershey* Hot Cocoa Mix)	120
(*Nestlé* Hot Cocoa Mix)	110
(*Ovaltine* Hot Cocoa Mix)	120
(*Superman* Hot Cocoa Mix), 1 pouch*	70
(*Swiss Miss*)	110
(*Swiss Miss*—sugar-free), .5 oz. serving	50
(*Swiss Miss* Double Rich)	110
freeze-dried (*Mountain House*)	110
chocolate marshmallow	
(*Alba* Hot Cocoa Mix), 1 pouch*	60

cocoa, continued

chocolate, w/mini-marshmallows
  (*Carnation* Instant Hot Cocoa Mix) 109
chocolate, w/marshmallows
  (*Nestlé* Hot Cocoa Mix) 110
chocolate, w/mini-marshmallows (*Swiss Miss*) 110
milk chocolate (*Alba* Hot Cocoa Mix), 1 pouch* 60
milk chocolate
  (*Carnation* Instant Hot Cocoa Mix) 112
mocha (*Alba* Hot Cocoa Mix), 1 pouch* 60
rich chocolate
  (*Carnation* Instant Hot Cocoa Mix) 112
  dietetic (*Estee*) 8
malted flavor:
  (*Ovaltine*), ¾ oz. 80
  chocolate (*Carnation* Instant), ¾ oz. 85
  natural (*Carnation* Instant), ¾ oz. 90
strawberry flavor:
  (*Alba '77 Fit 'N Frosty*), 1 pouch* 70
  (*Nestlé Quik*), 2 tsp. 90
  (*Ovaltine*), .54 oz. 60
vanilla flavor (*Alba '77 Fit 'N Frosty*), 1 pouch* 70

*As packaged

COFFEE, six fluid ounces

calories

plain:
  ground roasted, prepared* (*Brim*) 2
  ground roasted, prepared* (*Maxwell House*) 2
  ground roasted, prepared* (*Sanka*) 2
  ground roasted, prepared* (*Yuban*) 2
  ground roasted, w/grain, prepared*
    (*Mellow Roast*) 8
  instant* (*Kava*) 2
  instant* (*Maxwell House*) 4
  instant* (*Nescafé*) 4
  instant* (*Nescafé* Decaffeinated) 4
  instant* (*Sanka*) 4

Coffee, plain, continued

  instant* (*Yuban*) 4
  instant*, freeze-dried (*Brim*) 4
  instant*, freeze-dried (*Maxim*) 4
  instant*, freeze-dried (*Mountain House*) 0
  instant*, freeze-dried (*Sanka*) 4
  instant*, freeze-dried (*Taster's Choice*) 4
  instant*, freeze-dried
    (*Taster's Choice* Decaffeinated) 4
  instant*, w/grain (*Mellow Roast*) 8
flavored, prepared*:
  Amaretto
    (*General Foods* International Coffees *LeCafé*) 4
  café Amaretto
    (*General Foods* International Coffees) 50
  café Français
    (*General Foods* International Coffees) 60
  café Irish Creme
    (*General Foods* International Coffees) 60
  café Vienna
    (*General Foods* International Coffees) 60
  cinnamon
    (*General Foods* International Coffees *LeCafé*) 4
  Irish Mocha Mint
    (*General Foods* International Coffees) 50
  mocha
    (*General Foods* International Coffees *LeCafé*) 4
  orange cappuccino
    (*General Foods* International Coffees) 60
  Suisse mocha
    (*General Foods* International Coffees) 60
  imitation (*Celestial Seasonings Roastaroma*) 10

Prepared according to package directions

TEA, six fluid ounces, except as noted

---

calories

regular, loose or bags*:
almond (*Lipton Almond Pleasure*), 1 cup   4
Amaretto (*Lipton*), 1 cup   2
apple, spicy (*Lipton*), 1 cup   2
(*Bigelow Constant Comment*)   1
(*Bigelow* Earl Grey)   1
(*Bigelow* English Teatime)   1
(*Bigelow* Orange Pekoe)   1
(*Lipton*)   2
(*Tetley*)   3
blackberry (*Lipton*), 1 cup   2
cherry almond (*Lipton*), 1 cup   2
cinnamon (*Bigelow Cinnamon Stick*)   1
cinnamon (*Lipton*)   2
citrus (*Lipton Citrus Sunset*), 1 cup   4
lemon (*Bigelow Lemon Lift*)   1
lemon and spice (*Lipton*)   2
mint (*Bigelow Peppermint Stick*)   1
mint (*Bigelow Plantation Mint*)   1
mint (*Lipton*)   2
mint (*Lipton Roasty Mint*), 1 cup   4
orange and spice (*Lipton*)   2
spice (*Lipton Toasty Spice*), 1 cup   6
herbal, loose or bags*:
almond
    (*Celestial Seasonings Almond Sunset*), 1 cup   6
almond orange (*Bigelow*), 1 cup   1
apple (*Bigelow Apple Orchard*), 1 cup   5
apple
    (*Celestial Seasonings Country Apple*), 1 cup   4
apple spice (*Bigelow*), 1 cup   1
(*Bigelow Early Riser*)   3
(*Bigelow Feeling Free*)   1
(*Bigelow Looking Good*)   1
(*Bigelow Mint Medley*)   1
(*Bigelow Nice Over Ice*)   1

Tea, herbal, loose or bags, continued

(*Bigelow Sweet Dreams*) 1
(*Bigelow Take-A-Break*) 3
(*Celestial Seasonings Diet Partner*), 1 cup 5
(*Celestial Seasonings Emperor's Choice*), 1 cup 4
(*Celestial Seasonings Morning Thunder*), 1 cup 3
(*Celestial Seasonings Mo's 24*), 1 cup 2
(*Celestial Seasonings Pelican Punch*), 1 cup 3
(*Celestial Seasonings Red Zinger*), 1 cup 5
(*Celestial Seasonings Sleepytime*), 1 cup 2
(*Celestial Seasonings Sunburst C*), 1 cup 3
chamomile (*Celestial Seasonings*), 1 cup 2
chamomile (*Lipton*), 1 cup 4
chamomile mint (*Bigelow*), 1 cup 1
cinnamon
   (*Celestial Seasonings Cinnamon Rose*), 1 cup 3
cinnamon apple (*Lipton*), 1 cup 2
cranberry
   (*Celestial Seasonings Cranberry Cove*), 1 cup 3
ginseng
   (*Celestial Seasonings Ginseng Plus*), 1 cup 3
hibiscus and rose hips (*Bigelow*), 1 cup 1
lemon (*Bigelow I Love Lemon*), 1 cup 1
lemon (*Bigelow Lemon & C*), 1 cup 1
lemon (*Celestial Seasonings Lemon Mist*), 1 cup 2
lemon (*Lipton* Lemon Soother), 1 cup 4
mandarin orange spice
   (*Celestial Seasonings*), 1 cup 8
mint (*Bigelow Mint Blend*), 1 cup 1
mint (*Celestial Seasonings Grandma's Tummy Mint*),
   1 cup 2
mint (*Celestial Seasonings Mellow Mint*), 1 cup 2
mint (*Celestial Seasonings Peppermint*), 1 cup 2
mint (*Celestial Seasonings Spearmint*), 1 cup 5
orange (*Bigelow Orange & C*), 1 cup 1
orange (*Lipton* Tangy Orange), 1 cup 4
orange (*Lipton* Gentle Orange), 1 cup 4
orange spice (*Bigelow*), 1 cup 1
roasted grain and carob (*Bigelow*), 1 cup 3
canned or dairy pack:
lemon flavor, presweetened (*Hood*) 55

Tea, canned or dairy pack, continued

lemon flavor, presweetened (*Lipton*), 8 fl. oz.	80
lemon flavor, sugar-free (*Lipton*), 8 fl. oz.	2

instant and mixes*:

plain (*Lipton*)	2
plain (*Nestea*)	0
herbal, lemon, instant (*Celestial Seasonings Iced Delight*), 1 cup	6
herbal, lemon, mix (*Celestial Seasonings Iced Delight*), 1 cup	9
herbal, orange, instant (*Celestial Seasonings Iced Delight*), 1 cup	6
herbal, orange, mix (*Celestial Seasonings Iced Delight*), 1 cup	6
lemon-flavored (*Lipton*), 8 fl. oz.	4
lemon-flavored (*Nestea*)	2
lemon-flavored, presweetened (*Lipton* Iced Tea Mix), 8 fl. oz.	60
lemon-flavored, presweetened (*Nestea*)	70
lemon-flavored, presweetened (*Wyler's*), 8 fl. oz.	80
lemon-flavored, sugar-free (*Lipton*), 8 fl. oz.	2

*Prepared according to package directions

SOFT DRINKS & MIXERS,
eight fluid ounces, except as noted
See also "Fruit & Fruit-Flavored Drinks,"
"Flavored Milk Beverages"
and "Cocktail Mixes, Nonalcoholic"

---

	calories
apple (*Welch's* Sparkling Soda)	120
bitter lemon (*Schweppes*)	112
blended flavors (*Shasta* Fruit Punch)	112
(*Bubble Up*)	97
cherry:	
(*Crush*)	120
(*Fanta*)	117

Soft Drinks & Mixers, cherry, continued

  black (*Shasta*) 105
chocolate (*Yoo-Hoo*), 9 fl. oz. 170
club soda (all brands) 0
coconut shake (*Yoo-Hoo*), 9½ fl. oz. 150
cola:
  (*Coca-Cola*) 96
  (*Pepsi Cola*) 104
  (*Royal Crown*) 109
  (*Shasta*) 95
  cherry-flavored (*Shasta*) 91
cream:
  (*Schweppes* Red Creme) 112
  (*Shasta*) 100
  brown (*Crush*) 107
  red (*Crush*) 107
(*Dr Pepper*) 96
fruit punch, *see "blended flavors," above*
ginger ale:
  (*Canada Dry*) 93
  (*Schweppes*) 88
  (*Shasta*) 78
  sugar-free (*Canada Dry*) 3
ginger beer (*Schweppes*) 96
grape:
  (*Crush*) 120
  (*Schweppes*) 128
  (*Shasta*) 115
  (*Welch's* Sparkling Soda) 120
grapefruit (*Shasta*) 105
lemon, bitter, *see "bitter lemon," above*
lemonade (*Shasta*) 95
lemon-lime (*Shasta*) 93
lime (*Canada Dry*) 130
mineral water (*Schweppes*) 0
orange:
  (*Crush*) 120
  (*Schweppes* Sparkling Orange) 120
  (*Shasta*) 115
  (*Welch's* Sparkling Soda) 120
pineapple (*Crush*) 120

root beer:

(*Barrelhead*)	106
(*Dads*)	111
(*Hires*)	106
(*Schweppes*)	104
(*Shasta*)	100
(*Welch's*)	113
sugar-free (*Barrelhead*)	5
seltzer (all brands)	0
seltzer, flavored, all flavors (*Canada Dry*)	0
(*7-Up*)	97
(*Squirt*)	104

strawberry:

(*Crush*)	120
(*Shasta*)	95
(*Welch's* Sparkling Soda)	120
shake (*Yoo-Hoo*), 9½ fl. oz.	150

tonic water:

(*Canada Dry*)	93
(*Schweppes*)	88
(*Shasta*)	79
sugar-free (*Canada Dry*)	5
vanilla shake (*Yoo-Hoo*), 9½ fl. oz.	150
vichy water (*Schweppes*)	0

Chapter 25

BONUS SECTION: "FAST-FOOD" CHAINS AND RESTAURANTS

Note: The listings in this section—which are broken down by restaurant rather than by food category—are based on an "average" or a "standard" serving. The caloric content of a serving may vary slightly according to restaurant location. And, of course, individual orders that result in a change of ingredients or quantity of ingredients will alter the caloric value. Wherever possible, the weight of a serving has been included as a guide.

ARBY'S*

---

                                                          calories

Sandwiches:
  Arby's Sub, without dressing, 9.5-oz. sandwich 484
  Beef and Cheddar, 6-oz. sandwich 484
  Chicken Breast, 7¼-oz. sandwich 584
  Croissants:
    Bacon and Egg, 4.5-oz. croissant 420
    Butter, 2-oz. croissant 220
    Ham and Swiss, 4-oz. croissant 330
    Mushroom and Swiss, 4-oz. croissant 340
    Sausage and Egg, 5¾-oz. croissant 530
  French Dip, 5.5-oz. sandwich 386
  Ham and Cheese, 8¼-oz. sandwich 484
  Roast Beef, 5-oz. sandwich 350
  Roast Beef, Deluxe, 8¼-oz. sandwich 486
  Roast Beef, Junior, 3-oz. sandwich 220
  Roast Beef, Super, 9¾-oz. sandwich 620

*See note above

Arby's, continued

Side Dishes and Desserts:

Apple Turnover, 3-oz. turnover	310
Arby's Sauce, 1 oz.	34
Blueberry Turnover, 3-oz. turnover	340
Cherry Turnover, 3-oz. turnover	320
French Fries, 2½-oz. serving	216
Horsey Sauce, 1 oz.	120
Potato Cakes, 3½-oz. cake	95

BASKIN–ROBBINS*

calories

Ice Cream:

Butter Pecan, 1 scoop	136
Chocolate, 1 scoop	165
Chocolate Fudge, 1 scoop	178
Chocolate Mint, 1 scoop	162
Chocolate Mousse Royale, 1 scoop	183
Jamoca, 1 scoop	146
Pralines 'N Cream, 1 scoop	177
Rocky Road, 1 scoop	182
Strawberry, 1 scoop	141
Vanilla, 1 scoop	147
Vanilla, French, 1 scoop	181
Ice, Daiquiri, 1 scoop	84
Ice, Pineapple, 1 scoop	94
Ice Cream Cones, cake, 1 cone	19
Ice Cream Cones, sugar, 1 cone	57

Frozen Dairy Dessert:

Mountain Coffee, low-fat (*Special Diet*), 1 scoop	90
Sunny Orange, low-fat (*Special Diet*), 1 scoop	90
Wild Strawberry, low-fat (*Special Diet*), 1 scoop	80
Sherbet, Orange, 1 scoop	99

See Note on page 291

BURGER KING*

calories

Sandwiches:
Cheeseburger, 1 sandwich	350
Chicken Sandwich, 1 sandwich	690
Double Cheeseburger, 1 sandwich	530
Double Cheeseburger w/Bacon, 1 sandwich	600
Hamburger, 1 sandwich	290
Veal Parmigiana, 1 sandwich	600
Whaler, 1 sandwich	540
Whopper, 1 sandwich	630
Whopper w/Cheese, 1 sandwich	740
Whopper, Double Beef, 1 sandwich	850
Whopper, Double Beef w/Cheese, 1 sandwich	950
Whopper Jr., 1 sandwich	370
Whopper Jr. w/Cheese, 1 sandwich	420

Side Dishes and Dessert:
Apple Pie, 1 piece	240
French Fries, 1 regular serving	210
Onion Rings, 1 regular serving	270

Beverages:
Chocolate Shake, 1 serving	340
Vanilla Shake, 1 serving	340
Coca-Cola, 1 medium serving	121
Diet Pepsi, 1 medium serving	7

*See Note on page 291

CHURCH'S FRIED CHICKEN*

calories

Chicken, boned, dark meat, 3½-oz. piece	305
Chicken, boned, white meat, 3½-oz. piece	327

*See Note on page 291

DAIRY QUEEN/BRAZIER*

calories

Dairy Queen:
Banana Split, 13½-oz. serving 540
Buster Bar, 5¼-oz. bar 460
Double Delight, 9-oz. serving 490
Cone, 3-oz. small cone 140
Cone, 5-oz. regular cone 240
Cone, 7½-oz. large cone 340
Cone, Dipped**, 3¼-oz. small cone 190
Cone, Dipped**, 5½-oz. regular cone 340
Cone, Dipped**, 8¼-oz. large cone 510
Dilly Bar, 3-oz. bar 210
DQ Sandwich, 2.12-oz. sandwich 140
Float, 14-oz. serving 410
Freeze, 14-oz. serving 500
Hot Fudge *Brownie Delight,* 9⅓-oz. serving 600
Malt**, 10¼-oz. small serving 520
Malt**, 14¾-oz. regular serving 760
Malt**, 20¾-oz. large serving 1060
Mr. Misty, 8¾-oz. small serving 190
Mr. Misty, 11.7-oz. regular serving 250
Mr. Misty, 15½-oz. large serving 340
Mr. Misty Float, 14½-oz. serving 390
Mr. Misty Freeze, 14½-oz. serving 500
Mr. Misty Kiss, 3.14-oz. serving 70
Parfait, 10-oz. serving 430
Peanut Butter Parfait, 10¾-oz. serving 740
Shake**, 10½-oz. small serving 490
Shake**, 14¾-oz. regular serving 710
Shake**, 20¾-oz. large serving 990
Strawberry Shortcake, 11-oz. serving 540
Sundae**, 3¾-oz. small serving 190
Sundae**, 6¼-oz. regular serving 310
Sundae**, 8¾-oz. large serving 440
Brazier:
Chicken Sandwich, 7¾-oz. sandwich 670
Fish Sandwich, 6-oz. sandwich 400

Dairy Queen/Brazier, continued

Fish Sandwich w/Cheese, 6¼-oz. sandwich 440
Hamburger, "Single,"
   ⅙ lb. precooked, 5.2-oz. sandwich 360
Hamburger, "Double,"
   ⅓ lb. precooked, 7.4-oz. sandwich 530
Hamburger, "Double" w/Cheese,
   8.4-oz. sandwich 650
Hamburger, "Triple,"
   ½ lb. precooked, 9.6-oz. sandwich 710
Hamburger, "Triple" w/Cheese,
   10.6-oz. sandwich 820
Hot Dog, 3½-oz. sandwich 280
Hot Dog w/Cheese, 4-oz. sandwich 330
Hot Dog w/Chili, 4½-oz. sandwich 320
Hot Dog, Super, 6.2-oz. sandwich 520
Hot Dog, Super w/Cheese, 6.9-oz. sandwich 580
Hot Dog, Super w/Chili, 7.7-oz. sandwich 570
French Fries, 2½-oz. regular serving 200
French Fries, 4-oz. large serving 320
Onion Rings, 3-oz. serving 280

*See Note on page 291
**Chocolate

HARDEE'S*

calories

Egg and Biscuit Dishes:
  Bacon Biscuit w/Egg, 4-oz. serving 405
  Biscuit, 2.9-oz. biscuit 275
  Biscuit w/Jelly, 3½-oz. serving 324
  Biscuit w/Egg, 5.6-oz. serving 383
  Fried Egg, 1¾-oz. medium egg 108
  Ham Biscuit, 3.8-oz. serving 349
  Ham Biscuit w/Egg, 6½-oz. serving 458
  Sausage Biscuit, 4-oz. serving 413
  Steak Biscuit w/Egg, 5.7-oz. serving 527

Hardee's, continued

Sandwiches:

Bacon Cheeseburger, 8.6-oz. sandwich	686
Big Deluxe, 8.7-oz. sandwich	546
Big Roast Beef, 5.9-oz. sandwich	418
Cheeseburger, 4.1-oz. sandwich	335
Chicken Fillet, 6.8-oz. sandwich	510
Fisherman's Fillet, 6.9-oz. sandwich	469
Hamburger, 3.9-oz. sandwich	305
Hot Dog, 4.2-oz. sandwich	346
Hot Ham 'N Cheese, 5.2-oz. sandwich	376
Mushroom 'N Swiss, 7.2-oz. sandwich	512
Roast Beef Sandwich, 5-oz. sandwich	377
Turkey Club, 6.8-oz. sandwich	426

Side Dishes:

Biscuit Gravy, 1 oz.	60
French Fries, 2½-oz. small serving	239
French Fries, 4-oz. large serving	381

Beverage and Dessert:

Apple Turnover, 3.07-oz. turnover	282
Big Cookie, 1.9-oz. cookie	278
Milkshake, 11½-oz. serving	391

*See Note on page 291

KENTUCKY FRIED CHICKEN*

calories

Chicken Breast Fillet Sandwich, 5.5-oz. sandwich	436

Chicken Pieces, Original Recipe:

Drumstick, 1.66-oz. piece**	117
Keel, 3.35-oz. piece**	236
Rib, 2.45-oz. piece**	199
Thigh, 3.1-oz. piece**	257
Wing, 1.5-oz. piece**	136

Chicken Pieces, Extra Crispy:

Drumstick, 2.05-oz. piece**	155
Keel, 3.7-oz. piece**	297
Rib, 3-oz. piece**	286
Thigh, 3.8-oz. piece**	343

Kentucky Fried Chicken, Chicken Pieces, Extra Crispy, continued

Wing, 1.9-oz. piece** 201

Extras:

Potatoes, 3-oz. serving 64

Gravy, 1/2-oz. serving 23

Potatoes and gravy, 3.5-oz. serving 87

Roll, 3/4-oz. roll 61

Corn, 43/4-oz. piece 169

Cole Slaw, 3.2-oz. serving 121

Kentucky Fries, 3.5-oz. serving 184

Dinners***, Original Recipe:

#1—Wing and Rib, extras, 11.4-oz. dinner 604

#2—Wing and Thigh, extras, 12-oz. dinner 661

#3—Drumstick and Thigh, extras,
12.2-oz. dinner 643

Dinners***, Extra Crispy:

#1—Wing and Rib, extras, 12.3-oz. dinner 755

#2—Wing and Thigh, extras, 13.1-oz. dinner 902

#3—Drum and Thigh, extras, 13.2-oz. dinner 765

See Note on page 291

**Average edible serving weight*

****Dinner consists of 2 pieces of chicken, with potatoes and gravy, cole slaw and a roll*

LONG JOHN SILVER'S*

calories

Entrees and Sandwich Platters:

Baked Fish (fish fillet w/sauce, slaw, mixed vegetables)
1 serving 387

Battered Shrimp
(6 shrimp**, fryes, slaw), 1 serving 709

Breaded Shrimp Platter
(shrimp, fryes, slaw, 2 Hush Puppies),
1 serving 962

Catfish Fillet Dinner
(2 fillets, fryes, slaw, 2 Hush Puppies),
1 serving 980

Chicken Planks (4 planks, fryes), 1 serving 662

Long John Silver's, Entrees and Sandwich Platters, continued

Chicken Planks Dinner
(4 planks, fryes, slaw), 1 serving 844
Chicken Sandwich Platter
(sandwich, fryes, slaw), 1 serving 989
Chilled Seafood Combo
(seafood salad, 8 shrimp**, lettuce, tomato, crackers),
1 serving 437
Chilled Shrimp Dinner
(20 shrimp**, lettuce, slaw, crackers),
1 serving 354
Fish & Chicken
(1 fish, 2 chicken planks, fryes, slaw),
1 serving 838
Fish Dinner
(3 fish, fryes, slaw, 2 Hush Puppies),
1 serving 1,180
Fish Dinner, Kitchen-breaded
(2 fish, fryes, slaw, 2 Hush Puppies), 1 serving 816
Fish Dinner, Kitchen-breaded
(3 fish, fryes, slaw, 2 Hush Puppies), 1 serving 938
Fish & Fryes (2 fish, fryes), 1 serving 651
Fish & Fryes (3 fish, fryes), 1 serving 853
Fish & More
(2 fish, fryes, slaw, 2 Hush Puppies), 1 serving 976
Fish Sandwich Platter
(sandwich, fryes, slaw), 1 serving 984
Fried Clams (clams, fryes, slaw), 1 serving 955
Oysters (6 oysters, fryes, slaw), 1 serving 787
Peg Legs (5 peg legs**, fryes), 1 serving 703
Seafood Platter
(1 fish, 2 battered shrimp**, 2 scallops, fryes, slaw,
2 Hush Puppies), 1 serving 974
Seafood Salad
(seafood salad, lettuce, tomato, crackers),
1 serving 471
Scallops (6 scallops, fryes, slaw), 1 serving 746
Treasure Chest
(2 fish, 2 peg legs**, fryes, slaw), 1 serving 1,015
Children's Menu:
1 piece fish, fryes 449
2 chicken planks, fryes 455

Long John Silver's, Children's Menu, continued

   3 peg legs**, fryes 521
   1 piece fish, 1 peg leg**, fryes 540
Individual Pieces and Sandwiches:
   Baked Fish w/sauce, 5.5 oz. 151
   Battered Shrimp, .6-oz. piece** 47
   Breaded Clams, 1 order or 4.7 oz. 526
   Breaded Oyster, .7-oz. piece 60
   Breaded Shrimp, 1 order or 4.7-oz. 388
   Catfish Fillet, 2.7-oz. piece 203
   Chicken Plank, 1.4-oz. piece 104
   Chicken Sandwich, 6.1-oz. sandwich 562
   Chilled Shrimp, .2-oz. piece** 6
   Fish w/batter, 3-oz. piece 202
   Fish, Kitchen-breaded, 2-oz. piece 122
   Fish Sandwich, 6.4-oz. sandwich 555
   Peg Leg w/batter, 1-oz. piece** 91
   Seafood Salad, 5.8-oz. salad 386
   Scallop w/batter, .7-oz. piece 53
Soup and Side Dishes:
   Clam Chowder, 6 fl.-oz. serving 128
   Cole Slaw, drained on fork, 3.5-oz. serving 182
   Corn on the Cob, 5.3-oz. ear** 176
   Fryes, 3-oz. serving 247
   Hush Puppies, 2 pieces 145
   Mixed Vegetables, 4-oz. serving 54
Condiments:
   Catsup, .4-oz. serving 12
   Crackers, 4 pieces 50
   Seafood Sauce, 1.2-oz. serving 34
   Tartar Sauce, 1-oz. serving 119
   Thousand Island, .4-oz. serving 141
Desserts:
   Apple Pie, 4-oz. serving 280
   Cherry Pie, 4-oz. serving 294
   Lemon Meringue Pie, 3.5-oz. serving 200
   Pecan Pie, 4-oz. serving 446
   Pumpkin Pie, 4-oz. serving 251

  *See Note on page 291
  **Edible portion

McDONALD'S*

calories

Breakfast Dishes:
  Egg McMuffin, 4.86-oz. sandwich 327
  English Muffin, Buttered, 2.2-oz. muffin 186
  Hot Cakes w/Butter and Syrup,
    7.54-oz. serving 500
  Pork Sausage, 1.9-oz. sausage patty 206
  Scrambled Eggs, 3.45-oz. serving 180
Sandwiches and Entrees:
  Big Mac, 7.2-oz. sandwich 563
  Cheeseburger, 4-oz. sandwich 307
  Chicken McNuggets, 3.9-oz. serving 314
  Filet-O-Fish, 4.9-oz. sandwich 432
  Hamburger, 3.6-oz. sandwich 255
  Quarter Pounder, 5.84-oz. sandwich 424
  Quarter Pounder w/Cheese, 6.8-oz. sandwich 524
Side Dishes:
  Chicken McNuggets Sauce:
    Barbecue, 1.1-oz. serving 60
    Honey, .5-oz. serving 50
    Hot Mustard, 1.1-oz. serving 63
    Sweet and Sour, 1.1-oz. serving 64
  French Fries, 2.4-oz. serving 220
  Hashbrown Potatoes, 2-oz. serving 125
Beverages:
  Chocolate Shake, 10¼-oz. serving 383
  Strawberry Shake, 10¼-oz. serving 362
  Vanilla Shake, 10¼-oz. serving 352
Desserts:
  Apple Pie, 3-oz. pie 253
  Cherry Pie, 3.1-oz. pie 260
  Chocolate Chip Cookies, 2.43-oz. serving 342
  Ice Cream Cone, 4.1-oz. cone 185
  McDonaldland Cookies, 2.36-oz. serving 308
  Sundaes:
    Caramel, 5.8-oz. serving 328
    Hot Fudge, 5.8-oz. serving 310

McDonald's, Sundaes, continued
    Strawberry, 5.8-oz. serving 289

*See Note on page 291

PONDEROSA*

---

calories

Entree**:
    Chopped Beef, 5.3-oz. serving 324
    Prime Rib, 4.2-oz. serving 286
    Prime Rib, Extra-Cut, 5.99-oz. serving 409
    Rib-Eye, 3.8-oz. serving 259
    Strip Sirloin, 4.7-oz. serving 277
    T-Bone, 6.7-oz. serving 374
    Shrimp, 2.2-oz. or 4 pieces 139
    Shrimp Dinner, 3.5 oz. or 7 pieces 220
    Filet of Sole Dinner, 6 oz. or 2 pieces 251
Sandwiches**:
    Filet of Sole, 1 piece fish 125
    Junior Patty, 1.6 oz. 98
    Single Deluxe, 5.9 oz. 362
Rolls, 4" average roll 118
Side Dishes and Condiments:
    Baked Potato, 7.2-oz. potato 145
    Catsup, 1 tbsp. 18
    Cocktail Sauce, 1½ oz. 57
    Dill Pickle, 3 slices 2
    French Fries, 3-oz. serving 230
    Lemon Wedge, 1 piece 5
    Lettuce, 3 oz. 12
    Lettuce, .5 oz. 2
    Mustard, 1 tsp. 4
    Onion, chopped, 1 tbsp. 4
    Salad Dressings:
        Blue Cheese, 7/16 oz. 56
        Creamy Italian, 7/16 oz. 60
        French, 7/16 oz. 56
        Thousand Island, 7/16 oz. 51

Ponderosa, Side Dishes and Condiments, continued

Oil and Vinegar, 7/16 oz.	54
Steak Sauce, 7/16 oz.	10
Tartar Sauce, 1 tbsp.	95
Tomato, 3.5-oz. tomato	22
Tomato Slices, 2 slices	6

*See Note on page 291
**Meat or fish portion only—does not include bun, condiments and/or side dishes

---

WENDY'S*

calories

Breakfast Dishes:	
Bacon, 2 strips	110
Breakfast Sandwich, 4.5-oz. sandwich	370
Danish, 3-oz. piece	360
French Toast, 2 slices	400
Ham and Cheese Omelet, 4-oz. serving	250
Ham, Cheese and Mushroom Omelet, 4.2-oz. serving	290
Ham, Cheese, Onion and Green Pepper Omelet, 4.4-oz. serving	280
Home Fries, 3.6-oz. serving	360
Mushroom, Onion and Green Pepper Omelet, 4-oz. serving	210
Sausage, 1.6-oz. patty	200
Scrambled Eggs, 3.2-oz. serving	190
Toast w/margarine, 2 slices	250
Chicken Sandwich, on wheat bun, 4.5-oz. sandwich	320
Chili, 8-oz. serving	260
Hamburgers:	
Single, on wheat bun, 4.2-oz. sandwich	340
Single, on white bun, 4.1-oz. sandwich	350
Double, on white bun, 6.9-oz. sandwich	560
Bacon Cheeseburger, on white bun, 5.2-oz. sandwich	460
Kid's Meal, 2-oz. hamburger	220

Wendy's, continued

Condiments:

American cheese, 1 slice 70
Bacon, 3 half strips 90
Ketchup, 1 tsp. 6
Lettuce, 1/2-oz. piece 2
Mayonnaise, 1 tbsp. 100
Mustard, 1 tsp. 4
Onion, 1/3-oz. slice 4
Pickles, Dill, 4 slices 1
Relish, 1/3 oz. 14
Tomato, 1 slice 2

Salad Bar:

Alfalfa Sprouts, 2-oz. serving 20
American Cheese, 1-oz. serving 70
Bacon Bits, 1/8-oz. serving 10
Banana Peppers, 1 tbsp. 18
Bell Peppers, 1/4-cup serving 4
Blueberries, fresh, 1 tbsp. 8
Breadstick, 1 piece 20
Broccoli, 1/2-cup serving 14
Cantaloupe, fresh, 2 pieces or 2 oz. 4
Carrots, 1/4-cup serving 12
Cauliflower, 1/2-cup serving 14
Cheddar Cheese, 1-oz. serving 90
Chow Mein Noodles, 1/4-cup serving 60
Cole Slaw, 1/2-cup serving 90
Cottage Cheese, 1/2-cup serving 110
Croutons, 18 pieces 30
Cucumbers, 1/4-cup serving 4
Eggs, 1 tbsp. 14
Green Peas, 1/2-cup serving 60
Jalapeño Peppers, 1 tbsp. 9
Lettuce, Iceberg, 1-cup serving 8
Lettuce, Romaine, 1-cup serving 10
Mozzarella Cheese, 1-oz. serving 90
Mushrooms, 1/4-cup serving 6
Onions, Red, 1 tbsp. 4
Oranges, fresh, 2 pieces 10
Pasta Salad, 1/2-cup serving 134
Peaches in Syrup, 2 pieces 17
Pepperoncini, Mild, 1 tbsp. 18

Wendy's, Salad Bar, continued

Pineapple Chunks in Juice, 1/2-cup serving 80
Saltine Crackers, 4 pieces 45
Sunflower Seeds and Raisins, 1-oz. serving 80
Swiss Cheese, 1-oz. serving 80
Tomatoes, 1-oz. serving 6
Turkey Ham, 1/4-cup serving 46
Watermelon, Fresh, 2 pieces or 2 oz. 3

Salad Dressings:
Bleu Cheese, 1 tbsp. 60
Celery Seed, 1 tbsp. 70
Golden Italian, 1 tbsp. 45
Oil, 1 tbsp. 130
Ranch, 1 tbsp. 80
Red French, 1 tbsp. 70
Thousand Island, 1 tbsp. 70
Wine Vinegar, 1 tbsp. 2
Reduced-calorie Bacon & Tomato, 1 tbsp. 45
Reduced-calorie Creamy Cucumber, 1 tbsp. 50
Reduced-calorie Italian, 1 tbsp. 25
Reduced-calorie Thousand Island, 1 tbsp. 45

Side Dishes:
French Fries, 3.5-oz. serving 280
Hot Stuffed Potatoes:
Plain, 8.8-oz. serving 250
Bacon and Cheese, 12.3-oz. serving 570
Broccoli and Cheese, 12.9-oz. serving 500
Cheese, 12.3-oz. serving 590
Chicken à la King, 12.6-oz. serving 350
Chili and Cheese, 14.1-oz. serving 510
Sour Cream and Chives, 11-oz. serving 460
Stroganoff and Sour Cream, 14.3-oz. serving ... 490
Pick-up Window Side Salad, 18-oz. serving 110
Taco Salad, 12.6-oz. serving 390

Beverages and Desserts:
Chocolate Milk, 8 fl.-oz. serving 210
Coffee, 6 fl.-oz. serving 2
Cola, 12 fl.-oz. serving 110
Frosty Dairy Dessert, 12 fl.-oz. serving 400
Fruit Flavored Drink, 12 fl.-oz. serving 110
Hot Chocolate, 6 fl.-oz. serving 100
Iced Tea, 12 fl.-oz. serving 0

Wendy's, Beverages and Desserts, continued

Milk, 8 fl.-oz. serving 150
Noncola, 12 fl.-oz. serving 100
Orange Juice, 6 fl.-oz. serving 80
Tea, 6 fl.-oz. serving 0

*See Note on page 291

Chapter 26

SPIRITS, WINES, LIQUEURS, BEER AND RELATED DRINKS

> **DISTILLED SPIRITS***, one fluid ounce
> Unlike other products in this book, distilled spirits are not listed by brand name. The calorie content in *any* distilled spirit is determined entirely by the amount of alcohol it contains. The higher the proof (alcoholic content), the more calories in the spirit. Different brands of liquor may not taste the same, but if they are the same proof there is no difference in their caloric content. This applies only to distilled spirits. The calories in other kinds of alcoholic beverages— wines, liqueurs, etc.—are likely to vary by brand, depending on proof and sugar content.

	calories
80 proof	67
84 proof	70
86 proof	72
86.8 proof	72
90 proof	75
90.4 proof	75
94 proof	78
94.6 proof	79
97 proof	81
100 proof	83
104 proof	87

**Applejack, bourbon, brandy, gin, rum, tequila and vodka; blended Canadian, Irish and rye whiskey; Scotch whisky*

COCKTAILS, BOTTLED, ALCOHOLIC, one fluid ounce
See also "Cocktail Mixes, Nonalcoholic"
and "Distilled Spirits"

calories

daiquiri (*Calvert*), 60 proof 63
mai-tai (*Lemon Hart*), 48 proof 60
Manhattan (*Calvert*), 60 proof 54
Margarita (*Calvert*), 55 proof 59
martini, gin (*Calvert* Martini), 70 proof 59
martini, vodka (*Calvert* Vodka Martini), 75 proof 63
screwdriver, vodka (*Old Mr. Boston*), 25 proof 39
sour, gin (*Calvert*), 60 proof 65
sour, tequila (*Calvert*), 55 proof 61
sour, whiskey (*Calvert*), 60 proof 65
Tom Collins (*Calvert*), 60 proof 65

COCKTAIL MIXES, NONALCOHOLIC*
See also "Cocktails, Bottled, Alcoholic"
and "Soft Drinks & Mixers"

calories

liquid, bottled:
   Amaretto (*Holland House*), 1 fl. oz. 79
   apricot sour (*Holland House*), 1 fl. oz. 48
   black Russian (*Holland House*), 1 fl. oz. 92
   blackberry sour (*Holland House*), 1 fl. oz. 50
Bloody Mary:
   regular (*Holland House*), 1 fl. oz. 10
   extra tangy (*Holland House*), 1 fl. oz. 10
   smooth 'n spicy (*Holland House*), 1 fl. oz. 6
bullshot cocktail (*Steero* Original), 8-oz. can 33
cocktail host (*Holland House*), 1 fl. oz. 47
daiquiri (*Holland House*), 1 fl. oz. 51
dry martini (*Holland House*), 1 fl. oz. 10
gimlet (*Holland House*), 1 fl. oz. 40

Cocktail Mixes, Nonalcoholic, continued

mai-tai (*Holland House*), 1 fl. oz. 33
Manhattan (*Holland House*), 1 fl. oz. 33
Margarita (*Holland House*), 1 fl. oz. 39
old-fashioned (*Holland House*), 1 fl. oz. 36
piña colada (*Holland House*), 1 fl. oz. 60
sip 'n slim (*Holland House*), 1 fl. oz. 9
strawberry sting (*Holland House*), 1 fl. oz. 35
Tom Collins (*Holland House*), 1 fl. oz. 67
whiskey sour (*Holland House*), 1 fl. oz. 55
instant mixes, dry:
  Alexander (*Holland House*), 1 packet 69
  banana daiquiri (*Holland House*), 1 packet 66
  Bloody Mary (*Holland House*), 1 packet 56
  daiquiri (*Holland House*), 1 packet 69
  gimlet (*Holland House*), 1 packet 69
  grasshopper (*Holland House*), 1 packet 69
  mai-tai (*Holland House*), 1 packet 69
  Margarita (*Holland House*), 1 packet 69
  mint julep (*Holland House*), 1 packet 67
  piña colada (*Holland House*), 1 packet 66
  pink squirrel (*Holland House*), 1 packet 69
  screwdriver (*Holland House*), 1 packet 69
  strawberry Margarita (*Holland House*), 1 packet 62
  strawberry sting (*Holland House*), 1 packet 74
  tequila sunrise (*Holland House*), 1 packet 63
  Tom Collins (*Holland House*), 1 packet 69
  vodka sour (*Holland House*), 1 packet 65
  wallbanger (*Holland House*), 1 packet 65
  whiskey sour (*Holland House*), 1 packet 69

When using a drink mix, be sure to include the caloric content of the alcoholic beverage (see page 306) for the total calories per drink.

> **TABLE WINES,** four fluid ounces
> See also "Aperitif & Dessert Wines"

calories

Beaujolais, *see "Burgundy, red," below*
Bordeaux, red *(see also "Claret," below)*:
    (Château La Garde) 108
    (Château Olivier) 108
    (Château Pontet-Canet, Crus & Fils Frères) 96
    Bordeaux Rouge *(Chanson Père & Fils)* 108
    Bordeaux Rouge *(Crus & Fils Frères)* 84
    Margaux *(B & G)* 84
    Médoc *(Crus & Fils Frères)* 96
    St. Emilion *(B & G)* 84
    St. Emilion *(Crus & Fils Frères)* 92
    St. Julien *(Crus & Fils Frères)* 92
Bordeaux, white, Graves *(Château Olivier)* 108
Bordeaux, white, Graves *(Crus & Fils Frères)* 92
Burgundy, red:
    domestic *(Gold Seal)* 109
    domestic *(Italian Swiss Colony)* 86
    domestic *(Taylor)* 96
    imported, Beaujolais *(Crus & Fils Frères)* 96
    imported, Beaune
      (Chanson Père & Fils St. Vincent) 108
    imported, Gevrey Chambertin
      (Crus & Fils Frères) 96
    imported, Nuits St. George *(B & G)* 92
    imported, Pommard
      (Chanson Père & Fils St. Vincent) 108
    imported, Pommard *(Crus & Fils Frères)* 96
Burgundy, sparkling, domestic *(Gold Seal)* 116
Burgundy, sparkling, domestic *(Taylor)* 104
Burgundy, white:
    domestic, Chablis *(Gold Seal)* 108
    domestic, Chablis *(Italian Swiss Colony)* 86
    imported, Chablis
      (Chanson Père & Fils St. Vincent) 108
    imported, Chablis *(Crus & Fils Frères)* 88

Table Wines, continued

Moselle Bernkasteler (*Dienhard & Co.*) 92
(*Pink Carousel*) 167
Pouilly Fumé (*B & G*) 80
(*Red Carousel*) 139
Rhine:
   domestic (*Gold Seal*) 108
   domestic (*Italian Swiss Colony*) 86
   domestic (*Taylor*) 92
rosé:
   domestic (*Italian Swiss Colony*) 86
   domestic (*Taylor*) 92
   imported (*Crus & Fils Frères* Vin Rosé) 96
Sancerre (*B & G*) 80
sauterne:
   (*Gold Seal*) 116
   dry (*Gold Seal*) 108
   dry (*Taylor*) 108
Sauternes, *see "Aperitif & Dessert Wines," page 312*
(*White Carousel*) 167
zinfandel (*Italian Swiss Colony* Gold Medal) 86

APERITIF & DESSERT WINES, two fluid ounces
See also "Table Wines"

---

                          calories

Asti Spumante (*Gancia*) 84
(*Dubonnet* Blonde) 76
(*Dubonnet* Rouge) 95
Madeira:
   (*Hiram Walker*) 84
   (*Leacock*) 80
   (*Sandeman & Co.*) 84
muscatel (*Gold Seal*) 105
port:
   (*Hiram Walker Porto Branco*) 92
   (*Partners* Port) 94
   all varieties, domestic (*Gold Seal*) 105
   ruby (*Hiram Walker*) 92

Aperatif & Dessert Wines, port, continued

ruby, domestic
(*Italian Swiss Colony* Gold Medal) 86
ruby, domestic (*Taylor*) 100
ruby, imported
(*Robertson Bros. & Co.* Black Label) 92
ruby, imported (*Sandeman & Co.*) 92
tawny (*Hiram Walker*) 92
tawny, domestic (*Taylor*) 96
tawny, imported (*Sandeman & Co.*) 92
Sauternes (*B & G*) 64
Sauternes (*Château Voigny*) 64
sherry:
(*Hiram Walker* Armada Cream) 82
domestic
(*Gold Seal* Private Reserve New York State) 93
domestic (*Taylor* New York State) 88
domestic (*Taylor* New York State Cream) 100
imported (*Williams & Humbert* Dry Sack) 80
sherry, dry:
(*Hiram Walker* Cocktail) 70
domestic
(*Gold Seal* Private Reserve
New York State Cocktail) 81
domestic
(*Taylor* New York State Pale Dry Cocktail) 76
imported (*Sandeman* Cocktail) 72
vermouth, dry:
domestic (*Lejon* Extra Dry) 68
domestic (*Taylor* Extra Dry) 68
imported (*C & P* Extra Dry) 74
imported (*Gancia* Dry) 84
imported (*Noilly Prat* Extra Dry) 68
vermouth, sweet:
domestic (*Lejon*) 88
domestic (*Taylor*) 88
imported (*C & P*) 94
imported (*Gancia* Bianco) 88
imported (*Gancia* Rosso) 102
imported (*Noilly Prat*) 86
white tokay (*Taylor*) 96

LIQUEURS & OTHER FLAVORED SPIRITS,
one fluid ounce

	calories
Amaretto (*Hiram Walker*)	76
Amaretto and cognac (*Hiram Walker*)	62
anise-licorice liqueur:	
(*DuBouchett Absant*)	84
(*Pernod*)	79
anisette liqueur:	
red or white (*Bols*)	111
red or white (*DuBouchett*)	85
red or white (*Hiram Walker*)	92
white (*Dolfi*)	102
white (*Garnier*)	82
white (*Old Mr. Boston*—60 proof)	90
white (*Old Mr. Boston* Connoisseur—42 proof)	64
apricot brandy, *see "brandy, flavored," below*	
apricot liqueur:	
(*Bols*)	96
(*Dolfi*)	100
(*DuBouchett*)	63
(*Hiram Walker*)	79
(*B & B*)	94
Benai (*DuBouchett*)	110
Benai and brandy (*DuBouchett*)	89
(*Benedictine*)	112
blackberry, *see "brandy, flavored," below*	
blackberry liqueur:	
(*Bols*)	96
(*Dolfi*)	93
(*DuBouchett*)	70
(*Hiram Walker*)	93
bourbon, peach-flavored (*Old Mr. Boston*)	100
brandy, flavored:	
apricot (*Bols*)	100
apricot (*DuBouchett*)	81
apricot (*Garnier*)	86
apricot (*Hiram Walker*)	88

Liqueurs & Other Flavored Spirits, continued

triple sec:
  (*Bols*) 113
  (*Dolfi*) 107
  (*DuBouchett*) 61
  (*Garnier*) 83
  (*Hiram Walker*) 107
  (*Leroux*) 105
  (*Old Mr. Boston*—60 proof) 105
  (*Old Mr. Boston* Connoisseur—42 proof) 97
vodka, flavored:
  cherry, wild (*Old Mr. Boston*) 100
  grape (*Old Mr. Boston*) 100
  lemon (*Old Mr. Boston*) 100
  lime (*Old Mr. Boston*) 100
  orange (*Old Mr. Boston*) 100
  peppermint (*Old Mr. Boston*) 90
yellow plum (*Dolfi* Mirabelle) 78
yellow plum (*Dolfi* Cordon d'Or Mirabelle) 83

BEER, ALE & MALT LIQUOR, 12 fluid ounces

---

                                                   calories
ale (*Red Cap*) 159
beer:
  (*Blatz*) 150
  (*Brauhaus*) 150
  (*Budweiser*) 157
  (*Busch Bavarian*) 157
  (*Carling Black Label*) 162
  (*Carlsberg Light de Luxe*) 153
  (*Falstaff*) 150
  (*Grand Union*) 150
  (*Heidelberg*) 147
  (*Heidelberg Light Pilsner*) 130
  (*Heileman Grain Belt*) 150
  (*Heileman National Bohemian*) 150
  (*Heileman National Premium*) 170
  (*Heileman Old Style*) 150
  (*Heileman Special Export*) 170

Beer, Ale & Malt Liquor, beer, continued

(*Michelob*) 160
(*Old Dutch*) 150
(*Old Ranger*) 150
(*Pabst*) 150
(*Pearl*) 147
(*Pilsner's Original*) 150
(*Rainier*) 150
(*Rupert-Knickerbocker*) 158
(*Schaefer*) 160
(*Schlitz*) 153
(*Schmidt*) 150
(*Schmidt Extra Special*) 190
(*Stag*) 150
(*Sterling*) 150
(*Tudor*) 150
(*Wiedemann*) 150
light (*Blatz*) 96
light (*Heileman*) 96
light (*Rainier*) 96
malt liquor:
(*Champale*) 156
(*Colt 45*) 160
(*Country Club*) 163
(*Malt Duck Apple*) 250
(*Malt Duck Grape*) 210
(*Mickeys*) 160
near beer:
(*Kingsbury*) 60
(*Maltcrest*) 70
(*Metbrew*) 70
(*Schmidt Select*) 60
(*Zing*) 60

WHAT YOU SHOULD WEIGH

height (with shoes—2-in. heels)	WOMEN small frame	medium frame	large frame
4 ft. 10 in.	92– 98	96–107	104–119
4 ft. 11 in.	94–101	98–110	106–122
5 ft. 0 in.	96–104	101–113	109–125
5 ft. 1 in.	99–107	104–116	112–128
5 ft. 2 in.	102–110	107–119	115–131
5 ft. 3 in.	105–113	110–122	118–134
5 ft. 4 in.	108–116	113–126	121–138
5 ft. 5 in.	111–119	116–130	125–142
5 ft. 6 in.	114–123	120–135	129–146
5 ft. 7 in.	118–127	124–139	133–150
5 ft. 8 in.	122–131	128–143	137–154
5 ft. 9 in.	126–135	132–147	141–158
5 ft. 10 in.	130–140	136–151	145–163
5 ft. 11 in.	134–144	140–155	149–168
6 ft. 0 in.	138–148	144–159	153–173

For girls 18–25, subtract 1 pound for each year under 25.

WHAT YOU SHOULD WEIGH

height (with shoes — 1-in. heels)	MEN small frame	medium frame	large frame
5 ft. 2 in.	112–120	118–129	126–141
5 ft. 3 in.	115–123	121–133	129–144
5 ft. 4 in.	118–126	124–136	132–148
5 ft. 5 in.	121–129	127–139	135–152
5 ft. 6 in.	124–133	130–143	138–156
5 ft. 7 in.	128–137	134–147	142–161
5 ft. 8 in.	132–141	138–152	147–166
5 ft. 9 in.	136–145	142–156	151–170
5 ft. 10 in.	140–150	146–160	155–174
5 ft. 11 in.	144–154	150–165	159–179
6 ft. 0 in.	148–158	154–170	164–184
6 ft. 1 in.	152–162	158–175	168–189
6 ft. 2 in.	156–167	162–180	173–194
6 ft. 3 in.	160–171	167–185	178–199
6 ft. 4 in.	164–175	172–190	182–204

Prepared by the Metropolitan Life Insurance Co. from data of the Build and Blood Pressure Study, Society of Actuaries.

HOW MANY CALORIES TO MAINTAIN
YOUR DESIRABLE WEIGHT?

Desirable weight	18–35 years	35–55 years	55–75 years
	WOMEN DAILY MAINTENANCE CALORIES*		
99	1,700	1,500	1,300
110	1,850	1,650	1,400
121	2,000	1,750	1,550
128	2,100	1,900	1,600
132	2,150	1,950	1,650
143	2,300	2,050	1,800
154	2,400	2,150	1,850
165	2,550	2,300	1,950
	MEN DAILY MAINTENANCE CALORIES*		
110	2,200	1,950	1,650
121	2,400	2,150	1,850
132	2,550	2,300	1,950
143	2,700	2,400	2,050
154	2,900	2,600	2,200
165	3,100	2,800	2,400
176	3,250	2,950	2,500
187	3,300	3,100	2,600

*Based on moderate activity. If your life is very active, add calories; if you lead a sedentary life, subtract calories. Prepared by the Food and Nutrition Board of the National Academy of Sciences, National Research Council.